W9-AJK-944

The Sultana Tragedy

The
Sultana
Tragedy

America's Greatest Maritime Disaster

JERRY O. POTTER

973.771
P867s

92-1220

PELICAN PUBLISHING COMPANY
Gretna 1992

HARTFORD PUBLIC LIBRARY

Copyright © 1992
By Jerry O. Potter
All rights reserved

The word "Pelican" and the depiction of a pelican are trademarks of Pelican Publishing Company, Inc., and are registered in the U.S. Patent and Trademark Office.

Library of Congress Cataloging-in-Publication Data

Potter, Jerry O.
　The Sultana Tragedy : America's greatest maritime disaster / by Jerry O. Potter.
　　p.　cm.
　Includes bibliographical references and index.
　ISBN 0-88289-861-2
　1. Sultana (Steamboat) 2. United States—History—Civil War, 1861-1865—Prisoners and prisons. 3. Steamboat disasters—Mississippi River—History—19th century. I. Title.
E595.S84P68 1992
973.7'71—dc20　　　　　　　　　　　　　　　　　91-29521
　　　　　　　　　　　　　　　　　　　　　　　CIP

Manufactured in the United States of America

Published by Pelican Publishing Company, Inc.
1101 Monroe Street, Gretna, LA 70053

To my wife, Janita; my children, Kelly and Jeff; my parents, Elvis and Frances Potter; my brother, Larry E. Potter; my father-in-law, C. M. Lampley; and in memory of my mother-in-law, Alma Lampley. Lastly, a special dedication to the passengers aboard the *Sultana* on April 27, 1865.

Contents

How many visions of happiness were then disappointed? How many pleasures departed? The soldiers were there; the fortunes of war had long made him a prisoner; now he was returning home; he had laid down to rest; he dreamed of the bright eyes flashing with joy; as he slept he dreamed of the smiling infant, the snug dwelling, the farm, the workshop, and the village church; he calls around him his family and his friends; he tells of his suffering, his hair breadth escapes, the booming cannons, the rattle of musketry, of the blood and carnage of the field, the warm gushing tears of his mother, as she presses her son to her bosom. The bride and bridegroom were there; they talked of future plans, of the paradise of happiness laid in store for them; the mother had hushed her sweet babe to sleep and committed the little thing to the care of God. All was still; no one thought of danger by the resistless power of that clement which has enabled men to triumph over the mighty force of wind—the steamer was on her way, when suddenly the passengers are aroused to find themselves encompassed by fire. Who can tell the agony of that hour? What were the struggles of that hour; charred bodies, torn limbs, the agonizing cries; think of the loud shrieks ringing wildly over the Mississippi; cries for assistance from persons who had clung to such fragments of the wreck as they had grasped. Why attempt to describe such a scene, we are compelled to exclaim. Then arose that wild fearful shriek, then all was hushed save the wild wind and the remorseless dash of water, at intervals the solitary shrieks, the bubbling cry of some strong swimmer in his agonies. . . . *

---

*A portion of a sermon delivered by the Rev. Dr. George White on April 30, 1865, at the Calvary Episcopal Church in Memphis, Tennessee, which appeared in the Memphis *Argus*, on May 2, 1865, p. 3.

Preface

The *Titanic* on the night of April 14, 1912, steamed across the North Atlantic on her maiden voyage toward her destination of New York. She was the largest ship in the world—eleven stories high and over 882 feet long. At 11:40 P.M., Frederick Fleet, one of the *Titanic*'s lookouts, spotted a massive, glistening mountain of ice floating directly in the path of the speeding liner. "Iceberg right ahead," Fleet told the bridge, but the steamer continued on her collision course with the mammoth piece of ice. Slowly the ship's bow began to swing to the port and the iceberg glided past the *Titanic*'s starboard side. The watchman breathed a sigh of relief, believing that he had just witnessed a "close shave." But he was wrong. The iceberg had ripped a 300-foot gash in the *Titanic*'s hull, and the ship, which was believed to be unsinkable, was now sinking. Shortly after two o'clock on the morning of April 15, 1912, the queen of the White Star line vanished beneath the dark waves.

Forty-seven years earlier, another marine disaster occurred, which unlike that of the *Titanic* has never been the subject of novels or movies. In fact, even today this earlier tragedy is but a small footnote lost in the pages of history. The boat involved in this prior disaster was a 260-foot wooden-hulled steamboat, small in comparison to the gigantic *Titanic*. At 2:00 A.M. on April 27, 1865, the steamer *Sultana* exploded on the Mississippi River near Memphis, Tennessee. The incredible fact of this disaster is that at the time of the explosion, the *Sultana* carried more passengers than were aboard the *Titanic*. The *Titanic* had 2,227 passengers; the *Sultana*, over 2,400. This number was more than six times the *Sultana*'s legal carrying capacity of 376. As a result, more lives were lost on the *Sultana* than were lost on the *Titanic*. The number of deaths on the *Titanic* totalled 1,522 as compared to approximately 1,800 on the *Sultana*. The *Sultana* disaster still stands as the worst marine tragedy in American history and one of the worst in world history.

Shelby Foote in his noted trilogy on the American Civil War wrote:

> En route for Cairo with an outsized cargo of surplus army mules and discharged soldiers who had crowded aboard at Vicksburg and Helena after their release from Deep South prison camps, the sidewheel steamer *Sultana*, one of the largest on the Mississippi, blew her boilers near Paddy's Hen and Chickens, north of Memphis two hours before dawn. Although her authorized capacity was less than 400 passengers, she had about six times that number packed about her decks and in her hold—mostly Ohio, Illinois, and Indiana veterans, men who had fought perhaps the hardest war of all, sweating out its finish in stockades beyond reach of the various columns of invasion. So sudden was the blast and the fire that followed, those who managed to make it over the side had to dive through flames into muddy water running swift and cold as any millstream. A body count put the official death toll at about 1238, but there was really no way of telling how many troops had been aboard or were consumed by shrimp and gars before all those hundreds of other blue-clad corpses bobbed up downstream in the course of the next month. Estimates ran as high as 1800 dead and presumed dead, with 1585 as the figure most generally agreed on. That was more than the number killed on both sides at First Bull Run and Wilson's Creek combined, and even by the lowest count the loss of the *Sultana* went into the books as the greatest marine disaster of all time.*

---

*Shelby Foote, *The Civil War—A Narrative* (New York, 1986), Vol. III, pp. 1026-1027.

Acknowledgments

I am indebted to many individuals and institutions for assistance in one form or another in the researching and writing of this book. I owe everything to my family who followed me on the trail of this story for over ten years. Without the loving support of my wife and children, I could never have written this book.

Deep gratitude is expressed to Gene Salecker of Chicago, who loves the story as much as I do. Without Gene's help, the writing of this book would have been difficult if not impossible. Gene worked for years on compiling a list of the Union soldiers who were passengers aboard the *Sultana* and was kind enough to give me the benefit of his efforts. Any errors in the list are mine.

Special thanks must be given to Leonard Gill whose careful editing made this book readable. Dr. Lonnie Maness, Dr. Charles Crawford, J. Alan Hanover, Judge Robert Lanier, David M. Cook, Roger Easom, Larry E. Killebrew, and Janita Potter have all read the manuscript and given me the benefit of their suggestions. I am indebted to Tony and Maureen Bernot, Sam and Peggy Oliver, and Dr. Hugh Berryman for their encouragement.

I have received much help and encouragement from my law firm in this endeavor. I owe much to the lawyers and staff of The Hardison Law Firm. Special thanks must be given to Mary E. Manning who typed the manuscript through several revisions and to my secretary, Cindy Migliore, who had the difficult task of keeping up with all my correspondence on this project.

I also acknowledge the gracious cooperation of the staffs at the Memphis State University Library, the Memphis and Shelby County Public Library, the United States Army Military History Institute, the Public Library of Cincinnati and Hamilton County, the West Point Museum and Archives, the Library of Congress, and the National Archives.

There are hundreds of individuals who have given me encouragement and information regarding this project. I owe much to Phyllis Tickle for her timely advice. To the people across the nation whose ancestors were the passengers on the *Sultana* on her final trip, and to a special group of these descendants who meet each April in Knoxville, I owe special thanks. Finally, I must say thanks to Norman Shaw, the Knoxville attorney, who has given me information and encouragement.

All of these have helped me tell the story which must not be forgotten.

Jerry O. Potter
Memphis, Tennessee

The
Sultana
Tragedy

CHAPTER ONE

"One of the Largest and Best Steamers Ever Constructed"

ON THE EARLY morning of April 27, 1865, the steamer *Arkansas* plowed northward on the flooded Mississippi River, which spread beyond its western banks across the flatlands of Arkansas. Louis Rosche leaned against the rail keeping watch. Suddenly spotting something floating toward the boat, Rosche shaded his eyes to get a clearer view of the object as it drew closer. What he had initially taken to be a piece of driftwood gradually took on a more recognizable shape—the body of a small boy. Rosche believed that the unfortunate youngster must have been carried away by the spring flood. Rosche was about to signal the pilot, when he discovered the body of a woman also in the river. By this time, several passengers on the *Arkansas* had crowded to the rail. Rosche had only to glance further upriver to view a multitude of bodies floating like cordwood, and all of them dressed in the blue uniform of Union soldiers. The decks of the *Arkansas* were soon littered with the victims of some as yet unknown disaster.[1]

These bodies were not flood victims, as Rosche had first thought. At approximately two o'clock on that morning in April 1865, the steamer *Sultana* exploded just north of Memphis, Tennessee, with the loss of over 1,800 lives. The vast majority of those killed were Union soldiers on their way home after release from the infamous Confederate prison camps at Andersonville and Cahaba.

To say that the explosion on board the *Sultana* was purely accidental or unpreventable does not take into account the irresponsible conduct and criminal negligence that characterized

3

the actions of an entire chain of army command and the profit-making schemes of various civilians. The *Sultana* tragedy is much more than a record of a steamboat. The deeper record is one of greed and the lengths to which men will go to achieve personal gain, even if that gain means endangering the lives of others.

The story of the *Sultana* began on January 3, 1863, when two hulls were launched into the icy Ohio River from the Litherburg Shipyard at Cincinnati. One was the *Luminary*, designed for Capt. John A. Williamson, and the other was the ill-fated *Sultana*. Built for Capt. Preston Lodwick, a prominent steamboat owner in Cincinnati, at a total cost of $60,000, the *Sultana* joined several other boats belonging to Lodwick, including the *Northern Belle*, the *Northern Light*, and the *Prince of Wales*.[2]

Captain Lodwick's choice of a name for his new steamer was a sinister omen. The word "sultana" refers to a sultan's wife, sister, or mother, and three steamboats had previously carried it.[3] With this shared name they shared a common fate. The first *Sultana* ran down the *Marie* in the Natchez Island chute on November 21, 1846, with the loss of several lives. The second *Sultana* burned at St. Louis on June 12, 1851, taking with her a number of passengers. And the third *Sultana* caught fire at Hickman, Kentucky, on March 25, 1857.[4]

In February 1863, the Cincinnati *Daily Commerce* reported that the *Sultana* was one of the largest and best business steamers ever constructed. The boat was 260 feet in length, with a 42-foot beam and a hold seven feet deep. She had a capacity of 1,000 tons but trimmed on only 34 inches of water. This made her ideally suited for trade on the Ohio and the Mississippi rivers.[5]

On the steamer's main deck were four high-pressure tubular boilers, built by Moore and Richardson of Cincinnati, measuring 18 feet long and 46 inches in diameter.[6] Tubular boilers, not commonly found on steamboats of the period, were lighter in weight and smaller in bulk but were designed to generate more steam than the conventional type.[7] The boilers powered two engines with cylinders 25 inches in diameter with an eight-foot stroke. The engines, in turn, worked a pair of water wheels 34 feet in diameter. The wheels, mounted on the sides of the *Sultana*, had 11 feet length of bucket.[8]

The steamer's cabin consisted of a long, narrow saloon flanked on each side by a row of staterooms, which were luxuriously furnished by the Marine Railway Company. The saloon was illuminated by chandeliers manufactured by McHenry and Carson; fine china, glassware, and tableware by Hunnerwell graced the dining hall. The Harcourt Company prepared the steamer's rigging and blocks, while the copper, tin, and sheet iron used in the *Sultana*'s construction were produced by the Lape Company.[9] The *Sultana* provided accommodations for 76 cabin passengers and 300 deck passengers. This number combined to form the steamer's legal carrying capacity.[10] The crew numbered 80 to 85 men and women.[11]

During her first year of operation, the *Sultana* plied the Mississippi, Ohio, and Tennessee rivers. The first crew consisted of Preston Lodwick, master; W. H. Cropper and Charles Matthews, in charge of business affairs; and J. W. Keniston and Mr. McClain, engineers. Robert Curnish was the mate and Mr. Sanderline the steward.[12] Several captains commanded the steamer during her first year, including William Lodwick, William Thompson, James Mason, B. Switzer, and Jim Case.[13]

From February 1863 to March 1864, Capt. Preston Lodwick netted earnings nearly double the initial cost of the steamer, much of which came from transporting freight and men for the Federal government.[14] This very profitable business, however, was not without hazards. On May 18, 1863, in a convoy with four other boats, the steamer was fired upon by a Rebel battery near Island No. 82 on the Mississippi River.[15] On July 15, 1863, the *Sultana* was again fired upon by Confederate soldiers near Memphis and sustained heavy damage to her upper works.[16] The *Eastport*, a Union ironclad, reported on August 3, 1863, that the *Sultana* was fired upon below Buck Island on the Mississippi.[17]

On March 7, 1864, Lodwick sold the steamer to three investors for $80,000. The group was composed of William A. Thornburg, J. Cass Mason, and Namson, Damerson & Company. Thornburg owned a one-quarter interest; Mason, three-eighths; and Namson, Damerson & Company, three-eighths.[18]

Namson, Damerson & Company, a St. Louis commission house formed in 1860, was owned by Capt. Joseph S. Namson and Logan D. Damerson. Namson had already owned several steamboats, all of which proved to be bad investments. The steamer *Banner State*, purchased in 1857, sank on her third trip out and was a total loss. Namson then built the *N. J. Eaton,* but this boat was destroyed on her first trip. The *Kate Howard* sank in 1859. These failures almost bankrupted Namson, but his partnership with Damerson proved to be financially successful.[19]

J. Cass Mason was not only part owner of the *Sultana* but served as her captain and master as well. At only thirty-four years of age, Mason was already a skillful navigator of the Mississippi River. Before purchasing a share of the *Sultana* he had owned and operated the *Herald,* which traveled the Missouri River. Mason had also been an officer on the *William Campbell* and the *A. B. Chambers.*[20] In 1860, Mason married Mary Rowena Dozier, daughter of James Dozier, a successful St. Louis businessman with several steamboats under his control. After his marriage into the Dozier family, Mason became master of the *Rowena.*[21] He lost command of the *Rowena* on February 13, 1863, when the steamer was seized by the U.S. Navy. The crew of the gunboat *New Era* had boarded her near Island No. 10 on the Mississippi River and discovered 200 ounces of quinine bound for the Confederate-controlled city of Tiptonville, Tennessee, in addition to 3,000 pairs of Rebel uniform pants. While Mason was not arrested, his boat was enlisted in the navy's river fleet. Dozier was never to regain the *Rowena* because on April 18, 1863, she sank (while still under control of the navy) near Cape Girardeau, Missouri, after striking a snag. It is not clear whether Dozier blamed his son-in-law for the loss of the *Rowena,* but within weeks of her seizure, all business association between the two ended. By March 1863, Mason was captain of the *Belle Memphis,* a steamer engaged in the Memphis/St. Louis trade. A riverman respected by his peers, Mason was considered one of the clearest-headed men on the river and an ideal choice to captain the *Sultana.*[22]

CHAPTER TWO

The Prisoners

THE VAST MAJORITY of the passengers who would board the *Sultana* on her final trip were Union soldiers from Tennessee, Virginia, Indiana, Kentucky, Ohio, and Michigan.[23] Most were already veterans of Gettysburg, Missionary Ridge, Chickamauga, Stones River, and Franklin, but the carnage that they had witnessed on the battlefield did little to prepare them for what lay ahead — capture, imprisonment, and the *Sultana*'s final voyage.

Fighting ended for most of these soldiers in the latter part of 1864. By early September, Gen. William Tecumseh Sherman had taken Atlanta and was ready to continue his march to the sea. To the rear of Sherman's ranks snaked a system of railroads. Confederate Lt. Gen. Richard Taylor (commander of the department of Alabama, Mississippi, and east Louisiana) ordered Nathan Bedford Forrest to destroy these vital Union supply lines.[24]

A branch of this system of railroads ran through northern Alabama, where Union forces stood guard at Athens and at Sulphur Branch trestle. The fort at Athens was considered by Union authorities to be the strongest fortification between Nashville, Tennessee, and Decatur, Alabama.[25] A quarter of a mile in circumference, the fort was surrounded by a ditch 15 feet wide; the elevation measured 17 feet from the bottom of the ditch to the top of the parapet. The whole was further encircled by a palisade and an abatis of felled trees. Supplies of water, rations, and ammunition were sufficient to withstand a siege of ten days.[26] Under Lt. Col. Wallace Campbell, Federal commander at Athens, the garrison

7

included 150 east Tennesseeans with the 3rd Tennessee Cavalry (Union).[27]

Forrest, with a force of 4,500 men, arrived on the outskirts of Athens at sunset on September 23rd in preparation for a dawn assault. Shortly after sunrise, two of Forrest's batteries opened fire and for two hours Confederate shells rained on the fortification. Little damage was done, however, and at eight o'clock the firing stopped. General Forrest sent a soldier equipped with a white flag to demand surrender, but Campbell refused. In an effort to avoid an "effusion of blood," Forrest requested an interview with the Union commander. At this meeting, the Confederate general told Campbell that "for the sake of humanity," he would do everything in his power to avoid a "collision." Forrest allowed Campbell and another officer to review the Confederate force to satisfy themselves that Forrest had sufficient men to take the fort. Campbell concluded that there were at least 10,000 men and nine pieces of artillery poised to make the assault. What the Union colonel did not know was that the 10,000 men he claimed to have seen were actually Forrest's 4,500 Confederates cleverly mounted, dismounted, remounted, and moved about to convey a force of infantry and cavalry more than twice its actual size. Convinced that he was facing certain defeat, Campbell informed his officers, "The jig is up; pull down the flag." The flag was lowered, and 571 men marched out of the gate and into the hands of the waiting Confederates.[28]

While Colonel Campbell was negotiating the surrender of the fort, a relief column was attempting to fight its way to his rescue. This force was composed of the 18th Michigan Infantry and the 102nd Ohio Infantry—a total of 700 men. The column soon found itself surrounded by Forrest's troops but continued to fight toward the earthwork. When the would-be rescuers were within sight of the ramparts, they were shocked to see the fort's gates open and their comrades marching out. Since further resistance was futile, the relief column surrendered as well.[29]

Forrest then moved toward Sulphur Branch trestle. Standing 72 feet high and 300 feet long, the trestle was defended by two double-cased blockhouses (with walls 40 inches thick) and an earthen fort. These fortifications were garrisoned by 1,100 men, including 300 members of the 9th Indiana Cavalry and 400 soldiers with the 3rd Tennessee Cavalry. As with the fort at Athens, Forrest used his formidable artillery to force the surrender of the Federal units in these blockhouses.[30]

General Forrest captured almost 2,300 Union soldiers on September 24th and 25th.[31] Rank during the Civil War had its privileges, and under the terms of the surrender, the officers were to be paroled and later exchanged. Enlisted men were "to be turned over to the Confederate States Government as prisoners of war, to be disposed of as the War Department of the Confederate States shall direct."[32] These prisoners were sent to the Cahaba prison camp on the banks of the Alabama River, 12 miles from Selma.[33]

While the captured troops endured their first weeks of imprisonment, two armies prepared for battle. Gen. John Bell Hood, leading 30,000 Confederates, faced 34,000 men of the Army of Tennessee under command of Union Gen. John McAllister Schofield. On the afternoon of November 30, 1864, at Franklin, Tennessee, the two forces met in what was to be one of the bloodiest battles of the western theater. Hood's losses were about 7,000 men, with approximately 1,750 killed on the field, 4,500 wounded, and another 702 taken prisoner.[34] All told, the Union casualties were 2,326.[35] Union prisoners captured at Franklin were sent south to either the Cahaba or Andersonville prison camps.

December 1864 was unseasonably cold, and many prisoners were forced to march, unfed, through ice and snow in bare feet. J. Walter Elliott, captured near Nashville on December 2, 1864, recalled witnessing his fellow prisoners finally being fed raw corn thrown to them from a moving wagon. Several men died after eating the corn. Elliott sadly looked at the bodies on the frozen ground, as he and the remaining prisoners slowly made their way toward a chain of railroad cars. Crowded into an unheated boxcar lined with a half-foot of horse manure, the soldiers were shipped to Cahaba, near-dead from exposure and malnutrition.[36]

Others, captured in the latter part of 1864, arrived at Andersonville to join prisoners who had been confined there and at other Rebel prisons for months, even years. For example, after his capture on June 2, 1862, at Cold Harbor, Virginia, Chester Berry (with the 20th Regiment of the Michigan Volunteer Infantry) was confined at the Pemberton prison in Virginia and later transferred to Andersonville on June 16, 1864.[37] Alexander C. Brown and Michael Brunner (both members of Ohio units) were taken prisoners during the battle of Chickamauga in September 1863. Placed in Belle Isle and Libby prisons in Virginia, they too endured the infamous Andersonville before their release at war's end in 1865.[38]

One of the greatest tragedies of the Civil War was the creation of a system of prison camps. Early in the war, prisoners had been exchanged. The exchange, patterned after the cartel that Great Britain and the United States had agreed upon during the War of 1812, provided for a rate of exchange that ranged from sixty men for a general to one man for a private.[39] Unfortunately, the cartel between the Union and Confederacy was discontinued shortly after its inception. By the summer of 1863, prisoner exchanges had virtually ceased, and General Grant officially ended the cartel in August 1864. In a letter to Maj. Gen. Benjamin F. Butler, the commissioner of exchange, Grant explained his decision:

> It is hard on our men held in Southern prisons not to exchange them, but it is humanity to those left in the ranks who fight our battles. Every man we hold, when released on parole or otherwise, becomes an active soldier against us at once either directly or indirectly. If we commence a system of exchange which liberates all prisoners taken, we will have to fight on until the whole South is exterminated.[40]

The fact that a soldier was captured and placed in a prison camp did not mean he had escaped the horrors and dangers of the battlefield. In fact, a soldier during the Civil War had a better chance of survival in battle than he had as a prisoner of war. Historian Bruce Catton illustrated this point when he wrote:

> To become a prisoner in the Civil War, on either side, was no short cut to survival—Quite the opposite; and to understand how appallingly lethal were the prison camps, North and South, one need only reflect on this bit of simple arithmetic; about two and a half times as many soldiers were subjected to the hunger, pestilence and soul-sickening of the prison camps as were exposed to the deadly fire and crossfire of the guns of Gettysburg—and the camps killed nearly ten times as many as died on the battlefield.[41]

Conditions within the prison camps during the Civil War claimed the lives of approximately 26,436 Confederate and 22,576 Union soldiers.[42]

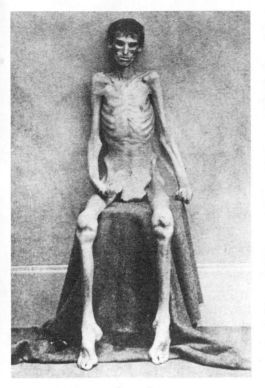

A prisoner of war from Andersonville. The inmates of Andersonville suffered from severe malnutrition and a host of diseases. (Library of Congress)

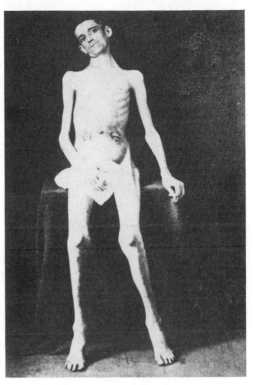

A Union soldier at the time of his release from Andersonville. (Library of Congress)

The Andersonville prison camp. Many of the Sultana's *passengers had been housed at this infamous prison. (Library of Congress)*

Disease, malnutrition, and violence marked prison life. And Andersonville, perhaps the most famous of all the camps, became, in the eyes of the Northern people, a great symbol of the needless suffering engendered by the war. The cry for retribution among Unionists was so strong that E. M. Stanton, then secretary of war, ordered Northern prison authorities to reduce the food, fuel, shelter, and clothing supplies of the Confederate prisoners to levels that he and others contended were parallel to conditions in the Southern prisons. Much of the suffering in Northern prisons was a direct result of this order.[43]

While many of the stories circulating throughout the North concerning Andersonville were grossly exaggerated, there can be no doubt that inmates suffered terribly. A Confederate surgeon in October 1864 reported 5,000 seriously sick prisoners in its hospital and stockade, and further stated that "the deaths ranged from 90 to 130 each day." He also provided the following grim statistics:

> Since the establishment of this prison on 24th of February, 1864, to the present time (October 1864) over 10,000 Federal prisoners have died, that is, nearly one third of the entire number have perished in less than seven months.[44]

Andersonville was established near Americus, Georgia, in the spring of 1864. It consisted of 27 acres enclosed by a pine stockade 20 feet in height. Around this main stockade were two additional wooden fences, 16 feet and 12 feet in height. Beyond the outer stockade were rifle pits and cannon emplacements.[45] Within the enclosure, the Confederate government crowded as many as 32,899 prisoners, which meant that each man had less than four square yards of living space. But the camp was even more crowded than the above figure suggests since areas of swamp and accumulated human waste made habitation impossible.[46]

The few tents issued to prisoners at Andersonville offered little real protection from the elements. The great majority of the men were forced to endure all types of weather without any shelter at all. Furthermore, the prisoners were clothed in rags, since the Confederate government distributed few garments to replace those that had been taken by captors or stolen by fellow prisoners.[47]

Most, if not all, of the prisoners suffered some degree of malnutrition, despite the fact that, according to Confederate regulations, they were to receive the same rations as Confederate soldiers.

These rations consisted of one pound of beef or one-third pound of bacon, and one and a quarter pound of corn meal per day. In reality, the Confederacy could not even provide such rations to its own fighting men.[48]

Malaria, smallpox, typhoid, diarrhea, dysentery, scurvy, and hospital gangrene killed thousands of men during the period Andersonville was in operation.[49] And the unsanitary conditions that prevailed in the camp greatly augmented the incidence of disease. It is known, for example, that a single drink from the water system (which was polluted with human waste) could lead to serious illness and even death. John Ransom, a prisoner at Andersonville, wrote of the conditions:

> Here we have the very worst kind of water. Nothing can be worse or nastier than the stream drizzling its way through this camp and for air to breathe, it is what arises from this foul place. On all four sides of us are high walls and tall trees and there is apparently no wind or breeze to blow away the stench, and we are obliged to breathe and live in it. Dead bodies lay around all day in the boiling sun by the dozen and even hundreds, and we must suffer and live in this atmosphere. It's too horrible for me to describe in fitting language.[50]

Under such conditions, a scratch, a sunburn, a splinter under the skin, or a mere mosquito bite could result in gangrene and death.

Medical care, too, was totally inadequate. The need for doctors to treat Confederate soldiers was so great that few physicians were sent to the prison camps to treat the captured enemy. And those doctors who were sent to Andersonville were often poorly trained. Nursing duties were for the most part carried out by the prisoners themselves, who in many cases were more intent on stealing from the sick than on treating them.[51] The hospital at Andersonville, like the rest of the prison, was filthy, and little attempt was made to keep it or the patients clean. A Confederate surgeon, during his inspection of the hospital, noted to his horror that soiled bandages from one patient were used again on other patients.[52] Gangrene, resulting in amputation of a diseased limb, almost invariably reappeared due to the unsanitary conditions.[53]

Medical treatment at Andersonville was so substandard that a shared belief among prisoners had it that the doctors were actually executioners in disguise. The inoculation of between 2,000 and

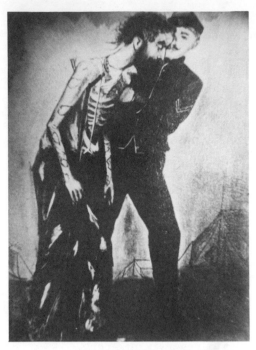

Pvt. Epenetus W. McIntosh, Company A, 14th Illinois Infantry, weighed only 80 lbs. at the time of his release from Andersonville. This soldier would survive the Sultana's *final trip.* (Courtesy of Gene Salecker)

Epenetus W. McIntosh as he appeared in 1890. (Courtesy of Gene Salecker)

The Cahaba Federal Prison. (Jesse Hawes, *Cahaba: A Story of Captive Boys in Blue*)

3,000 men in the spring of 1864 in an effort to stop the spread of smallpox merely served to reinforce this fear. Since many of the vaccinated prisoners already suffered from scurvy, gangrene of the arm frequently developed. The amputations and deaths following the vaccinations were so numerous that prisoners accused authorities of inoculating them with poison.[54]

Crime was another major problem. The Confederate government could not spare trained soldiers to guard the Union troops housed within the stockade, so boys or old men were often placed in charge. Moreover, few guards were willing to venture into the confines of the stockade itself to maintain order. As a result, bands of inmates preyed on their comrades. In July 1864, six prisoners were tried and executed by their peers for crimes ranging from robbery to murder. Eighteen other criminals who had escaped hanging were later beaten so badly that three of them died.[55] Authorities at Andersonville made little or no effort to interfere with the internal violence.

Soldiers who had survived the ordeals of battle watched, inside Andersonville, as disease and malnutrition, enemies as deadly as bullets or canister, continued to thin out their ranks: The red clay of Georgia would be the final resting place for over 12,912 Union men.[56]

Cahaba prison was named for the small Alabama town that lay nearby on the Alabama River, not far from Selma. Built as a cotton and corn shed measuring roughly 193 feet by 116 feet, Cahaba's walls were 8 to 10 feet high and only partially roofed over. The entire center area was left open. A stockade about 10 feet high was erected on one end of the shed for use by prison guards.[57] A little more than half of the roof remained on the shed during its use as a prison, and while it could protect some of the inmates from the summer sun, it gave little or no protection from the cold rains of winter. Into this small stockade the Confederates crowded over 3,000 men. Estimates suggest that each man in the prison had only six square feet of living space. (U.S. Army regulations at the time required that military posts allow at least 42 square feet of living space per soldier.)[58] Cahaba's chief surgeon, R. M. Whitfield, reported in March 1864:

HARTFORD PUBLIC LIBRARY

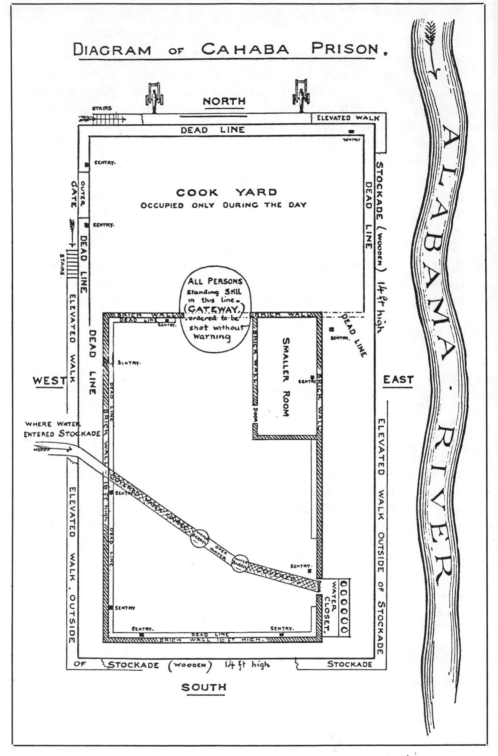

A diagram of the Cahaba Federal Prison. (Jesse Hawes, *Cahaba: A Story of Captive Boys in Blue*)

When you know the sanitary condition of the prison you cannot be surprised at the large number of cases reported. A brick
wall covered by a leaky roof, with sixteen hundred feet of open
space in its centre, four open windows, and the earth for the
floor, constitutes the prison.[59]

Surgeon Whitfield, in describing the prison's water supply,
wrote:

The supply of water for drinking, cooking, and bathing, as well
as for washing, is conveyed from an artesian well along an open
street gutter for two hundred yards, thence under the street
into the prison. In its course it is subjected to the washings of
the hands, feet, faces, and heads of soldiers, citizens, and ne-
groes; in it are rinsed buckets, tubs, and spittoons of groceries,
offices, and hospitals; in it can be found the filth from hogs,
dogs, cows, and horses, and filth of all kinds from the street
and other sources.[60]

The daily rations for the prisoners consisted of 10 to 12 ounces of
corn meal (including ground cobs and husks), and five to seven
ounces of bacon or beef. But in the warm months, the meat rations
often gave off such a nauseating smell that only a few of the men
could force themselves to eat it.[61]

In late February 1865, heavy rains caused the Alabama River to
flood the prison grounds at Cahaba. The water was so deep that on
the morning after the high water reached the stockade, the Confederates in charge floated through the prison gate in boats. For
four days and nights, prisoners were left to stand in freezing water,
which reached as far as the waist on some. Guards finally allowed
the prisoners to leave the compound to gather driftwood, which
was stacked to form platforms for the men. John Walker, a private
with the 50th Ohio Infantry, was one prisoner lucky enough to find
a few pieces of heavy timber and cordwood, which he and seven
comrades stacked high enough to clear the water. There they sat,
back to back, for two days. Finally, 700 prisoners were taken to
nearby Selma, while 2,300 waited in the flooded prison.[62]

By February 1865, the curtain was about to fall on the Confederacy as
Sherman prepared his move north. Ahead of him lay the remnants of a
tattered Rebel army, commanded by Gen. Joe Johnston, which, according to Johnston, could do no more than annoy the advancing Sherman.[63]

Pvt. Freeman L. Hume, Company C, 115th Ohio Infantry. Died. (Courtesy of Timothy R. Brookes)

Cpl. Benjamin Crew, Company F, 115th Ohio Infantry. Died. (Courtesy of Timothy Brookes)

Sgt. William H. H. Smith, Company F, 115th Ohio Infantry. Died. (Courtesy of Timothy Brookes)

Capt. Deming Norton Lowrey, Company G, 115th Ohio Infantry. Died. (Courtesy of Timothy Brookes)

Pvt. Thomas Laboyteaux, Company E, 9th Indiana Cavalry. Survived. (Courtesy of Kim Harrison)

Pvt. Lewis Johnson, Company G, 9th Indiana Cavalry. Survived. (Courtesy of Kim Harrison)

Pvt. Romulus Tolbert, Company H, 8th Indiana Cavalry. Survived. (Courtesy of Anne Tolbert Woodbury)

Pvt. Isaac Brown, Company K, 9th Ohio Cavalry. Survived. (Courtesy of Don Brown)

In the same month, the North began to exchange prisoners with the Confederacy. Grant ordered that disabled prisoners from Missouri, Kentucky, Arkansas, Tennessee, and Louisiana be the first released. Grant knew that these troops could not be sent back to the front lines as reinforcements.[64]

By March 1865, Gen. Robert E. Lee and his Army of Northern Virginia were facing a Union army nearly double in numbers at Petersburg. In North Carolina, Johnston faced even greater odds. Lee's (and the South's) last hope was for his men to slip past Grant's army at Petersburg, join Johnston in North Carolina, and crush Sherman. The combined armies could then face Grant on roughly even terms.[65]

On March 20, 1865, the Confederate authorities at Andersonville moved a group of prisoners who were to be exchanged for Southerners. The day these prisoners had been praying for came without ceremony. Told that their hour of deliverance had come, and without time to collect what few possessions remained to them, the men were marched to a railroad line to await the train to Montgomery, Alabama.[66] The Union soldiers were ecstatic when news of their impending release spread throughout Andersonville. J. Walter Elliott, a captain with the 44th Regiment of the U.S. Colored Troops, described the reaction of the prisoners in the following terms:

> "Get ready for exchange," came the order. Oh! the joyous shout that made the castle walls ring out. How each of us laughed and cried, shook hands with and hugged his fellows, and joining hands in a circle, in good old Methodist campmeeting-altar style, as we all joined in singing "Rally Round the Flag, Boys." The joy of that good hour more than repaid for all past tribulations.[67]

There were no bands playing or crowds cheering as the emaciated veterans slowly filed through the prison gates. Many depended on the abler arms of comrades to lead them. Lt. Joseph Taylor Elliott with the 124th Indiana Infantry recalled the scene:

> Coming like cattle across an open field were scores of men who were nothing but skin and bones; some hobbling along as best they could, and others being helped by stronger comrades. Every gaunt face with its staring eyes told the story of the suffering and privation they had gone through, and

*Pvt. Issac Van Nuys, Company D,
57th Indiana Infantry. Survived.*
(Courtesy of Patrick Kelley)

*Pvt. Isaac Battles, Company K, 3rd
Tennessee Cavalry. Died.* (Courtesy
of Eugene Eller)

*Pvt. Jessee M. Huffaker, Company
D, 3rd Tennessee Cavalry. Survived.*
(Courtesy of Edgar R. Keeble
and Norman Shaw)

*Pvt. John H. Simpson, Company I,
3rd Tennessee Cavalry. Survived.*
(Courtesy of Norman Shaw)

protruding bones showed through their scanty tattered garments. One might have thought that the grave and the sea had
given up their dead.[68]

These prisoners and a group from Cahaba were sent by train,
steamer, and on foot to Vicksburg, Mississippi, the city the Confederate Office of Exchange had designated as the point to which all
prisoners being held east of the Mississippi River would be delivered for shipment north.[69] The trip to Vicksburg was a difficult
one. (One train derailed three times, injuring several men.)[70] And
freedom came too late for many of the prisoners, who, due to poor
health, died in transit. Joseph Taylor Elliott would later write of this
too: "(A)nd there were others who barely escaped it, for there was
hardly a station on the road where we did not leave the remains of
some poor fellow to be buried by strangers."[71]

The U. S. Sanitary Agent in Vicksburg on April 4, 1865, filed the
following report to his superior regarding the surviving prisoners:

> There are now in camp four miles from here about 4,000 pris-
> oners, and more are coming in every day. Those who came in
> first were from Cahaba, and were in much better condition
> than those now coming in, who are from Andersonville. The
> latter are in very feeble and distressing condition; every train
> containing more or less who have died upon the road. Yester-
> day, an ambulance came in which started from Jackson with
> four sick men, and when it arrived they were all dead. Large
> trains of ambulances are running between Black River and
> Jackson, bringing more, who are too feeble to walk. The city
> hospitals are being emptied to make room for them and every-
> thing is being done that can be done, but still many will die for
> the succor has come too late.[72]

Most of these emaciated prisoners were forced to walk the thirty
miles from Jackson, Mississippi, to Vicksburg. It took Charles M.
Eldridge, suffering from scurvy and with sores covering his feet
and legs, one and a half days to reach the Union lines at Big Black
River, approximately four miles east of Vicksburg. Though Eldridge was far behind his column as they drew near the river, he
could hear shouting and saw several of the prisoners running and
throwing their hats into the air. On a small rise was the American
flag waving in the wind. This was the first time Eldridge had seen
the Stars and Stripes since his capture at Athens, Alabama, on

September 24, 1864. Eldridge, though, did not have the strength to go any farther and fell to the ground. Approached by a guard who told him it was only a short distance to his lines, Eldridge replied, "Oh! Let me alone. If I must die, let me die in sight of the flag." The guard placed him on a horse, which carried him across the Big Black River bridge to the Union lines.[73]

The prisoners were housed at a parole camp known as Camp Fisk (or Four Mile Camp), located four miles from Vicksburg. During March and April 1865, this camp received approximately 5,530 prisoners.[74] Though operated by the Union army, the men were still officially under the control of the Confederate government, since the two sides had not finalized a prisoner exchange. Once the exchange was finalized, these troops would go by steamer and train to Camp Chase near Columbus, Ohio, where they would be granted their discharge from the army. One of the first things many of these prisoners did when they arrived at the parole camp was to write to their families that they soon would be home.[75]

While men waited at Camp Fisk, a small town in Virginia named Appomattox was earning a place in American history. Near this town in early April, Grant's army was poised to deliver the final, crushing blow to the once-powerful, but still proud Army of Northern Virginia. Grant would never deal this blow because on April 9, a young Confederate officer galloped out of Lee's thin line with a white flag. Unable to join up with Johnston, Lee realized that further resistance would be futile. Within hours, Lee and Grant drafted documents that would put an end to the Civil War.[76]

Word of victory spread like wildfire among the men housed at Camp Fisk. Peace had finally come. But they were not yet free. Their lives were now in the hands of a few army officers at Vicksburg. These officers, however, wore Union blue, and the challenge to come for most of the soldiers on their homeward trip was to prove as great, and as deadly, as any they had faced during the war.

Maj. Gen. Napoleon Jackson Tecumseh Dana, Commander of the Department of Mississippi. (Library of Congress)

CHAPTER THREE

The Union Officers at Vicksburg

VICKSBURG AND CAMP FISK, as part of the Union's Department of Mississippi, were under the command of Maj. Gen. Napoleon Jackson Tecumseh Dana. Dana, a graduate of West Point, had previously served in the Mexican War, and at the battle of Cerro Gordo had been gravely wounded. After recovery and an assignment as a recruiting officer in Boston, Dana was appointed captain in the quartermaster department and sent to the frontier of Minnesota. In 1855, Dana resigned from the army and became a banker in St. Paul with the firm of Dana and Borup. But when the Civil War broke out, he reentered the army as a colonel with the 1st Minnesota Volunteer Infantry. Within a few months, Dana was appointed a brigadier general of volunteers and rose to brigade commander with the 2nd Corps of the Army of the Potomac. He participated in all the principal battles of the Peninsula Campaign in Virginia in 1862 and in the Maryland campaign. At the battle of Antietam, General Dana was seriously wounded and while recuperating was appointed major general. On December 8, 1864, Dana was made commander of the Department of Mississippi.[77]

Brig. Gen. Morgan L. Smith, commander of the Post and the District of Vicksburg, was a native of St. Louis and a riverboat captain for fifteen years prior to the war.[78] (Smith claimed that he had served in the regular army during the Mexican War, but no record of his service was ever found by the military. The army later theorized that Smith may have served under an assumed name.)[79] Shortly after the outbreak of the Civil War, Smith helped to

Gen. Morgan L. Smith, Commander of the Post and the District of Vicksburg. (United States Army Military History Institute)

Capt. George A. Williams, the Commissary of Musters at Vicksburg. (United States Military Academy Library)

organize the 8th Missouri Volunteer Infantry and served as its colonel.[80] On July 16, 1862, he became brigadier general of volunteers and assumed command of the 1st Brigade, 5th Division, of the Army of the Tennessee. On December 28, 1862, he received a severe wound to the left hip near Vicksburg and did not return to active duty until October 6, 1863, when he commanded the 2nd Division of the 15th Army Corps. His unit saw action in Alabama and Georgia during 1863 and 1864. General Smith assumed command of the Post and the District of Vicksburg on November 12, 1864, and held this position until the end of the war.[81]

In April 1865, Capt. William Franklin Kerns was the assistant quartermaster in charge of river transportation for the Department of Mississippi. Kerns, who was from St. Peter, Minnesota, had enlisted and served with the 9th Regiment of the Minnesota Volunteers, but in 1864, at the age of twenty-four, he accepted a commission as an assistant quartermaster of the United States Volunteers with the rank of captain. By July of the same year, Kerns was reassigned to the Department of Mississippi and stationed at Vicksburg.[82]

Capt. George Augustus Williams was the commissary of musters at Vicksburg for the Department of Mississippi in March and April 1865 and, as such, was in charge of the exchange of prisoners. Williams started his military career in July 1848, when at the age of seventeen he was appointed to the United States Military Academy from Newburgh, New York. At West Point, Williams studied alongside several classmates who would later gain fame during the Civil War, including Phillip H. Sheridan and George Crook. Williams graduated 34th out of a class of 43 in 1852. Following his graduation, Williams was commissioned as a second lieutenant in the 1st U.S. Infantry.[83]

After a short period of time at Fort Columbus, New York, Williams was transferred to Texas, where he served with the 1st Infantry until 1859. First Lieutenant Williams was then sent to Fort Cobb in the Indian Territory, but in 1860 he returned to West Point as an assistant professor of Spanish. With the outbreak of the war, Williams became an assistant professor of infantry tactics. Promoted to the rank of captain on May 14, 1861, Williams then served as acting commandant of the corps until the fall of 1861. Williams rejoined the 1st Infantry in the Department of Missouri and participated in the battles of New Madrid, Island No. 10, and Corinth.[84]

After the battle of Corinth, Williams was elected to the command of the 47th Illinois Volunteer Infantry with the rank of colonel. Thus, it appeared to this ambitious officer, who had watched many of his former classmates at West Point rise above him in rank, that he would finally reach the rank of colonel. For unknown reasons, however, Illinois governor Richard Yates refused to confirm Williams as colonel of the regiment, and he was forced to rejoin the 1st Infantry.[85]

Captain Williams evidently tried to use political influence to advance in rank. General Grant on November 2, 1862, and December 17, 1862, wrote on behalf of Williams in an effort to win him a promotion to the rank of brigadier general. Grant addressed the first letter to Maj. Gen. Henry W. Halleck. In a later letter to Elihu B. Washburne, a congressman from Illinois and friend of Lincoln, Grant described the captain as "one of the most efficient as well as one of the most experienced officers in my department." Grant's influence was apparently of no help because Williams remained a captain throughout the war.[86]

In March 1863, while in command of an expedition near Yazoo Pass, Mississippi, Williams suffered a hernia, which would plague him for the rest of his military career. Disabled as a result of this injury, he would never again serve in combat. The following month, Williams was ordered by General Grant to report to Memphis as the provost-marshal.[87] It was here that his military career almost came to an end. As the provost-marshal, Williams was in charge of the Irving Block military prison and hospital in Memphis. In early 1864, Lt. Col. John F. Marsh, an army inspector, made an inspection of this facility, which was used by the army for the detention of civilians, prisoners of war, and U.S. soldiers awaiting trial. Marsh was shocked at what he discovered and described the prison as "the filthiest place" he had ever seen. The inspector in his report to his supervisor dated April 28, 1864, reported:

> The whole management and government of the prisoners could not be worse. Discipline and order are unknown. Food sufficient, but badly served. In a dark, wet cellar I found twenty-eight prisoners chained to a wet floor, where they had been constantly confined, many of them for several months, one since November 16, 1863, and are not for a moment

released, even to relieve the calls of nature. With a single exception these men have had no trial.[88]

Marsh's report was forwarded to Edwin Stanton, the secretary of war, who on May 7, 1864, sent a telegram to Gen. C. C. Washburn, commander of the District of West Tennessee, ordering the dismissal of Williams from the army because of "excessive cruelty to prisoners and gross neglect of duty."[89]

General Washburn, after receiving Stanton's order, appointed a three-officer commission to investigate the charges and to make an inspection of the Irving Block prison. The military commission when it inspected the prison found it to be "absolutely filthy" and "without ventilation or light, badly policed, bed and clothing dirty, and everything in confusion." The officers on the commission, evidently reluctant to condemn a fellow officer, concluded their report by writing: "The building is unfit for the purpose for which it is used. Great improvements have been made in it during the administration of Captain Williams. . . ."[90]

But George Williams, who had spent his entire adult life in uniform, was not going to be drummed out of the army without a fight. He submitted a statement to the commission pointing out the improvements that had been made to the prison since it came under his supervision. Williams argued that he, a graduate of West Point in 1852, had never before been under charges and gave the names of U. S. Grant and William Sherman as character references. He also submitted several testimonials and letters supporting his management of the prison. Among the letters was one from General Washburn, the very officer who had appointed the commission to investigate the charges against Williams. Washburn, who after making it clear that in his opinion the War Department had "acted hastily and harshly," blamed Williams's subordinates for the abuses at the Irving Block prison.[91]

George Williams appealed his dismissal from the service and the entire file was turned over to Joseph Holt, the judge advocate general of the army. Holt, while impressed by the letters and testimonials Williams had submitted in his defense, was not persuaded by them. He evidently felt that the glowing testimonials of Williams's character were not sufficient to overcome the strong evidence of malfeasance and negligence contained in Marsh's report and the findings of the Washburn commission. Holt concluded:

> Upon the whole, however, it seems clear that gross mal-
> administration has been practiced at the Memphis prison; that
> Captain Williams is principally and directly responsible
> thereof, and that, in view of all the testimony, it must be left
> with the President to determine whether any good and suffi-
> cient reason is disclosed for reversing the action taken by the
> War Department.[92]

Thus, Holt refused to rescind the dismissal and it appeared that
Williams's future was in the hands of Abraham Lincoln. After Holt
prepared his report to Lincoln, however, he received a letter that
caused him to change his opinion. The letter was from Gen. U. S.
Grant, who asked for a revocation of the order of dismissal. Grant
also expressed a very high opinion of Williams's ability and services. While the other documents submitted by or on behalf of Williams had failed to convince Holt, the letter from Grant did. The
judge advocate general, after reviewing Grant's letter, added a
postscript to his report:

> In view of this strong testimonial (Grant's letter), it is conceived
> that the conclusion may be safely adopted that the accused was
> not personally responsible for the abuses complained of and
> that his character as an officer is amply established.[93]

On July 6, 1864, the secretary of war reversed his earlier decision
and ordered that Capt. George A. Williams be restored to the service.

Williams continued to serve as the provost-marshal in Memphis
until the early part of 1865 when he was ordered to Vicksburg to act
as the commissary of musters. In March of 1865, Gen. Morgan L.
Smith placed Captain Williams in charge of the prisoner exchange
to be conducted at Vicksburg. On April 7, Williams was ordered to
proceed to Cairo, Illinois to communicate with Grant concerning
problems that had arisen over the terms of the exchange. Williams
would also travel to New Orleans in an effort to resolve these difficulties.[94]

Capt. Frederic Speed, an assistant adjutant general at Vicksburg
in April 1865, volunteered to perform Williams's duties while the
latter was away from Vicksburg. Born in Ithaca, New York, on September 22, 1841, Speed was the youngest of five sons of John J. and
Anne Speed. In 1860, the family moved to Portland, Maine, where

Captain Frederic Speed. An Assistant Adjutant General at Vicksburg, Speed was the only person brought to trial following the Sultana *disaster.* (United States Army Military History Institute)

John Speed, a construction engineer, would later become president of the Independent Line of Telegraph, running from Maine to Washington.[95]

Shortly after Fort Sumter, Frederic Speed helped to raise the first company from Maine to serve in the war. Since he was too young to hold office, Speed enlisted as a private, but he was soon mustered into service as a sergeant major of the 5th Maine Infantry. Sergeant Speed served with this unit at the first battle of Bull Run and the siege of Port Hudson. He was later promoted to the adjutancy of the 13th Maine Regiment, and on August 21, 1862, Speed advanced to captain and assistant adjutant general of volunteers. In 1865, he became an assistant adjutant general for the Department of Mississippi and joined the staff of General Dana in Vicksburg.[96]

Lt. Col. Reuben B. Hatch was the chief quartermaster for the Department of Mississippi in April 1865. Prior to the war, Hatch had been a merchant in Griggsville, Illinois, near the town of Springfield. He started his military career on April 25, 1861, at the age of forty-one, when he enlisted in the 8th Regiment of the Illinois Infantry as a first lieutenant and regimental quartermaster. Hatch was promoted to captain on August 3, 1861. The following month, he was assigned to duty at Cairo, Illinois, as an assistant quartermaster.[97]

The quartermaster department kept the army supplied with food, fuel, and materials and, in general, acted as army storekeeper. Since the quartermaster controlled large sums of government funds, many men during the Civil War used this position for personal gain. Reuben Hatch was one such man.

In November and December 1861, vast quantities of war materials were being delivered to Cairo to supply Grant's army, which was preparing to launch an assault on the Confederate forts on the Tennessee and Cumberland rivers. It was at Cairo that charges of fraud were first leveled against Hatch. As quartermaster, Captain Hatch purchased large amounts of lumber for the army, with Henry Wilcox (Hatch's clerk) and B. W. Thomas (Wilcox's brother-in-law) acting as agents. There is persuasive evidence that these three men were involved in a scheme to defraud the government in these transactions. Thomas, acting on behalf of Hatch and the quartermaster department, entered into several contracts with lumber dealers in Chicago. The scheme was simple. Apparently, Thomas would purchase wood from a dealer at a set price but demand that the dealer write up a receipt at a higher sum. One dealer, Webster Batchelder, sold Thomas 100,000 feet of lumber at $9.50 per 1,000 feet but was forced to give Thomas a receipt showing the price at $10.00. Hatch was to draw from the government funds according to the higher price but pay the dealers the lower price. The difference was the illegal profit shared by the three men. Thomas later testified that Hatch had, indeed, shared in these profits.[98]

The scheme almost worked. But Hatch and his partners had failed to anticipate the integrity of the lumbermen. In December the dealers approached the *Chicago Tribune*, informed the paper of Hatch's illegal scheme, and requested that the *Tribune* investigate the quartermaster department at Cairo. On December 12, 1861, the paper reported that several of the "most respectable lumber dealers in the City" had stated that the quartermaster department would approach a dealer and purchase lumber at one price but would make the dealer prepare a receipt or invoice at a higher price.[99]

After the story appeared in the *Tribune*, Brig. Gen. U. S. Grant ordered Capt. William S. Hillyer, his aide-de-camp, to proceed to Chicago to investigate the allegations. Hatch must have been concerned with what Hillyer would find, because he requested and was granted permission by Grant to accompany Hillyer. Hatch's stated purpose was to aid Hillyer in his investigation, but his real motive was to cover himself. On the day after arriving in Chicago, Hatch secretly met with the lumbermen. During this meeting, he revoked all the prior contracts that Thomas had entered into and agreed to pay the dealers $10 per 1,000 feet of lumber. This was of course more than the dealers were to receive under the previous contracts.[100]

Hatch then asked the lumbermen to put an ad in the *Tribune* stating that he had not taken anything from the government and was an honorable man. Evidently, the dealers refused Hatch's request, because the ad never appeared.

Hatch did obtain an affidavit from his close friend Robert Foss, one of the dealers, that stated that the lumbermen had in fact been paid $10 per 1,000 feet of lumber and neither Hatch nor Wilcox had received any portion of the money. Hillyer was not satisfied by this affidavit and told Hatch that he intended to take sworn statements from all involved parties. Hatch, distressed that the affidavit did not terminate the inquiry, tried to protect himself by telling Hillyer that Wilcox "had done very wrong" and would be discharged when Hatch returned to Cairo. Captain Hillyer, meanwhile, continued his investigation and eventually learned of Hatch's secret meeting with the lumbermen and the new contract.[101]

Hatch realized by the time he returned to Cairo that his cover-up efforts in Chicago had failed. Knowing that Wilcox could give damaging testimony against him, Hatch took steps to get his clerk out of Cairo. Hatch told Wilcox that should he stay in Cairo, he would be arrested and placed in the guardhouse where the army would keep him "longer than he would wish." Hatch assured Wilcox that if he left, Hatch would fix matters up within a week or two and Wilcox could then return. Wilcox went to a farm belonging to Hatch's brother, where he was instructed to stay until matters were cleared up. After Wilcox left Cairo, Hatch claimed that Wilcox had absconded.[102]

Hatch faced yet another problem however: the department books. One was an invoice ledger of property purchased and prices to be paid; another ledger recorded Hatch's distribution of money. These two books were later found on the bank of the Ohio River and had obviously washed ashore after being thrown in the river.[103]

Captain Hillyer, after completing his investigation, reported to Grant that Hatch had intentionally hindered his inquiry. This report was forwarded to Brig. Gen. M. C. Meigs, the quartermaster general of the army. After reviewing the report, Meigs ordered Grant to place Hatch under immediate arrest. Grant, in a letter to Meigs dated January 13, 1862, informed the quartermaster general that Hatch had been arrested "upon what seemed to (him) probable evidence of guilt as an accomplice."[104]

Hillyer's findings were referred by General Meigs to Simon Cameron, who was then serving as secretary of war, and Cameron approved Hatch's arrest. Meigs also wrote to Grant and ordered that a court-martial be convened to try Hatch.[105]

On January 22, 1862, General Grant informed Meigs that a court-martial had not been convened because further investigation was needed to determine if additional charges should be brought against Hatch. Grant reported that his investigation into the lumber purchases had disclosed other irregularities involving Hatch and the quartermaster department. Evidence indicated that Hatch had also sold army clothing and various supplies for personal gain. Furthermore, it was clear that Hatch had awarded forage bids to the highest, rather than the lowest, bidder. General Meigs was informed by Frank Chapman, a reporter for the New York *Herald*, that Hatch had chartered the steamboat *Keystone* for the government for $1,200 per month but had reported to the government a fee of $1,800. Grant also informed Meigs that Hatch had hired other boats at one price and issued vouchers at a different rate.[106] In addition, A. M. Davidson, who had worked for Hatch in the quartermaster harness shop at Cairo, wrote to Meigs on January 19, 1862, and accused Hatch of operating the harness and saddle shops for his personal profit.[107]

The adjutant general for the U.S. Army, Brig. Gen. Lorenzo Thomas, on January 30 wrote to Maj. Gen. Henry W. Halleck and demanded that Hatch be tried immediately. The next day, Halleck telegrammed Thomas:

> . . . court martial already ordered on Capt. Hatch. It is said that he kept two sets of books—public and private. After his arrest an attempt was made to destroy the latter by throwing them into the Missippi (sic). Fortunately they were recovered. It will take some time to compare the books and prepare charges and specifications.[108]

On February 12, Thomas A. Scott, an assistant to Edwin M. Stanton, the newly appointed secretary of war, wrote to Stanton to express his firm conviction that Hatch was guilty:

> I spent the whole of this day in examination of matters connected with the Quartermaster's Department at Cairo—the condition of affairs under Qr.M. Hatch was about as bad as could well be imagined. From the evidence we have been able to procure (herewith enclosed) you will perceive that a regular system of fraud appears to have been adopted. Many transactions, large and small, have been used by the Qr. Master, and perhaps others under him, to promote his private interests. Hatch was placed under arrest in January and confined to the limits of Cairo, but he is now absent on parole of honor on a

visit to his family in Illinois; in my judgment it is doubtful of his return knowing as he must that the evidence against him is overwhelming.[109]

The evidence of Hatch's guilt *was* overwhelming. Moreover, Hatch's efforts to conceal his crimes tended only to incriminate him further. In the face of such strong evidence, the army was ready to bring Capt. Reuben Hatch before a court-martial tribunal, but he would never be tried. While Hatch had failed to cover up his guilt, his brother succeeded in stopping the investigation. Captain Hatch's brother was O. M. Hatch, who served as the Illinois secretary of state from 1857 to 1865. A personal friend and advisor to President Lincoln, O. M. Hatch had been one of Lincoln's most active supporters during the 1860 campaign. Hatch and nine other men formed the Sangamon County Finance Committee and provided much of Lincoln's financial support. O. M. Hatch maintained his close ties to Lincoln into the White House. In October 1862, for example, Hatch accompanied the president on an inspection tour of the Army of the Potomac in Western Maryland.[110]

On February 24, 1862, O. M. Hatch, along with Illinois governor Richard Yates and Illinois auditor Jesse K. Dubois, wrote Lincoln that the charges against Reuben Hatch were "frivolous and without the shadow of foundation in fact." Yates and Dubois, besides being officials in Lincoln's home state, had also worked for Lincoln's election.[111]

President Lincoln, on March 20, forwarded O. M. Hatch's letter to Maj. John F. Lee, a judge advocate general. Lincoln placed the following endorsement to the letter:

> The within is signed by our Illinois Governor, Secretary of State and State Auditor—all good and true men—I also personally know Captain R.B. Hatch, and never before heard any thing against his character. If the Judge Advocate has the means of doing so I will thank him to give me his opinion of the case.[112]

In a response clearly expressing disappointment over Lincoln's apparent willingness to halt any further action against Hatch, Brigadier General Meigs, the officer in charge of the quartermaster department and Hatch's ultimate superior, attached his own endorsement to this letter by writing on March 21:

> Charges prepared by the Judge Advocate were preferred

against him, and while he is certainly entitled to trial which the General Commanding should give him as soon as the interests of the service will permit, it would be in my opinion highly improper to pass over such charges, and restore an officer to duty until a trial cleared him. If convicted he ought to be dismissed from the service.[113]

Hatch must have known by late March that his problems would soon be over. On March 26, Meigs wrote to Secretary of War Stanton and advised him that Lincoln wanted a civilian commission appointed to investigate the Hatch case. The president went so far as to recommend members of the commission. In June, Stanton appointed George S. Boutwell, a future U.S. senator from Massachusetts; Stephen T. Logan, Lincoln's former law partner in Springfield; and Charles A. Dana, former editor of the *Chicago Tribune*, who would later be appointed assistant secretary of war in Lincoln's administration. Because of illness, Logan had to resign and was replaced by Shelby M. Cullom, a citizen of Springfield and later governor of Illinois.[114]

Between June 18 and July 31, the three commissioners investigated 1,696 claims at Cairo. It is not surprising that Lincoln's handpicked commission acquitted Hatch of all blame.[115]

O. M. Hatch on August 11, 1862, wrote to Lincoln requesting that his brother be released and returned to duty. Three days later, the president wrote to the secretary of war:

Mr. Cullom says that the commission at Cairo investigated the accounts of R.B. Hatch and utterly failed to find anything wrong and he thinks the charges against him and his arrest are wrong. I desire, if Gen. Meigs assents, to release R.B. Hatch from arrest and return him to duty.[116]

Even with help from the president, however, Hatch did not return to active duty until February 1, 1863, when he was appointed chief quartermaster for the eastern district of Arkansas.[117]

One week after Hatch returned to active duty, Maj. Gen. U. S. Grant wrote to Lincoln to recommend that Hatch be promoted and assigned to duty with General Prentiss. Grant believed Hatch was "in every way worthy and entitled to the promotion." One must question Grant's motivation and sincerity when he wrote the above letter, because shortly after the Cairo incident, Grant told a friend that he believed many of the stories about his drinking problems circulating at that time were started by Reuben Hatch, who was himself something of a sot.[118]

On March 4, three more letters were written to the president on behalf of Captain Hatch. O. M. Hatch sent one stating that his brother had been unjustly treated, and Gen. B. M. Prentiss requested that Lincoln make Hatch a colonel. The third letter came from Shelby Cullom, one of the commissioners who investigated the fraud allegations at Cairo. Cullom wrote, "I believe Capt. Hatch to be an honest man and an energetic and faithful officer and I therefore most cordially join in the recommendation that will be presented to you for his promotion."[119]

Jackson Grimshaw, one of Lincoln's active supporters during the 1860 Republican convention, wrote to the president on March 15 also recommending a higher rank for Hatch. Grimshaw concluded his letter by writing, "I have asked but few favors and have received none, but I do now ask as an act of justice that Capt. Hatch be promoted."[120]

These letters evidently did not achieve their desired end, because Hatch in August 1863 was still a captain. On August 8, Hatch wrote to Gen. Lorenzo Thomas, the adjutant general of the army, tendering his resignation after two lawsuits had been filed against him in Cairo and in Pike County, Illinois. Maj. Gen. S. A. Hurlbut, the commander of the District of West Tennessee, on August 10 recommended that Hatch's resignation be accepted. He stated that Hatch was forced to resign because "his disloyal neighbors in Pike County, Ills. have so annoyed his wife as to compel her to sell off their home at a great loss and remove elsewhere." Two days later, General Grant approved Hatch's resignation and forwarded it to the headquarters of the army.[121]

Hatch was apparently willing to be discharged and returned to civilian life, but in a sudden reversal of intent, Hatch informed General Thomas that he was withdrawing his resignation because the problems that had forced his resignation had been resolved.[122]

Captain Hatch soon discovered though that withdrawing his resignation was not going to be an easy matter. On December 11, General Thomas referred Hatch's letter to General Meigs, the quartermaster general. Meigs evidently still had a bad opinion of Hatch after the allegations of fraud in Cairo, because he recommended that Hatch not be allowed to withdraw his resignation.

Meigs further pointed out that Hatch had been absent without leave for nearly three months.[123]

When faced with Meigs's recommendation, Hatch did what he had done in the past—he sought his politically influential brother for help. And as in the past, O. M. Hatch's connections got Reuben Hatch what he wanted. On January 14, 1864, Lincoln wrote to his secretary of war advising him that "my Illinois Sec. of State, O.M. Hatch, whom I would like to oblige, wants Capt. R.B. Hatch made a QM in the Regular Army—I know not whether it can be done conveniently, but if it can, I would like it."[124]

Richard Yates, the governor of Illinois, and Jesse Dubois, the state auditor, joined several other politicians and military leaders in a petition to the president, recommending Hatch's promotion to lieutenant colonel. Governor Yates followed the petition with a telegram to Secretary of War Stanton recommending Hatch's promotion.[125]

Captain Hatch's resignation became effective on January 22, 1864, but Hatch would soon be back in uniform. It was John Nicolay, President Lincoln's private secretary, who came to his rescue this time. In 1860, Nicolay had been a clerk for the secretary of state for Illinois, and his boss was O. M. Hatch. During the 1860 campaign, Nicolay left Hatch's office to assist Lincoln with his correspondence. He was paid $75 per month by the Sangamon County Finance Committee, which O. M. Hatch had helped found. When Lincoln was elected, Nicolay became the presidential private secretary.[126]

Charles Dana, assistant secretary of war and one of the commissioners who had investigated the fraud allegations at Cairo, wrote Nicolay on February 6 that the commission had found no evidence of wrongdoing on the part of Hatch. Dana concluded his letter by writing, "With regard to the honesty of Captain Hatch, it was the unanimous conclusion of the commission that there was no evidence before it to prove him other than an honest man."[127]

Nicolay forwarded Dana's letter to General Meigs. Meigs then wrote to Lincoln's secretary on February 6 that Dana's letter "removed a painful impression from my mind in regard to Hatch." He ended the letter by informing Nicolay that he would have no objection to allowing Hatch to withdraw his resignation. Six days later, Nicolay on "Executive Mansion" stationery requested the secretary of war to allow Hatch to remain in the army. Hatch's resignation was quickly withdrawn. On March 24, 1864, Reuben Hatch, by direction of the president, was officially promoted to the rank of lieutenant colonel and assigned to duty as the chief quartermaster of the 13th Army Corps.[128]

Colonel Hatch held this position during the disastrous Red River campaign. Following this failure, the 13th Army Corps was disbanded in June 1864, and Hatch returned to his home in Illinois to await further orders.[129]

Dissatisfied with the army's delay in appointing him to another position, Hatch again sought the influence of his brother and others. On July 31, Maj. Gen. U. S. Grant wrote from Fortress Monroe, Virginia, to General Meigs recommending that Hatch be assigned to duty at New Orleans as the quartermaster in charge of river transportation or as the chief quartermaster for the Department of the Gulf. When Meigs received the letter on August 2, there was the following endorsement attached to it: "I personally and heartily concur with General Grant in the written recommendation." This endorsement was dated August 1 and was signed "A. Lincoln."[130]

Hatch sent copies of Grant's letter with Lincoln's endorsement to Stanton on August 6. He also wrote the secretary of war that he wished to be assigned as chief quartermaster for the Department of the Gulf. Hatch stated that he had intended to give Grant's letter to Stanton personally while he was in Washington but had been unable to meet with him.[131]

In support, O. M. Hatch and Jackson Grimshaw wrote to Lincoln on August 23 asking that Hatch be promoted to full colonel and assigned to the Department of the Gulf, "where he can best serve the interests of the Government on account of his knowledge of and influence with the officers and soldiers of the Department."[132]

Despite these efforts, however, Lieutenant Colonel Hatch was ordered on October 1 to report to the Department of Arkansas at Little Rock, and on November 1 he reached the mouth of the White River. One month later he reported from his home in Quincy, Illinois, that he had reported to Major Stelle at Little Rock but due to ill health had tendered his resignation and was awaiting action on it.[133]

On January 6, 1865, Hatch, again from Quincy, announced he had just received a copy of an order dated November 19, 1864, directing him to proceed to New Orleans to stand before an examining board. He stated in his report that he had withdrawn his resignation and was going to proceed to New Orleans, where he would determine whether or not he would retender it.[134]

Hatch evidently believed that his appearance before this board would be nothing more than a formality, but to ensure his continued military career, he again sought the political influence of his brother. On January 4, 1865, Hatch wrote to his relative and reported:

> I just saw Captain Flagg, who has just returned from before the examining board in Milwaukee. He says it is more of a historical sketch of Quartermaster lives than an examination—and advises me to go fortified with letters to New Orleans which he thinks with the papers I have will pass me without the least trouble. Therefore, will you write a letter to the examining board briefly giving the part I took in 1861—in raising troops and so on—it will take you but a few minutes to do it—get, if you can, Governor Yates to sign it with you—I want to pass rather than be dismissed from the service.[135]

Hatch soon discovered that his appearance before this board was going to be more than just a formality. He appeared before the military examining board on February 1, dressed in civilian clothing, which greatly upset the officers on the board. Hatch defended his attire by informing the board that he had lost his uniform in May 1864 during the Red River campaign and had not acquired another.[136]

During the examination, he was tested on accounting principles and forms used in the quartermaster department. Board members found that Hatch had an almost total ignorance not only of the accounting systems, but of the regulations and orders governing the quartermaster department as well. The board, in concluding that Hatch was mentally unqualified to be an assistant quartermaster, held that

> Of the 60 officers who have appeared before this board not more than 1 or 2 can compare with Capt. Hatch in degree of deficiency. His accounting deficiency, in view of his long period of service, must be ascribed either to culpable

negligence, or to incapacity. In either case he is totally unfit to
discharge the duties of assistant quartermaster.[137]

In a critical delay of several months, however, the report submitted by this board was not approved by the quartermaster general
until June 3, 1865, when it was forwarded to the secretary of war
for action by the president.[138]

Only ten days after the examining board had found him totally
unfit to be an assistant quartermaster, Hatch was ordered to report
to General Dana as the chief quartermaster for the Department of
Mississippi. In early April, President Lincoln and General Grant
recommended that Hatch be promoted to full colonel and assigned
chief quartermaster of the Department of the Gulf. No action,
however, was ever taken on this recommendation.[139]

CHAPTER FOUR

The Final Trip

As the Army of Northern Virginia was furling its battle flags on April 9 at Appomattox, the *Sultana* was docking at St. Louis for the final time. The steamer had arrived at her home port with a full load of passengers. An advertisement in the *Daily Missouri Democrat* on April 10 announced that the *Sultana* would be leaving the next afternoon at four o'clock.[140] The steamer, however, did not set out on the 11th. On April 12, John Schaffer and John Maquire, steamboat inspectors stationed at St. Louis, examined the *Sultana*, found the boat, including her boilers, to be structurally sound, and executed a certificate stating the following:

> We further certify, that the equipment of the vessel throughout, including pipes, pumps and other means to keep water up to the point aftersaid, hose, boats, life preservers, spark-arrestors, blocks, rigging, anchors, and other things are in conformity with the provisions of law; and that we declare it to be our deliberate conviction, founded upon the inspection we have made, that the vessel may be employed as a steamer upon the waters herein specified, without peril to life from imperfection of form, materials, workmanship, or arrangement of the several parts or from age or use. . . .[141]

Later that same day, the crew of the *Sultana* watched St. Louis disappear from sight as the steamer headed downriver. The boat reached her next stop at Cairo, Illinois, at one o'clock on the following morning. The steamer would remain docked here until April 15.[142]

Third —INSPECTION.

INSPECTOR'S CERTIFICATE.

Steamer *Sultana*

No.

ST␣␣ OF MISSOURI,
␣RICT OF ST. LOUIS. } ss

Application having been made in writing to the subscribers, Inspectors for␣␣␣ District to inspect the Steamer ␣␣␣␣ of ␣␣␣␣ in the State of ␣␣␣␣ whereof ␣␣␣␣ is Master, we having performed that service, now, on this ␣␣ day of ␣␣␣ A. D. 186␣, Do Certify that she was built at ␣␣␣␣ in the State of ␣␣␣ in the year 18␣␣; is of ␣␣␣ tons burthen, and is in all respects staunch, seaworthy, and in good condition for navigation having suitable means for escape from the main to the upper deck, in case of accident; that she is provided with ␣␣ State rooms, with ␣␣ berths to each; has ␣␣ permanent cabin and ␣␣ extra or movable cabin berths, and has suitable accommodations for ␣␣ cabin passengers. That she has also berths suitable for deck or other class passengers to accommodate ␣␣ persons. That she is a steamer sailing to and from inland ports a distance of five hundred miles or upward; and is permitted to carry ␣␣␣ deck passengers, except when making voyages between St. Louis and New Orleans, when the following rules shall govern to wit:

[A berth, bunk or hammock, shall have a space of at least 6 feet long, 2 inches wide, and 2 feet high, clear of obstruction, and easy of access for each passenger. Children one year old or less shall not be included in the calculation. Two Children, whose united ages shall not exceed sixteen years, shall be counted as one passenger. When there are four or more tiers of berths in height, ␣␣␣ square feet of deck-room shall be allowed for each passenger; when there are three tiers of berths in height, twelve square feet for each passenger; when there are two tiers of berths in height, fourteen square feet for each passenger. When there shall be one tier of berths, or where there are no berths, fifteen square feet shall be allowed each passenger. These spaces shall be calculated only in suitably enclosed deck-rooms, which shall be properly warmed in cold weather, and properly ventilated at all times.]

That she is provided with ␣␣ high pressure boilers, ␣␣ feet long, and ␣␣ inches in diameter, of cylindrical form, of iron, ␣␣ inch in thickness, with ␣␣␣ inch return flues in each, constructed of iron of ␣␣ of an inch in thickness; and made in the year 18␣␣; that they are in all respects conformable to law. That each boiler has been subjected to a hydrostatic pressure of ␣␣ pounds to the square inch; that the maximum working power allowed was ␣␣ determined by the rule prescribed by the Act of August 30th, 1852, the iron manufactured by and stamped ␣␣␣ ␣␣␣ That there are ␣␣ safety valves, with ␣␣ square inches area; that the load prescribed to each is such as to allow but ␣␣␣ pounds pressure per square inch, the whole left in charge of the Engineer, and withdrawn from interference of the officers of the boat, except the Engineer; has ␣␣ supply pipes of ␣␣ inches each in diameter, and has sufficient means to keep the water at all times and under all circumstances up to four inches over the flues; has ␣␣ steam pipes of ␣␣ inches in diameter each; has ␣␣ high pressure engines with cylinders ␣␣ inches in diameter each, and ␣␣ feet stroke; has ␣␣ forcing pumps of ␣␣ inches plunge and ␣␣ inches stroke each, worked by ␣␣␣ engine; has ␣␣ water gauges and ␣␣ steam gauges, all properly secured; uses the alloyed metal, with ␣␣␣ guards which fuses at ␣␣ pounds pressure; has ␣␣ fire forcing pumps of ␣␣ inches stroke each, worked ␣␣ inches in diameter of plunge, ␣␣ worked by hand; has ␣␣␣ feet of hose ␣␣ buckets and ␣␣ axes; has a metalic life-boat in good order, and ␣␣␣; has ␣␣ life-preservers, and ␣␣ floats, containing ␣␣␣ superficial feet; has additional steering apparatus.

We Further Certify, That the equipments of the vessel throughout, including pipes, pumps and other means to keep water up to the point aforesaid; hose, boats, life-preservers, spark-arresters, block, rigging, anchors and other things, are in conformity with the provisions of law; and that we believe it to be our deliberate conviction, founded upon the inspection we have made, that the vessel may be employed as a steamer upon the waters herein named, without peril to life from any imperfection of hull, materials, workmanship, or arrangement of the several parts, or from age or use and we further certify, that the said vessel is to run within the following limits, to wit:

From the Port of St. Louis to the Port of *New Orleans on Mississippi* touching at the intermediate places and back; and also to other ports, and on waters usually navigated by boats of the same class.

Signed,

John Schaffer (SEAL)

Wm Maguire (SEAL)

STATE OF MISSOURI,
District of St. Louis. Personally appeared before me, the undersigned, ␣␣␣ in and for the said District, ␣␣␣ Maguire and ␣␣␣ Schaffer ␣␣␣ duly appointed Inspectors of Hulls and Steam Boilers for the District of St. Louis, and made solemn oath that the annexed Certificate of Inspection is just and true.

Sworn and subscribed before me, on this ␣␣ day of ␣␣␣ A. D. 186␣

[Signed] ␣␣␣ (SEAL)

I Hereby Certify, that the above is a true copy of the original on file in this office.

Port of ␣␣␣ 13 day of ␣␣␣ 186␣ By ␣␣␣ Deputy

DAILY DISPATCH PRINT—ST. LOUIS.

The Sultana *was inspected on April 12, 1865, at St. Louis. The certificate certified that the vessel could be employed as a steamer on the Mississippi River without peril to life.* (National Archives)

While the *Sultana* was tied up at Cairo, tragic history was being made in Washington, D.C. On the evening of April 14, Abraham Lincoln and his wife were walking up the steps of Ford's Theatre; soon Lincoln would be carried down these same steps, mortally wounded. The president died early the next morning. News of Lincoln's death reached Cairo that same morning, and bells on the steamboats and in the churches were set ringing in memory of the fallen leader.[143] The *Sultana* was the first boat to steam southward on the morning of the 15th. Since all telegraph communications with the South had been cut off by order of Secretary of War Stanton, the steamer carried the grim news of the death of the president with her down the Mississippi River.[144]

By the morning of April 16, the boat's pilot was nosing the *Sultana* toward the cobblestoned levee at Memphis. The Memphis *Daily Bulletin*, describing the *Sultana* as a first-class boat, reported that the steamer would continue for New Orleans that same morning.[145]

As the *Sultana* backed away from the Memphis dock and headed toward Vicksburg, Captain Mason was aware that prisoners were waiting outside Vicksburg for transportation to Jefferson Barracks, Missouri, and Camp Chase, Ohio. Mason felt that his boat was entitled to a load of these men because she belonged to the Merchants' and People's line, which had contracted with the government for transporting freight and troops. This line, formed in February 1865, was a loose organization of independently owned steamboats, which included the *Henry Ames* and the *Lady Gay*, in addition to the *Sultana*.[146]

Mason, however, may have been driven by more personal reasons in his determination to secure a full load of troops at Vicksburg on his trip back upriver. The military was offering five dollars per enlisted man and ten dollars per officer for the transportation of the prisoners.[147] These revenues were desperately needed by Mason, who in April 1865 may have found himself in financial trouble. In March 1864, when he and other investors purchased the *Sultana*, Mason owned a three-eighths interest. By April 1865, Mason had sold one-eight of his share to his first clerk, William J. Gambrel. Furthermore, Mason evidently conveyed a one-sixteenth interest to William Shands and a one-eighth interest to De Bow & Company, thus leaving himself a minority owner with

The New Orleans waterfront. The Sultana started her ill-fated journey from here on April 21, 1865. (From the collection of the Public Library of Cincinnati and Hamilton County)

only a one-sixteenth interest. On this final trip downriver, everything Captain Mason owned was invested in this small share of the
Sultana.[148] Mason intended to use whatever influence he could to
ensure that the *Sultana* won a large number of prisoners for shipment out of Vicksburg.

As the *Sultana* pulled up to the wharfboat at Vicksburg, Col. Reuben B. Hatch was waiting. At a meeting with Hatch and Miles Sells,
the *Sultana*'s agent at Vicksburg, Mason demanded that his boat be
given a load of prisoners for his upriver journey. Hatch promised
Mason troops for his boat.[149]

Reuben Hatch was not the only officer Mason would meet. While
Mason was still at the Vicksburg riverfront, he was greeted by Brig.
Gen. Morgan L. Smith, a fellow citizen of St. Louis and former riverboat captain himself. Smith brought Mason and Sells into
Vicksburg. Mason informed the general that he understood there
was a good deal of government freight and prisoners waiting to be
shipped north, and Mason wanted assurance that he would be
granted a full shipment for his return trip. Smith guaranteed Mason a full load of the paroled troops when the *Sultana* arrived back
in Vicksburg. General Smith further instructed Captain Mason to
inform him if Hatch or Frederic Speed refused to turn the prisoners over to the *Sultana*. Confident of the deal struck with Smith
and Hatch, Mason reboarded his steamer and headed toward New
Orleans.[150]

The *Sultana* arrived at the Crescent City on April 19, and the next
day the New Orleans *Picayune* carried the following notice:

> The regular and unsurpassed passenger packet *Sultana*, in
> command of J.C. Mason, departs this evening at five o'clock for
> St. Louis, Cairo, Memphis and all way landings. The *Sultana* is a
> good boat, as well as a fleet one. Mr. Wm. Gambrel has control
> of the office while friend James McGinty will be found in the
> Saloon, where everything of the "spirit" order can be had in
> due time.[151]

On Friday, April 21, the newspaper updated its report and stated
that the steamer "having been unavoidably detained last evening
leaves this morning at 10 o'clock."[152] The following day the *Picayune* explained the delay as an effort to augment the *Sultana*'s load
of passengers and freight, but the postponed departure date did
little to attract further travelers.[153]

The last prisoner exchange at Camp Fisk, near Vicksburg, in late April, 1865. (Library of Congress)

The wharf at Vicksburg. (From the collection of the Public Library of Cincinnati and Hamilton County)

A few people, however, did take notice of the *Picayune* article and purchased passage on the *Sultana*—among them, twelve members of the Samuel Spikes family from Assumption Parish, Louisiana, on their way to establish a new home in the North.[154]

The steamer backed away from the Gravier Street dock, as scheduled, on the morning of April 21, 1865, carrying approximately 250 passengers and crew.[155] Besides Mason, the officers of the *Sultana* on her final trip were: William Jordan Gambrel, the first clerk; William Straton, the second clerk; William Rowberry, first mate; George Kayton and Henry Ingraham, the pilots; Nathan Wintringer, the chief engineer; Samuel Clemens, the assistant engineer; Henry Cross, the first stewart; and George Slater, the second stewart.[156]

Chief engineer Nathan Wintringer kept an especially close watch on the steamer's boilers. Wintringer's concern appears to have been warranted by later statements made by Henry J. Lyda. Lyda, a crewman who disembarked only two hours before the steamer left New Orleans for the final time, reported that the boilers had been patched or repaired at Natchez and Vicksburg on the two previous trips.[157] When the *Sultana* was ten hours south of Vicksburg this final time, Wintringer discovered steam escaping from a small crack on the middle larboard boiler.[158] The leak was serious enough to cause Wintringer to refuse to go any farther than Vicksburg unless the necessary repairs were made. The steamer continued up the Mississippi toward Vicksburg, but at greatly reduced speed.[159]

While the boat slowly plowed up the flooded river, events in Vicksburg were escalating the cost in human life to be paid in the *Sultana* disaster. The Confederates having finally agreed to parole the prisoners at Camp Fisk, General Dana ordered Captain Speed to prepare the rolls for the men as quickly as possible and send them north. Dana further instructed Speed to place 1,000 soldiers on each of the regular steamers docking at Vicksburg.[160]

In April 1865, the Atlantic and Mississippi Steamboat Line and the Merchants' and People's line were competing for transport of Federal prisoners out of Vicksburg. The first steamer to receive a portion of these men was the *Henry Ames*, a boat belonging to the Merchants' and People's line, which had officially contracted with the army to transport troops and freight. When this steamer arrived on April 22, the rolls for 800 men had been drawn up.

After a short delay, however, the number of prisoners loaded had risen to 1,300. General Dana, who stated at the time that he "had taken great interest in expediting the departure of these brave fellows to their homes," was present to watch the *Henry Ames* steam away from Vicksburg.[161] On board the *Henry Ames* was Epenetus W. McIntosh, a private with the 14th Illinois Infantry. This soldier, when captured on October 4, 1864, at Ackworth, Georgia, weighed 175 pounds, but when he was released from Andersonville, he weighed only 80 pounds.[162]

The *Olive Branch* pulled into Vicksburg at one o'clock on the morning of April 23. This steamer, a member of the Atlantic and Mississippi line, left later the same day with a cargo of 700 soldiers.[163] It was shortly after the *Olive Branch* left Vicksburg that allegations of bribery over the transporting of prisoners were first leveled. Captain Speed approached General Dana and requested authority to arrest Captain Kerns, the quartermaster in charge of river transportation. Speed informed Dana that he had ordered the quartermaster department to report immediately to him the arrival of all steamers. The *Olive Branch*, according to Speed, had arrived at 1 A.M., but Kerns had failed to advise him. Speed also told Dana that Kerns had been given "a pecuniary consideration" by the Merchants' and People's line to detain the prisoners until one of its boats could arrive to take them. The next boat to arrive would be the *Sultana*, which belonged to this line. General Dana refused to take any action against Kerns until a full investigation into the matter had been conducted.[164]

Frederic Speed was basing his allegations against Kerns on information he had received from Reuben Hatch. When Speed asked Hatch why the arrival of the *Olive Branch* had not been reported to him until 9 A.M. on April 23, Hatch informed him that Kerns had also failed to report to him the steamer's arrival and accused Kerns himself of accepting money to detain the prisoners at Vicksburg.[165] Thus, it was Hatch, Kern's superior, who had actually introduced the charges of bribery. A close examination of the evidence indicates that Kerns, in fact, had nothing to do with the *Olive Branch*. Kerns later testified that he had "timely reported" the steamer's arrival to Hatch, who was then supposed to inform Speed. Evidently Hatch failed to do this. Furthermore, it was Hatch and not Kerns who had made the arrangements with the captain of the *Olive*

Branch on April 23 to transport a portion of the prisoners.[166] One must wonder then if Hatch, by pointing the finger of guilt at Kerns, was merely trying to cover up his own illegal acts.

The *Sultana* finally docked at Vicksburg at 8:45 P.M. on April 23. Immediately after the steamer was safely moored, chief engineer Nathan Wintringer sought out R. G. Taylor, a local boilermaker, and informed Taylor that the *Sultana's* boilers had given out and that the boat could go no farther. Upon inspection, Taylor discovered a bulge on the middle larboard boiler. Taylor then asked Wintringer why he had not had the boiler repaired at New Orleans and was informed that there was no evidence of leaking at that time. Wintringer and Captain Mason instructed the boilermaker to repair the bulging seam and have the *Sultana* ready to leave Vicksburg as quickly as possible. Taylor told both Mason and Wintringer that for reasons of safety two sheets on the boiler needed to be replaced. He further stated that if he were not allowed to make the repairs he thought fit, he would have nothing more to do with the *Sultana*.[167]

Taylor walked off the steamer only to be followed close behind by Wintringer who convinced Taylor to do the best he could under the circumstances. Mason, evidently concerned about the time required to replace the two sheets, eventually persuaded Taylor to limit his repairs to a patch measuring only twenty-six by eleven inches. All the while, Mason assured Taylor that he would have the latter's full recommendations carried out when the steamer reached St. Louis. The boilermaker, who had only a short time before refused to take on responsibility for the boiler unless he was allowed to make thorough repairs, agreed in the end merely to patch the boiler. During his repairs Taylor told Wintringer that he first needed to force back the bulge on the boiler before applying the patch. This he was not allowed to do. The patch was fitted directly over the bulge. Even so, it would take Taylor over twenty hours to complete this operation. Wintringer hastily approved Taylor's work, stating that the repairs were adequate to continue upriver. But Taylor, the expert with twenty-eight years experience, did not consider the boiler safe after the limited repairs and is on record as stating that all the boilers on the *Sultana* appeared to him to have been burned by the time the boat reached Vicksburg owing to an insufficient supply of water.[168]

Since the *Sultana* had arrived so closely on the heels of the departing *Olive Branch*, the rolls for only 300 to 400 prisoners at the parole camp had been prepared. For this reason, Captain Speed informed Dana that no prisoners were to be loaded on the *Sultana*.[169] Mason, though, had received assurances from both General Smith and Colonel Hatch that the *Sultana* would secure a load of prisoners, and while the steamer was undergoing repairs, Mason was actively attempting to obtain as many prisoners as possible for his vessel.[170] Mason first called on Hatch at his Vicksburg boarding-house. Miles Sells, agent for the *Sultana*, joined him. Mason informed Hatch that he wanted all the men his boat could carry for the upriver trip.[171] Hatch told Mason that he had just been informed by Speed that only 300 men were ready for shipment. Mason replied that it would hardly pay him to wait until the next day for that number of men and reissued his claim to a larger share of the prisoners.[172] Hatch informed Mason that Speed indeed wanted to transport the remaining prisoners on a single boat, but he did not know if Speed could have the rolls for the men prepared in time for the *Sultana*'s scheduled departure. Hatch believed the rolls could be prepared by the next Tuesday (April 25); Speed calculated a later date (April 27).[173] Hatch commented that Speed was too slow in preparing the rolls and instructed Mason to check with Speed about obtaining more prisoners for his steamer.[174]

Later on the night of April 23, Captain Mason met with Frederic Speed for the first time.[175] Speed informed Mason that no men were ready to go the next day, as the rolls for only 300 of them had been completed. And he did not think it would be possible to get even that number checked and into Vicksburg before Mason would want to leave. Speed told Mason, however, that if he were prepared to wait, he would be given all the men that could be readied.[176] Mason, at this point, reiterated his claim to the prisoners because his boat belonged to the Merchants' and People's line. Speed then upped the number of prisoners to 700 men, and Mason agreed to wait until morning to pull out of Vicksburg. (Mason did not tell Speed that the *Sultana* would be detained at Vicksburg anyway because of repairs to one of her boilers.)[177]

Mason was not pleased with Speed's handling of the troop transfer and headed next for the office of General Smith. Mason was still determined on a full load of men for his trip upriver to St. Louis and was probably banking on Smith's influence to get them. It is certain that Mason had not forgotten Smith's promise of a major load of prisoners when the *Sultana* had last stopped at Vicksburg on her way downriver. As will be remembered, Smith had also instructed Mason to inform him if Speed refused to turn the men over to him.[178] According to Miles Sells, who joined Mason in the latest meeting with Smith, Mason simply told Smith that the *Sultana* was prepared to wait for the prisoners.[179]

At General Smith's office, Mason was introduced to Capt. George Williams, who had just arrived at Vicksburg. Mason expressed his disapproval of the way in which the Federal authorities at Vicksburg were handling the transfer of the prisoners north, and he informed Williams that he was planning to register a complaint in Washington against the Exchange Office. In Mason's view, the opposition line was being awarded the business of shipping troops that contractually belonged to his line. (The *Henry Ames*, a contract boat, had won 1,300 men, while the *Olive Branch*, belonging to the opposition line, had received 700.) Williams then told Mason that he was very anxious that the prisoners be shipped northward as soon as possible because they had been promised repeatedly that they were to be released. Williams followed with a statement that effectively sealed the fate of many of the prisoners waiting at Camp Fisk: There would be no trouble preparing the prisoner rolls because the men could be just as properly checked as they boarded the boat; the rolls did not have to be prepared, as Speed insisted, in advance of their departure from Camp Fisk. After this meeting, Mason confided to Miles Sells that "there would be no trouble about getting all the men he wanted."[180]

Captain Speed was finishing his supper when he was summoned by an orderly to the adjutant's office. When he arrived, he encountered George Williams and Captain Mason. Williams asked Speed if it was not possible to get all the remaining prisoners onto the *Sultana* the following day and stated that he was eager to have the whole matter concluded. Speed, objecting to the idea that all the men board Mason's boat before the preparation of the rolls, informed Williams that a list of only 400 men had been drawn up. As the meeting was concluding, Williams suggested to Speed that there was no reason to prepare the rolls in advance, that the names of the prisoners would be checked against the books maintained at

Pvt. James Hines, Company K, 58th Ohio Infantry. Twenty-two military guards boarded the Sultana *at Vicksburg. Hines and five other guards survived.* (Courtesy of Ron Chojnacki)

the parole camp, and that the rolls could be prepared after the *Sultana* left Vicksburg.[181]

Later that night, another meeting occurred in Colonel Hatch's room with Speed and Williams present. These officers again discussed whether or not all the prisoners then at Vicksburg could be shipped the next day on the *Sultana*. Speed continued with his argument that the rolls could not be prepared in time. Williams countered that there was no good reason to prepare the rolls in advance and that the men could be shipped the following day. In the end, Williams won over Speed. At the conclusion of this fateful meeting, it was agreed that all the prisoners then at Vicksburg were to be shipped on the *Sultana* the 24th of April.[182]

Speed issued Special Order No. 139, which instructed a detail of guards to be placed on the *Sultana* the next day. The detail was to consist of one officer, three noncommissioned officers, and eighteen privates with the 58th Ohio Infantry.[183] This order would later become a death warrant for 16 of these soldiers.[184] Meanwhile, Captain Williams ordered Lt. Edwin Davenport, an assistant commissioner of exchange, to Camp Fisk with instructions to ready the ragged Federal troops for shipment as quickly as possible.[185]

Frederic Speed then reported to General Dana that he and Captain Williams had decided to ship all the remaining prisoners at Vicksburg on the *Sultana*. Dana was also informed that the total number of prisoners to be shipped would be between 1,300 and 1,400. Dana expressed his satisfaction with this arrangement.[186]

On the morning of April 24, Colonel Hatch was evidently still concerned that Speed would not place all the prisoners on the *Sultana*, as had been agreed upon the previous evening. In order to reconfirm their agreement, Hatch visited Speed early that day, arriving before Speed or his roommate, Capt. H. H. Emmon, had been allowed time to dress. According to Emmon, Speed and Hatch talked for some twenty minutes, and at the conclusion of the meeting, they had once more agreed that all the prisoners were to go on the *Sultana*.[187]

Speed then joined George Williams and traveled with him by train to the parole camp. During the ride to Camp Fisk, the two officers discussed the impending prisoner transfer. Williams stated that as there were stories of bribery circulating around Vicksburg, the men had better be delivered to a boat belonging to the contract line. It then would be the responsibility of the quartermaster to see that they boarded the *Sultana* or another boat. Speed agreed that the soldiers should be given to the Merchants' and People's line as long as that line offered "equal facilities."[188]

Command of the prisoner transfer, however, had yet to be clearly established. According to Williams, the command belonged to Frederic Speed, who had been charged with keeping prisoner records. Williams later testified that when he arrived back in Vicksburg on April 23, he wanted to obtain these records but was informed by Speed that since there were only 1,300 to 1,400 men remaining, he would handle the final shipment himself.[189] Speed, on the other hand, would later testify that it was Williams who took active charge of the prisoner transfer at this point and that he was simply acting in conjunction with Williams.[190]

When Speed and Williams arrived at Camp Fisk, they immediately set about boarding the men on the trains to Vicksburg. Grouped according to their native states, the prisoners boarded the trains as their names were called.[191]

By April 24, 2,000 of these men had already been shipped north. The military, however, had not ascertained the number of prisoners remaining at the parole camp, and the exact number of soldiers to be shipped aboard the *Sultana* was yet to be determined. Captain Speed was under the impression that 1,300 to 1,400 prisoners were still housed at the camp and the army hospital.[192] His decision to load all the men on the *Sultana* on April 24 was based on this estimate. (Actually, the number was probably closer to 2,400.) Part of Speed's miscalculation must owe to his failure to prepare the rolls in advance. Had he done so, Speed might have anticipated the gross overcrowding of troops on the *Sultana*.

Williams and Speed were determined to get the prisoners into Vicksburg and onto the *Sultana* as quickly as possible, even if they endangered the men in the process. According to Edward D. Butler, the superintendent of railroads at Vicksburg, Speed placed more prisoners on the trains than could be safely carried. At one point, Butler cautioned Speed that one train had all the soldiers it could possibly transport, but Speed ordered on an additional 200 men.[193]

On the morning of April 24, Mason met with Kerns, who, recognizing that the *Sultana* had been docked at Vicksburg for an unusually long time, asked Mason why he was still in port. Mason informed Kerns that he was waiting for a load of prisoners. This was Kerns's first knowledge of the decision reached the night before. Mason also told Kerns that he was having a boiler on the *Sultana* patched and that he expected the repairs to be made by the time the prisoners were ready to board.[194]

After Mason left the quartermaster's office, Kerns received a written order from department headquarters stating that all prisoners remaining at Four Mile Bridge and the hospital at Big Black were to be organized and sent to Camp Chase, Ohio. The order further provided that the quartermaster's department was to furnish transportation. The remainder of the message was puzzling: "Copy furnished Captain of the *Sultana*." Kerns understood from this postscript that the *Sultana* had already been selected to carry the troops without his intervention. He later testified that it was unusual for a captain of a boat to be given a copy of such an order.[195]

Another steamer belonging to the Merchants' and People's line, the *Lady Gay*, arrived at Vicksburg at approximately 10 A.M. on April 24.[196] As has already been pointed out, Speed and Williams had both indicated that steamers from this line should be favored over boats of competing lines. One would think then that with the enormous number of prisoners scheduled to be shipped out of Vicksburg, the *Lady Gay*, with a capacity greater than that of the *Sultana*, could take on a sizeable share of the troops. (Captain Kerns, in fact, believed that action should be taken to divide the men.) It is interesting to note, too, that while Speed, who along with Williams had actual command of the prisoner transfer, was unsure of the exact number of men to be shipped that day, Kerns, who had little or no involvement with the prisoners, believed that there were too many for one steamer.[197]

Convinced that some of the prisoners should be placed on the larger *Lady Gay*, Kerns went to Reuben Hatch and inquired if the *Lady Gay* should not be detained and a portion of the troops loaded onto her. Hatch claimed that he knew nothing about the matter and requested that Kerns delay the steamer's departure until he could telegram Speed at the parole camp. Kerns then asked Captain Williamson of the *Lady Gay* to wait until he received further instructions. Hatch, despite his claim that he had nothing to do with the prisoner transfer, did telegram Speed at the parole camp to ask

The steamer Lady Gay. She steamed away from Vicksburg without a single prisoner. (From the collection of the Public Library of Cincinnati and Hamilton County)

if the *Lady Gay* should not take part of the prisoners. Later, Hatch showed Kerns a telegram he had received from Speed stating that all the men could be put on one boat—the *Sultana*. Speed, in answering Hatch's inquiry, was still figuring on a shipment of 1,300 to 1,400 men that day. General Smith and Captain Williamson of the *Lady Gay* went to Kerns's office shortly after Kerns had been shown Speed's telegram. Informed of Speed's determination to reserve all troops for the *Sultana*, Smith instructed Kerns to allow the *Lady Gay* to proceed upriver. The *Lady Gay* pulled out of Vicksburg around noon that day without a single prisoner on board.[198]

A few minutes after the departure of the *Lady Gay*, the first trainload of prisoners, accompanied by Captain Williams, pulled into Vicksburg. Williams had agreed to conduct the men onto the steamer and keep track of their number. Speed remained at Camp Fisk to supervise the loading of prisoners on the trains.[199]

William Boor, a private in Company D of the 64th Ohio Volunteer Infantry, was on this first trainload of men to board the steamer. As he and his comrades were being lead to the hurricane deck, he heard the sound of hammering near the boat's boilers. Curious over the noise, Boor went to investigate and discovered that repairs were being made to one of the *Sultana*'s boilers. Boor informed his friends that he did not believe the boilers were safe and that if there were an explosion "we would go higher than a kite." Boor and five of his fellow soldiers moved to relative safety on the boiler deck.[200]

Williams later estimated that 570 men arrived in Vicksburg on the first train. These prisoners joined 398 soldiers already placed on the steamer whom Williams thought probably came from the hospital.[201] Approximately 968 men had thus boarded a boat with a legal carrying capacity of only 376. This fact was later confirmed by the steamer's first clerk, William J. Gambrel. When Captain Kerns asked Gambrel how many men were aboard so far, Gambrel informed him that there were 1,000 on the boat and another 500 expected. Kerns asked the first clerk if he did not think that would be too large a load for the steamer. Gambrel told him that he thought the boat could safety accommodate all the men.[202]

Meanwhile, at the wharfboat, Captain Williams was meeting with Lt. William Tillinghast, an assistant quartermaster under Colonel Hatch. Tillinghast informed Williams that Speed was receiving 50 cents per head for furnishing prisoners to one of the steamboat lines. This news greatly angered Williams and firmly convinced him that Speed was being bribed. Williams also believed that the Atlantic and Mississippi Steamboat Line was behind the bribe, and he was determined that this line was not going to get a single prisoner.[203] There is no evidence to suggest that Speed had taken any bribes regarding the prisoner transfer. And while there is no proof that Speed was even offered money by either of the steamboat lines, there is evidence of bribery being used to win passengers. In fact, the army officer at Vicksburg who was offered money by the steamer line was not Speed, but Tillinghast, the very man who had accused Speed of taking bribes. It is known, for example, that William C. Jones, agent for the Atlantic and Mississippi line at Vicksburg offered Tillinghast 15 cents for every man he could secure for Jones.[204] And Jones was not the only man to present Tillinghast with a bribe. According to James P. McGuire, a steamboat passenger agent at Vicksburg, Tillinghast stated that Captain Mason had told him "that if he (Mason) had his (Tillinghast's) measure, it should cost him nothing for clothing for a whole year and that not having his measure, he had made it all right anyhow."[205] Tillinghast did not reveal that bribes had been offered to him until after the events of April 27.[206] Tillinghast's allegations of bribery on the part of Speed may have been an attempt on his part to ensure that the *Sultana* received all the prisoners remaining at Vicksburg.

A second train from the parole camp arrived at Vicksburg at approximately 2:15 P.M. carrying an additional 400 prisoners. George Williams, who had earlier agreed to count the soldiers as they boarded the steamer, was not at the dock and never counted these men as they walked across the gangplank.[207] In fact, Williams was never aware that this trainload of soldiers had boarded the *Sultana*.

At approximately 3 P.M., the *Pauline Carroll*, a boat belonging to the Atlantic and Mississippi line, tied up beside the *Sultana*. When the gangplank was lowered, Mr. Delgado, the steamer's first clerk, and William Geins, a passenger, went in search of passengers for the upriver trip. The first man they met was Reuben Hatch. Delgado told Geins that Hatch was just the man he wanted to see. Hatch and Delgado talked privately and then boarded the *Pauline*

William J. Gambrel. First clerk and part owner of the Sultana, *Gambrel would not survive his steamer's final trip.* (Courtesy of Allen Soper, Jr.)

Carroll to meet with his master, Capt. H. L. White. Geins understood that Delgado wanted some of the prisoners, since his steamer had few passengers for the journey to St. Louis.[208]

By the time the *Pauline Carroll* reached Vicksburg, Kerns was firmly convinced that the number of prisoners remaining at Camp Fisk was too large for one boat. Kerns informed Hatch, his superior, that the *Pauline Carroll* was in port and going upriver empty. He asked Hatch if this steamer should receive a portion of the prisoners.[209] Hatch again sent a telegram to Captain Speed at the parole camp that read: "Is there more prisoners than can go on the *Sultana*. If so the *Pauline Carroll* has arrived shall I detain her?" Speed, still mistakenly assuming that there were 1,400 prisoners remaining to be shipped, replied: "No they can all go on one boat." After reading Speed's response, Hatch told Kerns that he would now have nothing more to do with the matter. The chief quartermaster told Kerns that he could not detain the *Pauline Carroll*.[210]

One must admire the persistence of William Kerns, because after getting no help from Hatch, he sought out General Smith to protest against the number of men scheduled to board the *Sultana*. Kerns pleaded with Smith to "interpose his influence and have part of the prisoners go on the *Pauline Carroll*." Smith, however, informed Kerns that he would take no further part in the prisoner transfer, since the matter had been taken out of his hands by General Dana. Smith did state that if Kerns wanted to detain the steamer he could and that this would meet with his approval. Smith effectively washed his hands of the problem.[211]

Having failed with Smith, Kerns boarded the *Pauline Carroll* to meet with her master, Captain White and her agent, William C. Jones. Both men told Kerns that they wanted a load of prisoners. But White also said that he was behind schedule and did not want to wait unless he could be guaranteed a load of troops. Kerns told White that he could not guarantee anything but thought if White would wait, some troops would be placed on his boat. Unwilling to assume the responsibility of ordering White to remain at Vicksburg, Kerns gave him the option of voluntarily remaining.[212]

Captain Kerns went aboard the *Sultana* and asked Captain Mason the number of men on his boat. Mason answered that he was carrying 1,000 men and expected some 600 more. (In reality, the number then on board was approximately 1,400.) Kerns then asked Mason if he thought there was enough room for all of them and was assured that there was. Mason told Kerns that he had carried more men in the past than he expected to receive that day. He also claimed that the men were not equipped with gear and thus took up less room.[213]

Dr. George S. Kemble, the medical director for the Department of Mississippi, strongly disagreed with Mason on the number of passengers the *Sultana* could carry. During the early afternoon, Kemble had placed 23 prisoners confined to cots on the boat. Visiting the steamer shortly after the second trainload of prisoners had boarded, Kemble concluded that the *Sultana* was too crowded for the comfort and safety of the sick men. Shortly before 4 P.M., Kemble went to the home of General Dana and requested permission to remove his patients from the steamer. Dana told Kemble that the transfer of prisoners was in the hands of the proper officers, but he had no objection to the removal of the sick men. Kemble then returned to the boat. Captain Williams, though, objected to the removal of these soldiers because, he argued, their names had already been added to the rolls. Fortunately, the doctor did not listen to Williams and the 23 men were carried off. As Kemble left the gangplank, he also met a column of 278 soldiers released from the hospital and preparing to board the steamer. These men, whom Kemble had earlier ordered to report to the boat, were turned back to the hospital, their lives, inadvertently, saved.[214]

Around 4 P.M., George Williams entered the office of J. Warren Miller, the adjutant general on duty at the department headquarters. Williams informed Miller that Captain Speed had been induced to detain a sizeable number of prisoners at Camp Fisk that evening so that the men could be shipped on a boat other than the *Sultana*. Williams asked Miller to send Speed a telegram ordering him to send all remaining prisoners immediately to Vicksburg. Miller told Williams that the prisoner transfer was not his responsibility and that he did not wish to intervene. Miller also cautioned Williams against informing General Dana of his suspicions concerning Speed unless they could be proved. Miller did send Speed a telegram inquiring about his intentions. Speed, however, did not reply. Williams sent a telegram of his own to Lt. E. L. Davenport, assistant commissioner of exchange at the parole camp, and requested that Davenport hurry the men in as fast as possible.

Williams was careful not to send Speed the message.[215]

Captain Williams did report to General Dana his suspicions concerning Frederic Speed on the afternoon of the 24th. Dana informed him that Speed had earlier reported similar suspicions involving Captain Kerns. Persuaded by Dana that he was wrong, Williams concluded he was mistaken about Speed and later apologized to him.[216]

Notified that a third train would be bringing more soldiers to Vicksburg, Captain Kerns made yet another attempt to engage the services of a second boat. He again sought out Morgan L. Smith. Kerns insisted that too many men were being loaded on the *Sultana* and requested that Smith be present when the last train arrived to determine the possible use of the *Pauline Carroll*. Smith agreed to Kerns's request.[217] Kerns then approached Reuben Hatch, who agreed to be at the wharf to ascertain whether a portion of the prisoners should be loaded onto the *Pauline Carroll*.[218]

Before General Smith reached the riverfront, however, he encountered an officer associated with the quartermaster department who mistakenly informed Smith that only 300 men were left to board the *Sultana*. Smith concluded from this that all the men could go with comfort on the one steamer and so returned to his office.[219] Hatch too made his way toward the *Sultana* but, reminded that the shipment of prisoners had been taken out of his hands by General Dana, he turned and walked away from the steamer and her doomed passengers.[220]

H. C. Huntsman, the medical officer in charge of the Federal prisoners at the parole camp, was on hand as the men were called to board the trains for the trip to Vicksburg. He found 45 men he believed were too sick to leave the camp and ordered that they report to him that evening. But only 15 prisoners followed Huntsman's order; the rest had already boarded the *Sultana*.[221]

Capt. James McCowan of the 6th Kentucky Cavalry was in command of the third and last train out of Camp Fisk. On this train were loaded approximately 800 soldiers primarily from the states of Tennessee and Kentucky.[222] It was almost dark when the men arrived in Vicksburg, and Speed accompanied them to the *Sultana* and personally led them on board.[223] William C. Jones, the agent for the Atlantic and Mississippi line, witnessed this final column of paroled prisoners marching past the *Pauline Carroll* toward the

Sultana. Jones, noting the number of troops already on the steamer, thought it impossible for all these men to crowd onto the one boat.[224]

Kerns was also at the wharf when the men from the third train arrived. After observing the long column of troops stretching down the street toward the waiting steamer, Kerns found Speed, who was at the head of the column, and asked, again, if part of the men should not be put on the *Pauline Carroll*. Speed informed Kerns that he thought all the men should go on the *Sultana* since the rolls were prepared for all the troops to go together. Speed also stated that it was too late to divide the men. Since two majors commanded the prisoners, Kerns then questioned why the men could not be divided between the two boats with a major assigned to each. Speed remained adamant in his refusal to delegate soldiers to the *Pauline Carroll*, however, insisting that there was no time to alter the rolls. Why Speed should repeatedly make this argument is inexplicable since official rolls for most of the troops had yet to be drawn up.[225]

Captain Speed, however, offered a different version of his conversation with Kerns. As Speed approached the *Sultana* at the head of the last detachment of prisoners, Kerns asked him if indeed it would not be better for some of the men to go on the *Pauline Carroll*. According to Speed, Kerns said that he had the endorsement of General Smith in this recommendation. Speed then halted the column of prisoners and informed George Williams of Kerns's proposal. Again according to Speed, Williams answered, "No, I have been on board; there is plenty of room and they can all go comfortably."[226]

Failing to win Speed over to his plan, Kerns approached George Williams, who was counting the men from the final train. Kerns asked him if part of the troops should not be placed on the *Pauline Carroll*. Williams angrily replied: "No, that they could all go very well on the *Sultana*. That the *Pauline Carroll* had offered 20 cents per man to get those men and for that reason she could not have a single one of them."[227]

Maj. William Fidler of the 6th Kentucky Cavalry, a prisoner himself, was in command of the soldiers aboard the *Sultana*. As the last detachment of men boarded the steamer, this officer complained to Mason that too many men were on the boat. Mason replied that

Maj. William Fidler, 6th Kentucky Cavalry. This officer was in command of the soldiers aboard the Sultana. *It would be his last command, because he was among the lost.* (Courtesy of Gene Salecker)

he could not help it; all the men had to go on the *Sultana*. And in a none too convincing manner, Mason told Fidler "he thought he could carry them through."[228]

Fidler was not the only officer on the scene expressing concern. J. L. McHarg, an assistant quartermaster assigned to duty at the parole camp, asked Speed if all the men were to go on one steamer. Informed that they were, McHarg told Speed that there were too many men for one transport to carry. Speed harshly reminded McHarg that "officers sometimes get dismissed from the service for meddling with that which is none of their business."[229] Another officer, Lt. F. A. Roziene, an assistant adjutant general at the parole camp in charge of the prisoners' records, asked Speed about plans to send the men on separate boats. Roziene reported that he received "a humiliating reprimand for presuming the inquiry."[230]

Corp. Jeremiah Mahoney of the 2nd Michigan Cavalry was with the last group of prisoners who boarded the steamboat. Mahoney said that many of the men would have gladly transferred to another steamer, and some prisoners did attempt to go on the *Pauline Carroll*, but were told that smallpox was aboard and were ordered to stay off.[231]

Captain Kerns returned to the *Pauline Carroll* and reluctantly told William Jones, the steamer's agent, that the men would have to go on the *Sultana*. The *Pauline Carroll* by this time had her steam up and was ready to leave, but in one final effort to divide the men, Kerns asked the *Pauline Carroll*'s master, Captain White, to wait until all the troops had boarded the *Sultana*. Kerns still held out the hope that the *Sultana*'s overcrowding would convince the authorities that a second boat was necessary.[232]

Kerns then proceeded to the *Sultana*'s office where he met Captain Mason and William J. Gambrel. Kerns asked them if the passengers would be comfortable. Mason assured him that the men were comfortable and told him that the boat had carried more men in the past. Williams and Speed joined Kerns in the steamer's office and confirmed that conditions on board the *Sultana* were acceptable. The *Pauline Carroll* backed away from the wharfboat and steamed northward with a total of 17 passengers.[233]

Many observers did not share the opinion of Speed and Williams regarding the comfort of the prisoners. William C. Jones, agent for the *Pauline Carroll*, for example, reported hearing soldiers objecting to being herded onto the already crowded decks. Jones estimated that the steamboat now carried 2,000 men, with its human cargo extending as far as the forecastle.[234]

After watching the troops board the *Sultana,* William Butler, a cotton merchant from Springfield, Illinois, reported that

> When about one third of the last party that came in had got on board, they made a stop, and the remainder swore they would not go on board. They said they were not going to be packed on the boat like damned hogs; that there was no room for them to lie down, or place to attend to the calls of nature. There was much indignation felt among them, and among others who went about the boats. Some person on the wharf-boat, an officer I presume, ordered them to move forward and they went on board.[235]

Butler added:

> I only noticed the *Sultana* from where I stood on the *Pauline Carroll.* On every part of her the men seemed to be packed as thick as they could well stand. They were on the hurricane deck, on her wheel-house, forward deck and guard, and a person could go from one part of the boat to another only with much difficulty. A loyal gentleman who was standing by me, Judge Durwell, said it was a damned shame to crowd men on board a boat in that way; that he did not believe the men would have as much room to lie down as was allowed to slaves on slave-ships, or words to that effect.[236]

Capt. James N. McCowan stated that "the men were everywhere in the boat, any place where they could get a chance to hold on, to stand up or to sit down."[237] And James Brady, another prisoner, felt that he and his fellow troops had been packed more like hogs than men.[238]

Capt. William L. Friesner commanded the detachment of guards on the *Sultana,* and his duties required him to inspect all parts of the steamer. In his words: "The whole boat was crowded, overcrowded. On the boiler deck, forward of the cabin, the men were so crowded they could not well lie down; had to sit up against the racks, some of them. The hurricane deck was also crowded."[239]

The paroled prisoners were not the only passengers to board the *Sultana* at Vicksburg, however. Lt. Harvey Annis walked on board the steamer with his wife and small child. On January 16, 1865,

Annis had submitted a letter of resignation from the 57th U.S. Colored Infantry in order to return home where his presence was required. He had chosen the *Sultana* to carry him and his family. Ann Annis was very concerned about the crowded conditions on the *Sultana* and stated that "great fear was felt by everybody on account of the large number of passengers and the boat being top-heavy." William J. Gambrel, the *Sultana*'s clerk, pointed out to Mrs. Annis and her husband that the hurricane deck was sagging despite the extra supports that had been installed in many places.[240] Gambrel was so concerned about the upper decks, in fact, that he finally requested that no more troops be placed on the cabin roof.[241]

William H. Gaud, a passenger on the *Pauline Carroll*, talked with William Straton, the second clerk of the *Sultana*, while both boats were still docked in Vicksburg. Straton, with a premonition of future events, told Gaud "what a terrible thing it would be if the *Sultana* should burn up with so many prisoners on board."[242]

At least two civilian passengers on the *Sultana* decided to remain in Vicksburg precisely because of the number of soldiers being loaded on the steamer. They bought passage on the *Pauline Carroll*, but after hearing that this steamer too was going to get a portion of the paroled prisoners, they tried to get their money back. The clerk refused to refund their money and these men were two of the 17 passengers who went north on the *Pauline Carroll*.[243]

After all the troops had been loaded, Captain Speed was shocked when informed that 1,996 prisoners were on board. Speed then approached Mason to voice his concerns. Mason assured him that the men "would go through comfortably and safely."[244]

William D. Snow, a U.S. senator-elect from Arkansas and a passenger on the *Sultana*, was also alarmed over the density of the troops crowding the decks. Snow talked the matter over with the steamer's clerk, who showed him the boat's certificates and books. The clerk then informed him that the *Sultana* was transporting the largest number of passengers ever carried upriver on a single vessel.[245]

Alexander C. Brown, who had been captured at Chickamauga on September 20, 1863, expressed concerns similar to Snow's. When Brown asked William Gambrel about the number of passengers on board, the clerk remarked

... that if we arrived safe at Cairo it would be the greatest trip
ever made on the western waters, as there were more people
on board than were ever carried on one boat on the Mississippi
River. He stated that there were 2400 soldiers, 100 citizen passengers and a crew of about 80—in all over 2500.[246]

Prisoners were forced to crowd throughout the *Sultana*. Packed
around the boilers themselves were two companies of Kentucky
troops who sought warmth against the cool April air.[247]

The actual number of passengers placed on board the *Sultana* on
April 24 will perhaps never be known. Lt. F. A. Roziene, the assistant adjutant general in charge of the prisoners' records at the parole camp placed the number of prisoners at 2,146. This total
included 552 from Ohio; 420 from Michigan; 460 from Indiana;
180 from Kentucky; 522 from Tennessee; and 12 from West Virginia. This officer also reported that besides the prisoners there
were several Confederates going to Northern prisons, Union
guards, civilian passengers, and the steamer's crew.[248]

George Williams incorrectly estimated the number at 1,996.[249]
He later discovered an error in his addition and computed the new
figure to be 1,866.[250] Williams's estimate, though, was based on the
arrival of two, not three, trainloads of prisoners. Neither he nor
Speed had any knowledge of the men who had arrived on the second train at 2:15 on the afternoon of April 24. Williams's estimate
took into consideration the 398 men who were already on the
steamer when the first train arrived, the soldiers from the first
train, and those on the third. In order to arrive at a more accurate
total number of passengers, soldiers from the second train
(roughly 400), as well as the many soldiers who marched from the
parole camp, uncounted, must be added to Williams's tally of
1,866. Furthermore, Williams's count did not take into consideration the civilian passengers (100), the military guards (21), or the
crew (85). A truer estimate, then, of the number of passengers on
board the *Sultana* would probably run to more than 2,500.[251]

The *Sultana* also carried a large store of freight. In the hold were
250 hogsheads of sugar (each weighing over 1,200 pounds), 97
cases of wine, and on the main deck, toward the stern, were 70 to
100 mules and horses, and 100 hogs.[252] The strangest cargo on the
steamer was the crew's pet—a large alligator housed in a wooden
crate.[253]

At nine o'clock on the evening of April 24, the *Sultana* slowly backed away from the wharf at Vicksburg, her passengers thankful to be heading at long last out into the flooded river. The next morning, Captain Speed informed General Dana of the steamer's departure. Dana inquired as to the number of troops shipped on the boat and was astonished when Speed told him 1,900. Having never seen the boat, Dana asked about the capacity of the transport and the comfort of the men. Both Speed and Williams assured Dana that the load was not too large for the steamer and that the men were comfortable. They further added that few boats traveling the Mississippi were as well suited for shipping troops as was the *Sultana*.[254]

Pvt. William H. Peacock, Company G, 9th Indiana Cavalry. Survived. (Courtesy of Kim Harrison)

This photograph of the Sultana *and her doomed passengers was taken on April 26, 1865, at Helena, Arkansas.* (Library of Congress)

CHAPTER FIVE

"... We Would Be at Home in a Few Days ..."

THE PRISONERS ABOARD the *Sultana* were more than willing to suffer the crowded conditions on deck, believing that they were finally out of harm's way. Behind them lay the horrors of war and the deprivations of prison camp; ahead lay families and homes. One witness, Charles M. Eldridge, described the men as "singing and dancing on the boat, and telling each other what they were going to do when they got home."[255] And Lt. William Dixon with the 10th Indiana Cavalry wrote:

> We were all talking of home and friends and the many good things we would have to eat. We consoled ourselves that we had lived through it all and now were in the land of the free. We had no thought but that we would be at home in a few days feasting with our loved ones once more.[256]

The excitement generated by the prisoners, however, could not alleviate the severe hardships endured on board. Chronic diarrhea, malnutrition, scurvy, and a host of other diseases plagued the mass of Federal troops.[257] James K. Brady, a 16-year-old boy in the fall of 1862 when he enlisted in the 64th Ohio Volunteer Infantry, was among the recently released soldiers. Captured during the battle of Franklin, Brady was sent to Andersonville, where he is recorded to have weighed 154 pounds; as a passenger aboard the *Sultana*, he weighed a mere 96 pounds.[258] Six months of confinement at Cahaba had reduced Commodore Smith, a member of the 18th Michigan Volunteer Infantry, to the size of a skeleton. His recorded weight upon reaching Vicksburg: 94 pounds.[259] William

73

H. Peacock of the 9th Indiana Cavalry had weighed 197 pounds when captured at Athens, Alabama, on September 25, 1864. By the time of his release from Cahaba, Peacock weighed only 91 pounds.[260]

Despite the crying need for medical care, the army at Vicksburg did not provide a single doctor to minister to the health of the troops on board the *Sultana*. Witnesses did recall a civilian doctor who provided what care he could to comfort the sick.[261]

Since troops occupied every inch of the decks and roofs, many had no protection at all from the cool April air and rain. The army failed to issue a sufficient number of blankets for the soldiers, which forced many to sleep on the cold decks without any means of keeping warm. Moreover, the lone cooking stove on board was reserved mainly for civilians and crewmen. Prisoners ate hard bread and raw salt pork or bacon.[262]

As the *Sultana* continued upriver, safe navigation of the boat was a primary concern among the officers in charge. Reminded of the boat's legal carrying capacity of 376, William Gambrel, the first clerk, warned Major Fidler, who headed the prisoners, that with so many men on the roof of the cabin, any quick movement on the part of these soldiers might cause the roof to collapse. Gambrel also warned against the sudden shifting of soldiers from one side of the boat to the other, for fear the vessel could capsize or explode. Captain Mason, on the day before reaching Helena, Arkansas, expressed similar concerns to Major Fidler. Heeding the recommendations of these two men, Fidler mounted the pilot house and commanded the soldiers "to keep quiet especially in case of an accident, and not to change places when the boat was stopped."[263]

The worst fears of Mason and Gambrel were nearly realized when the *Sultana* landed at Helena. A photographer, who saw the mass of passengers piled aboard the steamboat, decided that such a scene should be captured by his camera. While he was setting up on the west bank of the river, word passed among the passengers that their picture was about to be taken. The prisoners quickly sought the port side of the boat in order to be featured in the photograph, thus bringing the *Sultana* dangerously close to capsizing. The resulting photograph is not only the only known picture of the *Sultana*; it is also the last photograph of many of her passengers.[264]

The *Sultana* pulled from the wharfboat at Helena shortly after being photographed and began to steam, without further incident, toward the next stop, Memphis. But her chief engineer, Nathan Wintringer, must have been a worried man. Lewis Bean, a member of the 6th Kentucky Cavalry, observed Wintringer walking about the boilers several times and checking the patch that had been applied in Vicksburg. The boiler was now a bomb and the small patch a lit fuse.[265]

Elbert J. Squire, a first lieutenant with the 101st Ohio Infantry, observed another of the *Sultana*'s officers, Captain Mason, frequently at the steamer's bar but never saw him drunk. Squire, in fact, wondered at the time how Mason could drink so much and not show it.[266] Capt. Lewis F. Hake of the 115th Ohio Infantry also witnessed Mason's drinking habits and, unlike Squire, observed occasions when Mason was having difficulty balancing himself.[267]

The *Sultana* docked at Memphis at 6:30 P.M. on April 26, the day John Wilkes Booth was killed by a platoon of New York Cavalry.[268] Members of the Chicago Opera Troupe were among the first to set foot on the cobblestoned riverbank at Memphis to open an engagement at the Atheneum Hall. No doubt, these passengers were relieved to escape the crowded conditions on the *Sultana* after having traveled up from Vicksburg.[269] But Epenetus W. McIntosh was gladdened by the arrival of the *Sultana*. McIntosh had gotten off the *Henry Ames* after she tied up at Memphis. When he arrived back at the wharf, however, he discovered to his dismay that the steamer had already left. Boarding the *Sultana*, he knew that he would soon be joining his fellow prisoners. What McIntosh didn't know was that within hours he would be struggling to survive in the flooded currents of the mighty river.[270]

While the *Sultana* was being emptied of her hogsheads of sugar and cases of wine, many prisoners took to the city to celebrate their newly won freedom at a local saloon.[271] Army guards from the *Sultana* were later to enter the city to round up the more inebriated of the soldiers. William A. McFarland, watching from the steamer as these drunken men were led aboard, reported the sight of a "seven-foot-tall" Tennessean, shouting and cursing at bayonet point, as he was escorted to the hurricane deck, where he continued to cause a considerable disturbance. This towering soldier may have been Pvt. Richard M. Pierce of Company D, 3rd Tennessee Cavalry.[272]

William H. C. Michael and some of his fellow officers from the gunboat *Tyler* walked aboard the *Sultana* while she was docked at Memphis. Michael later wrote of his visit that night:

> I . . . mingled with the living skeletons who had been rotting in southern prison-pens for months, but who were now happy at the prospect of soon meeting the dear ones at home. We cheered them with kindly words and rejoiced with them at the bright prospects before them. Some of the men were too weak to walk without being supported by more fortunate comrades. Others were compelled by sheer weakness to lie on cots or blankets spread upon the decks, while their wants were cheerfully provided for by devoted companions, who loved them because of the sufferings they had passed through together.[273]

The *Sultana* left Memphis at eleven o'clock that night and steamed across the river to Hopefield, Arkansas, where she took on over 1,000 bushels of coal. George Downing, a private with the 9th Indiana Cavalry, watched from the Memphis shore as the brightly lit *Sultana* docked at the coaling station. Downing had disembarked at Memphis to see some friends but failed to return in time for the steamer's departure. Downing reached into his pocket for the money his family had sent him at Vicksburg and paid a man with a skiff two dollars to carry him across the river to the *Sultana*. As he boarded the steamer and made his way over the crowded decks to an area near one of the wheelhouses, he met up with a friend, Henry J. Kline. Downing told Kline, "If I had not sent home for that money I would have been left." Within a few hours, Downing would pray that he had never received the money.[274] The cold river was his final resting place.

At midnight, Nathan Wintringer ended his shift and turned the *Sultana*'s boilers over to his second engineer, Samuel Clemens (not the Samuel Clemens who would later take on the name Mark Twain). Wintringer reported to Clemens that the boilers were operating properly.[275]

About this time, a passenger named Joseph Taylor Elliott was searching for a vacant space aboard the crowded decks to sleep. In an encounter with Captain Mason, who had finally grown concerned over the safety of his passengers, Mason told Elliott that "he would give all the interest he had in the boat if it was safely landed in Cairo."[276] Another passenger, William Fies also observed Mason

Pvt. Henry J. Kline, Company G, 9th Indiana Cavalry. Survived.
(Courtesy of Phylliss Harris)

early that morning as the latter attempted to reach his stateroom. Several soldiers joked at Mason's being forced to crawl along the rail to get by them.[277]

The *Sultana* pulled away from the coaling station at 1 A.M. on April 27. William B. Floyd, a sailor aboard the U.S. gunboat *Grossbeak* docked at Memphis, watched the *Sultana* steaming north. When he started his watch at midnight, Floyd had marveled at the sight of the large, brightly lit boat lying just north of the city and was reminded of the remarks being circulated concerning the crowded conditions on board.[278]

The Mississippi River in the latter part of April 1865 flooded, unchecked, across its Arkansas banks, since no system of levees served to channel its flow. The river measured more than four miles wide in places just north of Memphis. As the steamer was carefully steered through a series of islands known as Paddy's Hen and Chicks, only an occasional flash of distant lightning amid a cold drizzle of rain broke the darkness of the spring morning.[279]

On board the *Sultana*, passengers slept. In front of the pilothouse lay Stephen M. Gaston. Gaston and his friend William Block were contented with a full stomach after discovering a broken hogshead of sugar. Gaston, who had enlisted in the 9th Indiana Volunteer Cavalry at the age of 13, was captured by Forrest's men in Alabama in September 1864. At the time of his release from the Cahaba prison camp, Gaston was 15 years old.[280]

Another passenger, George F. Robinson of the 2nd Michigan Cavalry, was used to planning and executing escapes. Fifteen days after his capture on November 5, 1864, Robinson and seven other prisoners tunneled their way out of a prison at Meridian, Mississippi, and traveled 60 miles on foot before being caught by an elderly lady and her 15 dogs. On their way to Cahaba prison, Robinson and a fellow prisoner, John Corliss, jumped from the train, but the two soon heard the frightening sound of the tracking hounds. They escaped capture for five days but were eventually taken, half-starved and close to freezing, to Cahaba. Robinson's fierce desire for freedom had not been diminished though. After one month of internment, he and Corliss again managed an escape. Apprehended near Selma, Alabama, they succeeded in escaping from their captors one more time before being caught and returned to Cahaba, where they remained until the prisoner exchange in March 1865. Robinson and Corliss were asleep on the hurricane deck, between the smokestacks, on the morning of April 27.[281]

Ogilvie E. Hamblin of the 2nd Michigan Cavalry was near one of the wheelhouses as the steamer plowed northward. Hamblin had been wounded and captured at Muscle Shoals, Alabama, on October 30, 1864. In a Confederate hospital at Florence, Alabama, his left arm was amputated just below the shoulder, but Hamblin's wound did not receive proper medical attention and gangrene developed. He survived, however, and was shipped to Cahaba.[282]

Alexander Sackett also lay on the deck of the steamer and probably dreamed of the homecoming he believed lay in store with his wife and six children in Iowa. Destiny had other plans, however, for the 40-year-old farmer-soldier.[283]

George Kayton, the *Sultana*'s seasoned pilot, strained his eyes as he steered through the darkness veiling the countryside, guiding the vessel by memory, or as Mark Twain put it, "by the shape that's in your head, and never mind the one that's before your eyes."[284]

The pilothouse, where Kayton manned the wheel, crowned the steamer's superstructure. Beneath him were three decks: main, boiler, and hurricane, with the so-called texas rising from the hurricane. The pilothouse was situated directly above the texas. The *Sultana*'s upper decks, sagging under the mass of passengers, were not designed to carry such a load, because in an effort to reduce the weight of the steamboat's superstructure, light, flimsy wood served in the construction of floors and walls.[285] If the members supporting the superstructure were destroyed by fire or an explosion, these upper decks would collapse like a house of cards. The upper decks were also coated with a layer of paint composed of turpentine, benzine, and other highly combustible ingredients, which led one author to describe them as "an orderly pile of kindling wood."[286]

On the main deck and between the waterwheels lay a battery of four boilers, each measuring 18 feet in length, and filled with steam and boiling water. On the middle larboard boiler was the small patch Wintringer had eyed closely. The chief engineer must have been aware that this patch could fail at any moment. His concern was justified. According to one study, a boiler on a western steamboat contained, at 150 pounds of pressure, enough energy to hurl the boiler over two miles into the air. Furthermore, a cubic foot of heated water under pressure of 60 to 70 pounds had about the same energy as a pound of gunpowder. On the morning of April 27, these four boilers had approximately 135 pounds per square inch of pressure.[287]

Beneath the boilers was a coal-burning furnace running nearly the breadth of the steamer forward. Hard-firing was necessary to maintain the working pressure of steam in the boilers, making metalwork around the furnace, the furnace itself, and the boilers red hot. The risk of fire and the consequences to a steamboat's superstructure are only too easy to imagine. Louis Hunter, in *Steamboats on the Western Rivers*, wrote:

> Once a fire was started many conditions encouraged its rapid growth and spread: the partially open structure of the lower deck and the open galleries of the boiler deck, the abundant jigsaw- and fretwork of the superstructure on the larger boats, and the tinderlike quality of the wood. When, as was often the case, the fire started near the furnace or chimneys the draft created by the motion of the boat carried the flames quickly along its whole length . . . . With a fire well started on the main deck or above, however, there was usually little chance of stopping it. Often within a few minutes of the first flare up the entire superstructure would be enveloped.[288]

If a fire were to erupt on the *Sultana* then, the only hope was for George Kayton to steer the steamer immediately to shore. Passengers could not depend on the lifesaving equipment on board. The vessel carried only 76 cork-filled life preservers, one yawl, and a single metal lifeboat.[289]

CHAPTER SIX

The Visit of
the Death Angel

As Samuel Clemens kept close watch on the *Sultana*'s boilers on the morning of April 27th, the steady exhaust issuing from the boat's engines and the machinery laboring to drive the vessel were the only noises to be heard. Clemens also monitored the gauges to ensure that the boilers had enough water to maintain 135 pounds of pressure.[290] In the pilothouse stood George Kayton, ready at the wheel and preparing to steer the *Sultana* through a bend in the river just south of Island No. 41. The boat was seven miles out of Memphis, traveling at her normal speed of nine miles per hour. At Kayton's side was William Rowberry, chief mate and replacement for Captain Mason, who had retired to his room on the texas deck.[291]

Ben G. Davis of the 7th Kentucky Cavalry found sleep impossible and, shortly before 2 A.M., made his way to the main deck, where he lit his pipe at the boilers. He then returned to the hurricane deck to join other members of his regiment. The 38-year-old private sat on the deck and peacefully enjoyed his pipe. When, at approximately 2 A.M., Davis brought his canteen to his lips, the canteen was blown from his hands.[292] At this moment, and without warning, three of the steamer's four boilers erupted with a volcanic fury that resounded across the countryside.[293] William H. Wooldridge, asleep on the Tennessee shore, woke to the thundering noise of "a hundred earthquakes." The shattering sound, according to Wooldridge, "rolled and re-echoed for minutes in the woodlands."[294]

Arthur A. Jones of the 115th Ohio Volunteer Infantry described

Sgt. Arthur A. Jones, Company C, 115th Ohio Infantry. Survived. (Chester Berry, Loss of the Sultana *and Reminiscences of Survivors)*

Pvt. Jacob Helminger, Company B, 50th Ohio Infantry. Survived. (Chester Berry, Loss of the Sultana *and Reminiscences of Survivors)*

An artist's drawing of the disaster. (Harper's Weekly)

the blast in the following manner:

> What a crash! My God! My blood curdles while I write and words are inadequate; no tongue or writer's pen can describe it. Such hissing of steam, the crash of the different decks. As they came together with the tons of living freight, the falling of the massive smoke stacks, the death cry of strong-hearted men caught in every conceivable manner, the red-tongued flames bursting up through the mass of humanity and driving to death's door those who were fortunate enough to live though worse than a dozen deaths in the "damnable deaths pen" at Andersonville. We had faced death day by day while incarcerated there, but this was far more appalling than any scene through which we had passed.[295]

The explosion tore instantly through the decks directly above the boilers, flinging live coals and splintered timber into the night sky like fireworks. The entire center section of the *Sultana* was shot to fragments. Whole chunks of the upper decks, including most of the pilothouse, were blown clear of the boat. William Rowberry was hurled from the steamer, while George Kayton, at the wheel when the floor of the pilothouse crumbled beneath him, was dropped into the wreckage of the main deck.[296]

Jacob Helminger of the 50th Ohio Infantry was asleep on the hurricane deck when he was startled awake by the terrific jarring of the steamer; smoke and steam surrounded him like a thick fog. The soldier pulled his watch from his pocket and saw that the time was 2 A.M.[297]

The explosion hurled scores of passengers into the air. Many woke to find themselves tumbling high above the river; others woke up in eternity. Charles M. Eldridge, asleep on the hurricane deck, was whirled though the air and into the waters of the Mississippi.[298] Jotham W. Maes, a soldier with the 47th Ohio Volunteer Infantry asleep behind the left wheelhouse on the boiler deck, was convinced for a moment that a nightmare had him dreaming of falling through space. The dream became reality when he found himself in the cold water of the river gripping a three by ten foot section of deck. This small piece of wreckage would serve as a lifeboat for Maes and nine other survivors.[299] Samuel Pickens, a member of the 3rd Tennessee Cavalry, was also blown off the steamer. Pickens held to a horse as it struggled to remain afloat.[300]

The force of the explosion pitched Perry S. Summerville, who slept on the edge of the deck above the boilers, approximately 100 feet from the steamer. He thought at the time that the boat had been running too close to shore and that the limb of a tree had knocked him into the river. Afraid the *Sultana* would leave him in the dark water, Summerville started to swim toward the boat, all the while calling for help. He soon recognized the fire and columns of steam on board and heard the screams of passengers. Realizing then that the source of danger lay with the *Sultana*, Summerville turned and swam downriver, where he floated to safety on a wooden rail.[301]

The blast drove boiler fragments, pipes, bricks, and machinery through the upper decks like shrapnel, killing and maiming scores of sleeping passengers. When William Lugenbeal found his fellow infantryman Josephus Test (both of the 153th Ohio Volunteers) after the explosion, he was horrified to find that Test had been impaled by a piece of timber.[302]

Commodore Smith was asleep on one of the upper decks near the rear of the boat's stern when the disaster occurred. Smith was almost buried by dead or wounded comrades, and the dismembered bodies that littered the wreckage of the upper decks prevented him from reaching the relative safety of the lower deck.[303]

In addition to flying debris, the explosion caused a spray of scalding steam and boiling water to descend upon the boat's hapless passengers. George A. Clarkson (5th Michigan Cavalry) had encountered Samuel Clemens on the boiler deck minutes prior to the disaster and commented how smoothly the *Sultana* was running. Clarkson then bedded down in an area 12 to 15 feet forward of the boilers, wrapping a blanket around himself to keep off the chill. The blanket protecting Clarkson from the cold saved him from a shower of boiling water, which rained over this area of the boiler deck. Many of the men near Clarkson were scalded to death. Samuel Clemens was also critically burned.[304]

Andrew T. Peery from Tennessee graphically described the scene surrounding him on the boiler deck in the following terms:

> Then the fire shot up and I saw sights so terrible and heart-rending, I fail to have language to explain. Oh, the awful sight! The lower deck for a considerable distance all around the boilers was covered with the dead and wounded. Some were

scalded, some seemed to be blind, some of them would rise up partly and fall, and some were pinned down with the timbers of the wreck. I saw hundreds in this frightful plight, crying, praying, screaming, begging, groaning and moaning.[305]

Phillip L. Horn, a private with the 102nd Ohio Volunteer Infantry, was asleep on the second deck beside his bunkmate, Joseph McKelvy, when he was suddenly blown off the boat. Temporarily disoriented by the sensation of being lost in mid-air, Horn struck the water and went down twice. Horn survived by seizing hold of a piece of drifting wreckage, but his friend McKelvy was scalded to death.[306]

Daniel McLeod was reading in one of the steamer's cabins, when the blast blew him clear of the table at which he had been sitting. McLeod found himself on the edge of a crater within the boat, with both his ankles broken and the bones visible. Improvising with his suspenders, he fashioned a pair of tourniquets in order to check the bleeding.[307]

William H. Peacock of the 9th Indiana Cavalry left the boiler deck prior to the explosion because of the crowded conditions there and found a spot on the texas roof, in front of the pilothouse. Four members of Peacock's company were with him. The roof gave way beneath Peacock and his friends when the boilers blew, and the five soldiers fell into what remained of the lower deck. Peacock somehow survived; his four comrades did not.[308]

Pvt. Albert Norris of the 76th Ohio Volunteer Infantry lay on the boiler deck, immediately over the boilers, when the center section of the *Sultana* erupted. Norris fell to the main deck and landed on the hot irons of the furnace, severely burning his left arm and shoulder. Men from the hurricane deck rained down around Norris.[309]

Capt. William S. Friesner, officer in charge of the army guards on the *Sultana*, rushed to check on his men when it became clear that disaster had struck the boat. Friesner was horrified at the sight of the rubble where he knew his men had retired for the night. Of the 21 guards who marched aboard the steamer at Vicksburg, 16 would die on April 27.[310]

William T. Shumard, a member of the 7th Ohio Volunteer Cavalry, was asleep alongside 12 comrades in front of the boilers on the main deck. The force of the explosion blew Shumard forward

Pvt. Albert Norris, Company A, 76th Ohio Infantry. Survived. (Chester Berry, *Loss of the* Sultana *and Reminiscences of Survivors*)

Pvt. Commodore Smith, Company F, 18th Michigan Infantry. Survived. (Chester Berry, *Loss of the* Sultana *and Reminiscences of Survivors*)

Pvt. William H. Norton, Company C, 115th Ohio Infantry. Survived. (Chester Berry, *Loss of the* Sultana *and Reminiscences of Survivors*)

Capt. J. Walter Elliott, Company F, 44th United States Colored Troops. Survived. (Chester Berry, *Loss of the* Sultana *and Reminiscences of Survivors*)

toward the bow of the steamer. When he woke, he found himself clutching a chain attached to the bow. Although his face and feet were badly scalded, Shumard was alive. Eleven of his fellow soldiers were dead.[311]

Sgt. Christian M. Nisley of the 40th Indiana Infantry was lying on the cabin roof near the bow. When this soldier got to his feet and looked toward the stern of the dying steamer, he saw that the texas was gone and that the upper decks had given way and sunk to the level of the boilers.[312]

Joseph Taylor Elliott was stirred awake by the oppressive heat that swept through the cabins after the explosion and immediately discovered that the floor of his cabin had partially collapsed to form an incline to the lower deck. Peering down into the gaping hole, Elliott was later to compare the scene to the inside of a furnace. He also observed that the cots in that area of the steamer had completely disappeared, along with the men who occupied them.[313]

J. Walter Elliott, a member of the 44th United States Colored Troops, sprang to his feet when the blast shook the *Sultana* and rushed across the boiler deck until he came to a huge opening created by the explosion. Fire had already erupted in the wreckage of the main deck below, revealing a scene akin to Dante's vision of hell:

> . . . mangled, scalded human forms heaped and piled amid the burning debris on the lower deck. The cabin, roof and texas were cut in twain; the broken planks on either side of the break projecting downward, meeting the raging flames and lifting them to the upper decks.[314]

In the confusion immediately following the explosion, Elliott discovered Daniel McLeod calmly sitting on a cot near the gaping hole. Despite McLeod's pleas to be thrown into the river, away from the spreading flames, Elliott felt powerless to help McLeod once he hit the water since Elliott, like many passengers aboard the *Sultana*, could not swim. McLeod continued in his pleadings, and with the help of Captain Chapman, Elliott was persuaded to lift the injured man and throw him off the rear of the steamer.* As Elliott stood at

---

*This Captain Chapman was probably Capt. William L. Coleman of Company D, 40th Indiana Infantry, who perished in the disaster.[315]

the stern, a young girl ran past him, preparing to jump. Elliott grabbed the girl and fastened his own life preserver onto her.[316]

John L. Walker and four members of his company were lying on the hurricane deck, in front of the steamer's bell. With the explosion and resulting crash of timbers, Walker and his friends found themselves buried under a mound of debris. Walker managed to free himself and saw that the central portion of the boat had collapsed on top of the boilers, forming a funnel, which was filled with a mass of unfortunate soldiers.[317]

The upper decks of the *Sultana*, already sagging under the weight of the great load of passengers, crumbled when the blast ripped through the steamer's superstructure. The wreckage of these decks imprisoned hundreds, who, if they survived at all, suffered burns, lacerations, and broken limbs. Hot ashes and flaming coals rained across the entire length of the vessel. Soon the night sky was red with flames that fed on the pile of rubble that had only moments before been the passenger-ladened decks of the steamer. William H. Norton of the 115th Ohio Volunteer Infantry watched in disbelief as flames consumed the *Sultana* and later remarked on the "awful wail of hundreds of human beings burning alive in the cabin and under the fallen timbers."[318]

William Fies, a member of the 64th Ohio Volunteer Infantry, recounted the scene this way:

> The agonizing shrieks and groans of the injured and dying were heart-rendering, and the stench of burning flesh was intolerable and beyond any power of description.[319]

At the rear of the hurricane deck, William A. McFarland watched helplessly as fire quickly spread. He too was later to describe the scene:

> The wildest confusion followed. Some sprang into the river at once, others were killed, and I could hear the groans of the dying above the roar of the flames. . . I was on the hurricane deck clear aft. This part of the boat was jammed with men. I saw the pilot house and hundreds of them sink through the roof into the flames; at which juncture I sprang overboard into the river.[320]

The chaos that prevailed on the *Sultana* during the minutes following the explosion was also described by Arthur A. Jones:

Sgt. William Fies, Company B, 64th Ohio Infantry. Survived. (Chester Berry, *Loss of the* Sultana *and Reminiscences of Survivors*)

Comrades imploring each other for assistance that they might escape from the burning deck; officers giving orders for the safety of their men; women shrieking for help; horses neighing; mules kicking and making the terrible scene hideous with their awful brays of distress.[321]

Amid this chaos, Capt. J. Cass Mason, in shirtsleeves and bareheaded, was trying to restore order by asking for calm. Mason offered reassurances to several women kneeling on deck and praying for help. Jacob W. Rush reported that of the 17 female passengers on board, only one was saved; several of the wives of the deck hands were also lost. In all, 22 women on the *Sultana* died.[322]

Among the female passengers aboard the *Sultana* were several members of the Christian Commission. Chester Berry would later write the following about one of these brave ladies:

. . . When the flames at last drove all the men from the boat, seeing them fighting like demons in the water in the mad endeavor to save their lives, actually destroying each other and themselves by their wild actions, [she] talked to them, urging them to be men, and finally succeeded in getting them quieted down, clinging to the ropes and chains that hung over the bow of the boat. The flames now began to lap around her with their fiery tongues. The men pleaded and urged her to jump into the water and thus save herself, but she refused, saying: "I might lose my presence of mind and be the means of death of some of you." And so, rather than run the risk of becoming the cause of death of a single person, she folded her arms quietly over her bosom and burned, a voluntary martyr to the men she had so lately quieted.[323]

On the main deck near the hatchway to the *Sultana*'s hold stood Ogilvie Hamblin. Around him lay the remains of the upper decks. Hamblin could hear the cries of the soldiers trapped in the hold. With the aid of another soldier, the one-armed Hamblin opened the hatch, and the men "came rushing out . . . like bees out of a hive, followed by dense clouds of steam and smoke."[324]

George H. Young initially thought that lightning had struck the *Sultana*. Stretched out for the night on the boiler deck, along with David Muller and William F. Clancy (members of the Ohio regiments), these men soon found themselves trapped by pieces of the collapsed hurricane deck. Their narrow escape from immediate death was apparent to Young when he noticed that the man next to him had been crushed by a timber. Young and Clancy extricated themselves from the rubble, but Muller was pinned by a heavy beam. The two frantically worked to move the huge timber as flames threatened the trapped soldier. Young and Clancy were forced to abandon their rescue efforts, however, by the raging fire, which soon consumed their friend. In describing this man's death, Young would later recount:

> [I]t was agonizing to listen to the beseeching of our comrade while we were so helpless. We could not escape from his hoarse cries, and, cruel as it seems, we were relieved when death ended his horrible agony.[325]

The two soldiers turned their backs on the tragic scene and climbed down to the main deck, where they encountered further evidence of the explosion's destructive force. Again, in Young's words:

> We found few sound men on the boiler deck, but a large number of injured ones. Some of these were trying to get forward, crawling along with broken limbs or badly scalded, and many implored us for aid, as they could not swim. Some, in their agony, crawled to the edge of the boat and rolled themselves into the water to drown.[326]

George Robinson woke to find the body of John Corliss lying across his legs. He then looked out at the flooded river and saw the mass of drowning passengers, each desperately clinging to the other. He turned to the men trapped in the wreckage and to the fire spreading over the decks of the *Sultana*. Forced to leap into the cold river, Robinson floated toward an island but could not reach the trees, which were already full of soldiers. Robinson then spied a dark object floating near him, and with his remaining strength he swam to meet it. The object was a dead mule, which Robinson climbed upon and used as a float to reach Memphis, where he was finally rescued.[327]

The flames raced through the wreckage of the *Sultana* like an unchecked firestorm. William D. Snow, watching in horror as flames spread the entire length of the steamer, guessed that the entire boat was in flames within 20 minutes of the explosion. He also estimated that 500 men sought uncertain refuge on the bow of the boat, while winds drove the flames toward the stern. A sense of total helplessness must have filled Snow as he witnessed the two wheelhouses fall away from the boat, causing her stern to turn upstream, thus reversing the flames. The flames then swept across those huddled at the bow, forcing them into the rain-swollen river.[328]

John L. Walker, who could not swim, was among those seeking safety on the bow of the steamer. Having removed his clothing in the event he would be forced to enter the water, Walker decided instead to stay on the *Sultana* for as long as possible. But as the boat spun according to the current, the wind soon sent the flames in the direction of Walker and the other passengers at the bow. The raging fire caused a mad rush into the river. Walker, at the center of the crowd, pushed those in front of him, and was in turn shoved by those behind. At first, the water relieved his scorched skin, but Walker was soon fighting for his life. He later wrote of this struggle:

> While under water I was driven back two different times by others jumping on me. I could feel arms and legs and bodies of men all around me, but I was fortunate enough to know what I was doing all the time, and I struck out with the best effort I could make at swimming. After a few strokes I came to the surface.[329]

Pvt. Chester D. Berry of the 20th Michigan Volunteer Infantry was struck in the head by a piece of wood, a blow which fractured his skull. Thinking that the steamer had been hit by an artillery shell, he ran to the bow and discovered that the upper decks had collapsed. Wood from these decks instantly ignited upon reaching the hot bed of coals below. Berry then returned to his bunk, only to find his mate scalded to death. Grabbing what was left of a cabin door, he considered diving into the river but decided against jumping when he saw the water "literally black with human beings, many of whom were sinking and taking others with them." Berry waited until the river was relatively clear of men to make his leap. Once in the water, Berry heard a loud crash of breaking timbers and turned to see that one of the wheelhouses had partially broken away from the hurricane deck. He also saw one unfortunate soldier sandwiched between the deck and the wheelhouse; flames soon overtook this man. Berry would later write, "Even now, after the lapse of years, it almost seems as though I could hear the poor fellow's

Pvt. Chester Berry, Company I, 20th
Michigan Infantry. Survived.
(Chester Berry, *Loss of the* Sultana
and Reminiscences of Survivors)

Sgt. Alexander C. Brown, Company
I, 2nd Ohio Cavalry. Survived.
(Chester Berry, *Loss of the* Sultana
and Reminiscences of Survivors)

screams, as the forked flames swept around him."[330]

Another soldier adrift in the morning darkness, Charles M. El-dridge, chanced upon a ladder floating downstream. Much to his surprise, Eldridge discovered that two of his friends had caught hold of the same ladder. The three men watched the flames crowd-ing the remaining passengers toward the bow of the boat and could not escape the cries of those still on board. Eldridge wondered about the fate of those who only yesterday had been dancing and singing over their newly won freedom.[331]

When Alexander C. Brown, a sergeant with Company I, 2nd Ohio Volunteer Infantry, was struck on the head by a piece of de-bris and knocked into the water, he reached the surface only to be caught around the neck by a fellow passenger. Finally freeing him-self from the grasp of the drowning man, Brown managed to swim several hundred yards from the *Sultana* and take in the whole night sky, which was lit up by the flames leaping from the wreckage. "Hundreds of my comrades were fastened down by the timbers of the decks and had to burn, while the water seemed to be one solid mass of human beings struggling with the waves." Despite his at-tempts to recount the evening, Brown believed he could never ac-curately describe the light and the screams that issued from the burning steamer.[332]

Because of their injuries, many passengers were unable to join those who had jumped overboard and were left to endure the en-croaching fires. Commodore Smith was one who remained on the burning boat for 20 or 30 minutes, performing a task that he later described as the most difficult job of his life. Many of those left on the main deck, according to Smith, were rendered helpless by bro-ken bones; some were so badly scalded that the flesh literally fell from their limbs. These men begged to be thrown into the river, away from the holocaust. Smith complied out of pity and sent sev-eral poor souls to certain death in the flood waters of the Missis-sippi. Another soldier, Michael H. Sprinkle, estimated that he cast 50 wounded men off the steamer.[333]

Due to the flood conditions and the fact that the *Sultana* was midstream when the blast occurred, the safety of land was a consid-erable distance away. Furthermore, the distant riverbanks were blanketed by darkness, leaving many without any idea of where dry land lay.

As stated, the number of drowned passengers rose due to the fact that so few could swim. J. Walter Elliott overheard one Kentucky soldier tell another Kentuckian that he had never learned to swim. The other replied that he could not swim either. The two soldiers embraced, and Elliott heard one of them say, "Then let us die together." They jumped into the river, and as Elliott watched, the water closed over them.[334]

Wilson A. Fast, propped against the *Sultana*'s lifeboat on the hurricane deck, was jolted awake by a spray of hot water at the moment of the explosion. He immediately made his way forward from the stern and discovered that the front of the steamer had disappeared altogether and with it probably 500 men. He then jumped to the boiler deck and searched for a life preserver but was not able to find one. Peering down into the gaping hole that had been made in the deck, Fast could view the soldiers on the main deck below, whom he described as "pouring over the prow into the dark water like a flock of sheep through a gap in a fence." Fast also recounted the panic of those who delayed entering the river:

> I saw many men standing on the debris and on the edge of the boat, just ready for the final leap, indulging their vocal and oratorical powers in a great variety of ways. Some were praying, some singing, and some swearing a "blue streak." Some would curse Abe Lincoln, Jeff Davis, General Grant—any and everybody prominently connected with the war. Some were crying like children. Some muttered curses on everything in heaven above or on the earth below. Some prayed very loud, and most passionately; others were getting off very formal and graceful prayers—all in dead earnest.[335]

J. Walter Elliott later offered his own words:

> Women and little children in their night clothes, brave men who have stood undaunted on many a battle field, all contribute to the confusion and horror of the scene as they suddenly see the impending death by fire, and wringing their hands, tossing their arms wildly in the air, with cries most heartrending, they rush pell-mell over the guard into the dark, cold waters of the river.[336]

Manly C. White, asleep on the hurricane deck near the wheelhouse, had misinterpreted the explosion as a rebel battery firing on the steamer. Officers could be heard giving orders to remain quiet.

White soon realized, though, that it was up to each man to save himself as flames rose from the wreckage. In describing the horror of that morning, White would later write:

> Most of the boys stripped off their clothes and jumped into the river, which was cold and swift, and some three or four miles wide, and so dark that you could not see the shore. The scenes were heart-rending; the wounded and dying begging for help—some praying, and some swearing—while those in the water would catch hold of one another, and go down in squads. The fire was getting so hot that I soon saw that I must get into the water. I was quite an expert swimmer, and thought if I could get away from the crowd I might save myself, though I was quite weak, having been sick a good deal of the time I was in prison. I went to the gangway to go below, but found that it was gone, so I jumped down on the lower deck. What a sight— men dead and dying, parts of bodies, arms, legs, and the wreck of the boat, all in one mingled mass![337]

The odds were clearly against Ogilvie Hamblin when he jumped from the boat. Weakened by months of internment in Cahaba and left with only one arm, he nevertheless mustered sufficient strength to beat those odds. He floated down the river for several miles until he caught hold of a tree that had fallen into the water. He was eventually rescued by some woodsmen, who took Hamblin to their shelter and later loaded him on the steamer *Pocahontas*, destined for Memphis.[338]

Other passengers, meanwhile, were pulling down doors, shutters, pieces of deck, bales of hay, and anything else that would float to help them survive the swift currents and whirlpools of the Mississippi. Those who could not secure a float lined both sides of the flaming boat. In the words of Sgt. James H. Kimberlin:

> The water around the vessel for a distance of twenty to forty feet was a solid, seething mass of humanity, clinging one to another. The best or luckiest man was on top. I then, after partially dressing, went forward, climbing down on the wreckage to the lower deck on the west side, and when I looked out over the water where but a few minutes before there were hundreds of men struggling for supremacy, now there were but few to be seen. The great mass of them had gone down, clinging to each other.[339]

Another witness to survive the explosion, Joseph Taylor Elliott, stood on the hurricane deck and watched, helpless, as the fire quickly spread across the steamer. As he watched the flames jumping from one ceiling cross-piece to another, Elliott was reminded of "a lizard running along a fence." And as for those already overboard, Elliott later wrote:

> Such screams I never heard—twenty or thirty men jumping off at a time—many lighting on those already in the water—until the river became black with men, their heads bobbing up like corks, and then many disappearing never to appear again. We threw over everything that would float that we could get hold of, for their assistance; and then I, with several others, began tearing the sheeting off the sides of the cabin, and throwing it over.[340]

In the darkness of the spring morning, the basic instinct to survive took control. Men fought one another to stay alive. In the words of John L. Walker:

> I thought the sights on the battle-fields terrible, and they were, but they were not to be compared with the sights of that night when the animal nature of man came to the surface in the desperate struggle to save himself regardless of the life of others.[341]

The *Sultana*'s one lifeboat, beside which Wilson A. Fast had slept, itself caused the death of many passengers. When it was thrown into the water, an estimated 100 to 150 fought to grab hold. Five of Fast's friends lost their lives in the struggle, and as the small boat filled with anxious passengers, the overcrowding sent it below the dark water.[342]

In the meantime, Fast had torn a stateroom door from its hinges and thrown it onto the main deck. He jumped to the lower level and carried the door to the bow of the steamer, where he encountered several deck hands. The crewmen tried twice to seize the door from Fast, but the soldier pulled his jackknife and defended his crude raft. The determined soldier remained on the *Sultana* until the unbearable heat forced him to a decision. Several soldiers had climbed into the hold to escape the flames, but Fast chose the river as the only possibility for survival. Checking his pocket watch (the time was 2:30 A.M.), he cast the door into the river and leaped after it. Within minutes, a hysterical soldier also grasped hold of the door. And before long, five other men were struggling to gain

Sgt. Joseph Stevens, Company E, 4th Michigan Cavalry. Survived.
(Chester Berry, *Loss of the* Sultana *and Reminiscences of Survivors*)

possession of the makeshift raft. Fast fought to retain control of the door, but he was outnumbered. Exhausted, Fast allowed himself to drift. Fatigue and hypothermia forced him into a state of unconsciousness.[343]

J. W. Rush ran to the stern of the *Sultana* when the explosion occurred. When he reached the rear of the steamer, Rush saw the yawl being launched from the lower deck with four or five deckhands. A woman (apparently the wife of one of the crewmen) was begging to be allowed into the yawl but could not convince the men to take her on as well. The boat made its way without her.[344] Another soldier, Joseph Stevens, watched as the crewmen in the yawl kept others out by using a board on anyone who drew near the boat.[345] The army would later arrest and charge five of the surviving crewmen of the *Sultana* when they reached St. Louis for commandeering the steamer's yawl for themselves.[346] And despite the confusion and panic aboard the *Sultana*, some passengers prepared themselves for an imminent end. Benjamin F. Johnston, a private with the 5th Michigan Cavalry, for example, stuck an ambrotype likeness of his wife and son into his pants pocket so that his body might be identified.[347] Pvt. William A. Cruddis, a member of the 1st Virginia Cavalry from Wheeling, West Virginia, took the time to attach a name tag to his clothing. The body, later fished out of the river by rescue teams, carried the private's name inside the dead soldier's coat.[348]

Seth W. Hardin, Jr., and his new wife, who had bought passage on the *Sultana* for their return home to Chicago, were wakened by the sound of screams and the intense heat of the spreading flames. The couple rushed from their cabin and into a mass of people intent on escape. As the upper decks crashed around them, they leaped into the river. The Hardins were separated among the hundreds who followed them off the boat. Hardin never saw his wife again but was himself able to float to safety.[349]

Harvey Annis and his wife were shaken abruptly awake by a sound much like the rattling of iron. Shocked to find that his cabin was quickly filling with steam, Lieutenant Annis immediately fastened a life preserver onto his wife and himself. The soldier took up his child and led his wife to the stern of the boat. Holding the child, he let himself down by rope to the lower deck. Mrs. Annis followed but was knocked into the hold of the steamer by a man jumping from an upper deck. Rejoining her family, she then watched as her husband jumped overboard, still gripping their child. Mrs. Annis again followed. The *Sultana*'s rudder helped to keep her afloat when her life preserver began to slip free. It was in horror, though, that she watched her husband lose strength and disappear with their small child beneath the water. Forced to release her grip on the rudder because of the spreading fire, Mrs. Annis managed to secure a small board, which eventually carried her to safety.[350]

The flames leaping from the wreckage virtually transformed night into day as Pvt. Charles J. Lahue floated downstream. Around him passengers fought to keep their heads above surface. Lahue's attention was momentarily captured by a woman calling for help from another man nearby, who carried a small child on his back. Lahue watched as the man struggled and then disappeared beneath the muddy river. As the man and child slipped from view, he heard the frantic woman scream, "My husband and baby are gone!" The woman was Ann Annis.[351]

Capt. J. Walter Elliott waited until the water around the burning steamer had cleared of the mass of men before attempting his own escape. A mattress tossed over the side by Elliott was immediately claimed by several men already in the water, so Elliott tried a second mattress. Hardly had it touched the water when four others grabbed it. Forced to do without a float of any kind, Elliott entered the river. But as soon as he hit the water, a drowning man clutched his legs. He freed himself and swam to the second mattress, which had by now only one soldier holding to it. The other three men had disappeared. As he drifted alongside the steamer, Elliott was horrified to find that a burning wheelhouse was collapsing toward him. The wave created by the fallen wreckage caused him nearly to drown. In Elliott's words, "there seemed to be acres of struggling humanity on the waters, some on debris of the wreck, some on the dead carcasses of horses, some holding to swimming live horses, some on boxes, bales of hay, drift logs. . . ."[352]

William Lugenbeal searched the main deck of the *Sultana* for a loose board, door, window, shutter, anything he could find when he realized the fires aboard the boat had spread out of control. Lugenbeal then remembered the alligator housed inside a large wooden crate in the *Sultana*'s wheelhouse. (On the trip up from

Vicksburg, Lugenbeal had enjoyed teasing the animal.) Locating the alligator in a closet under the stairway, Lugenbeal dragged its crate onto the deck, killed the reptile with his bayonet, and threw the box overboard for use as a raft. Anyone attempting to join him on the crate received a sound kick from Lugenbeal, who was finally rescued three miles below Memphis by the gunboat *Essex*.[353]

Lugenbeal was not the only soldier to have the *Sultana*'s alligator in mind that morning. Several men were clinging to a log, floating toward Memphis, when from out of the darkness a horse swam up and stuck its head over the log. The soldiers nearest the animal mistook the horse for the alligator and rather than "keep his company they let loose and gave him full possession."[354]

When Joseph Taylor Elliott hit the water, he was shocked to find it "colder than Greenland's icy mountains." Elliott soon realized that despite his excellence as a swimmer, he would need some support and sought out any passing debris. He started away from the burning boat and came upon a set of stairs and joined another soldier who was already attached. Two more soldiers soon joined them. These four watched the burning steamer with a mixture of distress and fascination as she drifted parallel to them. Elliott, who could plainly see passengers overtaken by the flames, recalled the scene as the final day of judgment. Elliott clung to the stairs as the group drifted past the lights of Memphis and eventually passed out from exposure. Waking to the splashing of an oar, Elliott was stirred into consciousness. He tried to call out for help, but his voice was gone. He felt like someone calling out from a nightmare. His rescuers placed him in a boat and revived him with a shot of whiskey.[355]

When James and Jesse Millsaps, brothers belonging to the 3rd Tennessee Cavalry, were separated following the explosion, each clung to a log, with another person holding to the opposite end. Darkness concealed their identities from one other. Only after their rescue did the brothers realize that they had shared the same float.[356]

From out of the darkness of the Mississippi, Perry Summerville heard an unfamiliar noise as he floated on a piece of wood. When the noise drew closer, the soldier discovered that it was issuing from a horse. He paddled toward it in hopes that the horse would serve him as a better float but was surprised to find six or eight

Pvt. Perry S. Summerville, Company K, 2nd Indiana Cavalry. Survived. (Chester Berry, *Loss of the* Sultana *and Reminiscences of Survivors*)

soldiers already using the animal as a raft. Fearing these men might try to take his board, Summerville swam away beyond reach.[357]

Samuel Pickens of the 3rd Tennessee Cavalry was another passenger whose survival came to depend on one of the horses being transported on the *Sultana*. Pickens, after being blown off the steamer, had grabbed the first object he could find, which happened to be the tail of a horse swimming alongside the steamboat. Worried that the animal would stay too near the burning boat, Pickens caught hold of a dead horse drifting near him. He then traded the dead horse for a piece of wreckage and eventually reached land. Pickens would later recount that his trading a live horse for a dead one was the best bargain he ever made.[358]

It was only after resisting the desperate attempts of two passengers to grab hold of him that George H. Young was able to claim a small section of the *Sultana's* roof. And when the section of roof floated into still water, Young knew that he was nearing shore. The shapes of treetops, against the sky, filled him with hope. He grabbed a limb of a tree and pulled himself up onto it, but a numbing chill he sensed creeping over his body convinced Young to slide himself back into the river to avoid the cold air and there he prayed for the coming dawn.[359]

Young was finally rescued and taken to a cabin already full of survivors from the *Sultana*. Two soldiers who were badly burned lay on one bed and screamed in agony whenever wind blew its way through the cracks in the cabin's wall. Seated nearby were two women, their tattered clothing soaked. Young walked outside to discover a "one-armed comrade who was entirely naked, poor from a long prison life, and shivering in the wind." The man was Ogilvie Hamblin.[360]

As Truman Smith of the 8th Michigan Cavalry fought his own battle to stay afloat, the screams of his companions in the cold water were mixed with the unexpected, but unmistakable, sound of voices singing. What he had taken to be his dreaming became reality when Smith passed alongside a drifting tree with four soldiers locked in its roots belting forth "The Star Spangled Banner."[361]

Pleasant Keeble and his brother, John, both with the 3rd Tennessee Cavalry, were on different decks when the *Sultana's* boilers erupted. Pleasant, on the hurricane deck, was caught in a mass of men stampeding for the stairway. Initially forced down the stairs,

Pvt. John H. Keeble, Company A,
3rd Tennessee Cavalry. Died.
(Courtesy of Edgar R. Keeble
and Norman Shaw)

Pvt. Pleasant M. Keeble, Company
H, 3rd Tennessee Cavalry. Survived.
(Courtesy of Edgar R. Keeble
and Norman Shaw)

he somehow managed to climb to the top of the crowd and crawled over the shoulders of the men until he reached the texas. Pleasant Keeble searched for his brother but was shocked to find that the portion of the texas where he last saw him had been crushed by a fallen smokestack. Forced to give up his search, Pleasant Keeble finally found a small box and jumped into the river. As he passed the *Sultana*, a portion of one of its wheelhouses fell away. Keeble used it to clear himself from the vicinity of the steamer's hull.[362]

Another Tennessean, Andrew T. Peery, stood on the only area of the main deck (at the bow of the *Sultana*) that was not in flames. The rest of the steamer was burning down to the hull, fed by several large fallen timbers. Scattered at Peery's feet were piles of discarded clothing, which themselves had begun to catch fire. Realizing that the material would simply add fuel to the already spreading flames, Peery cast the clothing into the river and discovered to his horror the charred remains of two bodies among the rags. Alongside the hull was Pleasant Keeble. Peery watched as Keeble clubbed a mule that was fighting for space on Keeble's makeshift raft.[363]

At the moment disaster struck the *Sultana*, William B. Floyd was pacing the deck of the *Grossbeak*, docked at Memphis, trying to warm himself against a steady drizzle of rain. When Floyd's glance fell north, the sight filled him with alarm. An ominous red glow on the horizon indicated fire. He took up his field glasses and could plainly make out the smokestacks of a steamer over the tops of the trees. Floyd thought at first that the burning steamer was lying next to shore, which led him to believe the passengers could disembark safely. His concerns mounted, however, as he discovered that the steamer was apparently adrift. The explosion, in destroying the pilothouse, had also crippled the steering. The *Sultana* was moving with the current and the crew was powerless to maneuver the boat ashore. Floyd quickly summoned the senior master's mate to the deck. Since the captain of the *Grossbeak* was ashore, Floyd's superior refused to take the responsibility of ordering the gunboat upriver. The senior mate returned to his stateroom, leaving Floyd alone on deck.[364]

Another witness on shore, Charles Ackley, who was stationed aboard the U.S. gunboat *Tyler*, also failed to take immediate action when informed of the distant fire. Concluding that the burning steamer was too far away for the *Tyler* to provide any assistance, Ackley returned to his stateroom.[365]

Meanwhile, William Wooldridge, standing on the Tennessee shore, continued to view the grim spectacle. He later reported:

> Quite a distance out in the river we saw the steamer burning. She seemed a little more than two-thirds the way across—if anything, more toward the Arkansas shore. She was immediately opposite our house. The blaze was shooting far up into the sky when I first saw her. It was so light in our front yard I could have picked up a pin. We could see her timber falling and we heard the cries of hundreds for help. We saw many jumping into the water to save themselves from being burned. We could see them plainly as they struggled in the river. Their cries for help were pitiful. They were indescribable. The impression it made on my mind will never be erased.
>
> Finally the burning boat began to resemble a massive ball of fire. It was drifting down river, helpless against a wind and with a strong current back of it.[366]

Across the wide river, at Mound City, Arkansas, stood L. P. Berry. Like Wooldridge opposite him, Berry, and his parents, watched the flames erupting from the *Sultana* as she drifted past and heard cries of those still on board and the hundreds more struggling in the dark river.[367]

CHAPTER SEVEN

"... Would Morning Never Dawn on Night So Hideous."

By 3 A.M., the steamboat *Bostonia II* was plowing down the Mississippi River toward Memphis. William B. Alwood, the steamer's mate, was on watch when he noticed a fiery glow to the south. He wondered what building at Memphis was burning. Fifteen minutes after Alwood first sighted fire, the steamer rounded a bend and he looked upon the *Sultana* engulfed in flames. The river was now filled with the dead or dying. Capt. John T. Watson, the *Bostonia's* master, ordered that the yawl be lowered and directed that the crew pitch any item of cargo that would float (stage planks, chairs, tables, hay bales, and cordwood) into the Mississippi. The steamer's yawl made nine trips collecting survivors. The crew also threw out the boat's lines so that people might grab hold as the *Bostonia* drifted past them. Two of the steamer's passengers, a Mr. Deson and a Mr. Humphreys of Memphis, took one of the foot planks from the *Bostonia* and together rescued eight people.*[368]

Jacob W. Rush, a passenger on the *Sultana* who had recovered a small piece of wood once he entered the river, could not see which way to swim to reach land. Nor was he able to elicit any reply from a fellow soldier who joined him. The two drifted silently toward Memphis until the *Bostonia* came into view. Rush could make out

---

*In 1874, Congress passed an act giving Captain Watson the sum of $3,962 for property he had lost in rescuing survivors of the *Sultana*.[369]

the crew launching lifeboats and throwing bales of hay and other objects into the river. He then noticed a yawl coming toward him with a torch in its bow. As the small boat neared, a rope was tossed in Rush's direction. Rush reached for the rope, but in vain. The silent man on the other end of the plank suddenly came alive and grabbed Rush's hair. After being pulled beneath the water, Rush was finally able to break free. The lifeboat had by this time disappeared into the darkness, however, and Rush was again left to drift along with the current.[370]

William A. Hulit, afloat in the darkness, consoled himself with the knowledge that he was drifting "on the bosom of the broad Mississippi." He lost track of time as the cold river numbed his body. When Hulit was finally rescued by the *Bostonia*, he was barely conscious.[371]

In his slow drift down the Mississippi, John L. Walker was joined by another hapless passenger, a soldier already weak from prison and despairing of his slim chances of ever reaching home. The soldier cried out repeatedly, and Walker drew as far away from him as was possible on the piece of wreckage he had recovered. The man's crying eventually ceased and he sank beneath the dark water.[372]

Walker, however, could not entirely escape the voices of men struggling to survive. Out across the river, one man prayed for divine assistance. Another voice answered him "to quit his damned praying and go to swimming, that it would do him more good at that time." Walker held on, despite a sense of drowsiness growing inside him, for four hours. The *Silver Spray* arrived in time to fish him out of the river.[373]

J. Walter Elliott and another soldier were also fortunate enough to survive the night's ordeals. The mattress they clung to eventually struck a small drift near the Arkansas shore. Crawling onto a tree, Elliott could not at first stand up but did have sufficient strength to swallow three doses of quinine he had stored in his pocket. By vigorously rubbing his legs, he was able to stand. His companion, however, could not make it off the mattress and onto the drift unaided. In an effort to revive him, Elliott used a small branch to whip the soldier into consciousness. Smarting under the welts, the man was able to reach the drift. The two soldiers also pulled a young woman and two soldiers from the river, but the three died quickly afterward. Elliott later described the scene that night.

Shivering with cold, silently we paced back and forth on that floating cypress. Minutes seemed hours, as we kept our lonely vigil over the lifeless form of that beautiful girl and of the two brave men who had passed the perils of field and prison life only to die in this way just when all danger seemed past. There was no sound to break the oppressive silence save the splashing of the cruel waters and the gurgling moan of a poor fellow who had clasped his broken, scalded arms over a scantling and drifted, with his mouth just above the water, and lodged near us, dying. An occasional feeble cry of distress near by on the river side was answered by voices up the bank. Oh, would morning never dawn on night so hideous.[374]

Time was indeed running out. The diseased, malnourished, and exhausted soldiers stood little chance in the flooded river. What little heat remaining in their bodies was quickly drained by the cold currents of the Mississippi. Soldiers simply passed out and sank beneath the muddy river or died after they had been pulled onto land or rescue boats. Scores fell victim to hypothermia or exposure before dawn that day.

At approximately 3:20 A.M., William B. Floyd was pacing the deck of the *Grossbeak*. From far out across the river, Floyd suddenly heard a faint cry for help. He strained his eyes to locate the source of the mournful sound, which was soon joined by a chorus of similar pleas. Floyd ran to the pilot's stateroom and shouted that the *Sultana* was on fire. The *Grossbeak*'s cutters were immediately launched, and within minutes Floyd was at the stern of one of them as six sailors pulled on its oars in the direction of the distant cries. When the cutter drew near a piece of wreckage carrying 12 soldiers, the men panicked over the prospect of rescue. An old sailor in the cutter turned to Floyd and said, "For God's sake, Mr. Floyd, don't put us alongside that raft or they will swamp us." Despite the apparent danger, however, Floyd steered the boat around the wreckage, and the soldiers were taken on. One man had to be grabbed by the hair before the current could carry him downstream. With the 12 men safely in the small boat, Floyd navigated toward the Tennessee shore.[375]

Thomas G. Love, on watch aboard the U.S. gunboat *Essex* docked at Memphis, also heard the cries for help coming from the river and immediately reported to his commander. All boats were

U.S.S. Essex. The crew from this gunboat, which was docked at Memphis, helped in the rescue efforts. (From the collection of the Public Library of Cincinnati and Hamilton County.)

ordered to search for survivors. Love, in charge of one of the cutters, helped save 76 men that morning.[376]

Once informed that the *Sultana* had exploded, James H. Berry, acting ensign and executive officer of the *Essex*, himself took command of a cutter and headed it toward the middle of the river. Berry and his men could not make out anything since it was still an hour before sunrise and the sky was overcast. Their only guide was the sound of the drowning men.[377]

Berry's cutter eventually drifted down to Fort Pickering, just south of Memphis, where a sentry on shore actually fired at the small vessel. Berry was being forced ashore to explain his presence. While the boat slowly inched toward the Tennessee shore, Berry could hear men around him "crying out and imploring us for God's sake to save them; that they couldn't hold out much longer." The sentry insisted the boat come ashore. Informed that Berry and his crew were rescuing people from the river, the sentry responded that he was simply following orders. Berry again ordered the cutter toward the middle of the wide river, where the crew discovered a drift covered with men who seemed to their rescuers to be more dead than alive. A second shot, meanwhile, rang out from the bank, calling Berry and two other boats that had joined the cutter. Berry, determined to save as many lives as possible, refused to bring his boat in.[378]

A sailor aboard the gunboat *Tyler*, which was tied up at the navy yard at Memphis undergoing repairs, also heard the chorus of desperate cries. He quickly reported to Charles Ackley, acting ensign and executive officer of the *Tyler*, that the river was full of drowning people. Ackley later wrote in his log: "I immediately went on deck and of all the sounds and noises I ever heard that was the most sorrowful; some cursing, calling for help; and shrieking. I will never forget those awful sounds." Ensign Ackley ordered that the *Tyler*'s cutters be launched.[379]

Since most of the *Tyler*'s crew had been discharged, only a few men were on hand to board the boat's two cutters. Frances Ackley, wife of Charles, quickly realized this fact and, against the wishes of her husband, climbed into one of the boats to help in the rescue efforts. An officer in charge of the other cutter was surprised to discover Mrs. Ackley, with boat hook in hand, reaching toward a man in the water and successfully pulling him to safety. On seeing this rescue, the officer exclaimed, "Bless your brave and devoted soul." His crew joined him in unison with an "amen."[380] Frances Ackley helped to rescue 40 to 50 men that night. When she returned, exhausted, to the *Tyler*, she discovered its decks covered with the injured and the dying. Mrs. Ackley spend the next several days nursing these soldiers. (In 1902, Congress passed a private bill awarding a pension of $20 per month to Frances Ackley for her heroic efforts during the early morning hours of April 27.)[381]

Many observers, meanwhile, stood helpless on the Tennessee shore. Lt. William Bracken, with the 88th U.S. Colored Infantry, was on picket duty at Memphis. Bracken could hear the groans of the wounded and drowning soldiers coming from all across the river, but could do nothing.[382]

Steamboats docked at the riverfront spread news of the disaster by sounding their bells. The city, barely awake, quickly realized that something was wrong. Those citizens who ventured down to the riverfront viewed a northern sky still tinted by the glow of the dying steamer; the river before them swarmed with survivors. Already, on the levee, naked and helpless men lay suffering from exposure, innumerable injuries, and, in many cases, scalded flesh.

And meanwhile, cutters and small boats continued combing the Mississippi. These rescue crafts were soon joined by the *Pocohontas*, the *Silver Spray*, the *Marble City*, the *Essex*, the *Grossbeak*, and the *Rose Hambleton*.[383]

Nathan Wintringer was floating down the river with four other men, when, after over two hours, their 30-foot plank finally lodged onto a drift. The men could only wait and pray for rescue. Wintringer watched as one of his companions, numb from the cold, lost his grip and sank beneath the river. Within minutes, however, a cutter appeared from out of the darkness to rescue the remaining men.[384]

As Chester D. Berry floated on a small board through the predawn darkness, he too could feel the icy water draining him of any remaining energy. Concluding that survival was impossible, he decided that letting go of the board would only shorten his misery. Berry was about to push the board away when he heard the voice of his mother praying, "God save my boy." Berry vowed to his mother that he would survive. A creeping numbness and an overpowering desire for sleep induced him, though, to close his eyes.[385]

Arthur A. Jones likewise held fast to a plank despite the numbing effect of the river. Powerless to steer himself to safety, he drifted with the current around a bend in the river and came within sight of the lights of Memphis. Hope quickly turned to fear, however, when he realized that the strong current was pushing him past the city. Terrified at the thought of floating into the dark "wild region" below Memphis where he thought he would be beyond help, Jones assumed that his fate was sealed. Jones's spirits, however, were revived by the sound of oars, and he soon felt a powerful hand pulling him into a small cutter. The soldier was wrapped in a blanket and taken to Washington Hospital in Memphis.[386]

Shortly before dawn, the *Sultana* finally lodged at the head of Chicken Island, across from Fogelman's Landing, just north of Mound City, Arkansas. The once-mighty steamer, which had been entirely engulfed in flames within 20 minutes of the explosion, was now a furnace for the hundreds of passengers and crew trapped between its collapsed decks.[387]

At approximately 5 A.M., a messenger from the steamer *Marble City* rushed to the quarters of Lt. Col. B. T. D. Irwin, the medical director and superintendent of the government hospitals at Memphis, to inform him of the tragic explosion. He was also told that survivors were washing ashore at the riverfront. Dr. Irwin ordered ambulances and medical attendants to the wharf and joined in the treatment of victims pulled from the Mississippi.[388]

Dawn brought to an end a night that for many had now seemed an eternity. But with the sun came, for the first time, the true dimensions of the disaster: The dead littered a long stretch of the Mississippi both above and below Memphis. Ens. James H. Berry sadly observed that with the coming day "the cries of the sufferers had ceased, and all who had not been rescued had gone down. . . ."[389]

Daylight did bring some comfort for those who miraculously survived the long night, and it revealed the lengths to which some men had gone to escape the currents of the river. Many soldiers, stripped of their clothing, hung naked from bushes, sat perched in trees on flooded islands, or lay along the banks. Manly C. White, for example, sat atop a tree on the Arkansas side as the river raced beneath him. With the arrival of dawn, White found himself in the company of other soldiers, likewise positioned in trees or holding to driftwood. To add to their misfortunes, White and the others had to do battle with "buffalo gnats" (probably mosquitoes), which filled the air this time of the year. After fighting the gnats for three hours, White was finally rescued by the *Silver Spray*.[390]

With the rising of the sun, Alexander C. Brown was also able to gaze at the river surrounding him. This soldier had drifted into the flooded timber of an island and escaped up a tree from the ten feet of water racing beneath him. He later recalled the scene and the four hours he spent there:

> Now, when I hear persons talking about being hard up, I think of my condition at that time—up in a tree in the middle of the Mississippi River, a thousand miles from home, not one cent to my name, nor a pocket to put it in.[391]

Sgt. Wilson A. Fast, who had passed out while adrift, was revived by the sun's warmth. He woke to find himself caught in some bushes on an island approximately three-quarters of a mile from the Arkansas shore and in water so deep he could not touch bottom. All about Fast were naked men perched in trees, clutching bushes, or attached to drifts struggling to keep themselves above the river. Many of these men were celebrating their survival and, as Fast described,

> . . . indulging their humor in a great variety of ways. Some were singing old and familiar army songs and patriotic airs; some negro melodies; some mocking the birds; some sitting on rocks, and conscious of their ridiculous plight, raised a laugh among their companions by mimicking frogs—in fact, every living thing that raised its voice above the sound of the waters. . . .[392]

As he held on, Fast glanced downriver to see the hull of the *Sultana*, with all her upper decks burned away, slowly rotating in an eddy at the head of an island. Fast made his way from tree to tree toward the wreckage, and as he drew closer, he recognized several survivors huddled on the hull. Fast fell into the water twice and came close to drowning but finally pulled himself onto the deck of the *Sultana*. The time was approximately 7:30 A.M. The hull was covered with debris, all afire and alive with intense heat, except for a small area at the bow, where 25 men, five of them seriously injured, had grouped themselves.[393]

Robert N. Hamilton and Thomas Pangle, privates in the 3rd Tennessee Cavalry, were among those on the hull. They had earlier pulled aboard an injured crewman whose nose hung from his face by a piece of skin. The injured man, probably William Durkin (a deck hand on the *Sultana*), soon died. The Memphis *Argus* reported on April 28 that Durkin's body was taken aboard the *Pocohontas*; the body was "terribly burnt in the hands and face, and had a horrid gash on his face, the nose being completely severed."[394]

The men at the bow of the hull unsuccessfully fought the flames inching closer to them and soon realized that they would have to jump. At 8 A.M., three men appeared on the Arkansas shore and launched a crude raft composed of two hewn logs approximately 12 feet in length. These men were probably John Fogelman and his sons, Dallas and Leroy.[395] The men navigated the raft to within 30 yards of the burning wreckage but refused to come any closer for fear that those on the hull would overload the small raft. Fast and another soldier promised that only six of them would board the raft at a time. The rescuers pulled alongside the wreckage and the first six scaled down the side of the *Sultana* and got on the logs. The raft managed the trip to the Arkansas shore and immediately returned to the *Sultana* for another load. Fast and those left on the hull were ever watchful of the encroaching flames. Fire had burned a large hole through the deck near the bow, which sent flames sweeping under the hull and out this hole like a chimney.[396]

Those who remained hung wet blankets about themselves for protection from the unbearable heat. The five who were helpless from wounds and burns begged to be transported next. The raft made two final trips before flames overtook the entire bow. With only 30 yards between the raft and the flaming wreckage, the *Sultana*'s hull disappeared beneath the river, leaving a cloud of steam behind. John Fogelman and his sons succeeded in collecting all 25 soldiers and took them to their home, which had already been converted into a refuge for the victims of the disaster.[397]

Andrew Peery was fortunate to be rescued from the *Sultana* by an anonymous civilian and taken to the Arkansas shore, where he joined several fellow survivors around a large fire. As Peery warmed himself, he witnessed the small body of a young girl in a life preserver being brought up from the river. The dead child appeared to Peery to be asleep. A young man sitting near Peery cried as he too watched the child's body being placed on the cold ground. The youth was DeWitt Clinton Spikes and the dead girl was his sister.[398] Spikes was credited with saving 30 lives, but despite his herculean efforts, young Spikes was not able to save his father, mother, three sisters, two brothers, and a niece. The Spikes family also lost their life savings of $17,000 in gold, which was aboard the *Sultana*. (The Spikes family Bible was later recovered by the crew of the *Rose Hambleton*.)[399]

J. G. Berry, a discharged Confederate soldier, and his friend George Malone, both from Mound City, Arkansas, helped in the rescue of approximately 100 people from the river and the trees lining the flooded Arkansas shore. Frank Barton, a Confederate officer, saved several Union soldiers.[400] And on the Tennessee shore, William Wooldridge and a man by the name of Hill took a skiff out into the river and saved 45 passengers.[401]

Thomas Love, in charge of one of the *Essex*'s cutters, continued to search the shorelines for survivors throughout the early morning. One soldier had been so badly scalded that when Love took his arm, the man's skin came off in Love's hands "like a cooked beet."[402]

Robert Hamilton was among the group of men rescued from the hull of the *Sultana* and taken to the Fogelman home. Later, he and other survivors were taken to Memphis on the *Pocohontas*. As the steamer made her way toward Memphis, Hamilton discovered Jason M. Elliott of his company badly burned and lying on the deck. The dying soldier gave Hamilton his army badge and begged him to give it to his parents. Elliott died later that day at Gayoso Hospital.[403]

As the *Jenny Lind* slowly followed along the Arkansas shoreline in search of survivors, J. Walter Elliott stood on her deck, thankful to have been picked up shortly after daybreak. Elliott watched a civilian paddling a small dugout toward the steamboat, and as it pulled alongside, Elliott was shocked to see Daniel McLeod lying inside. This was the man Elliott had only a few hours earlier thrown off the *Sultana* to what he thought was certain death. Now Elliott helped to lift the injured McLeod to the deck of the *Jenny Lind*. McLeod was later taken to Adams Hospital in Memphis, where a surgeon amputated his right leg but saved his life.[404]

Winfield S. Colvin, a member of the 6th Kentucky Cavalry, had been rescued by a steamer shortly after 8 A.M. On board the steamboat, the soldier observed the *Sultana*'s pilot and second engineer. The pilot was not injured, but Samuel Clemens appeared to be near death. Colvin, in describing Clemens's condition, later wrote: "The engineer was the most pitiable object I ever beheld. Every particle of the skin was burnt from his face and breast, yet I could see that the heart was beating faintly."[405]

Hiram Allison of the 9th Indiana Cavalry survived the perils of the river by holding tight to a horse trough. Two other men, who prayed for divine help, held onto the same trough. Allison attempted to talk to these men, but they refused to stop their praying. At daybreak, Allison discovered that his companions had vanished. The trough finally drifted close enough to the flooded timber on the Arkansas shore for Allison to abandon it and climb onto a tree. He was later rescued and taken to Memphis.[406]

William A. McFarland sat on a log in the middle of the wide river as day slowly ushered in. Near him, on another log, were a woman and small child. A short time later, the three were met by a yawl belonging to the *Silver Spray*. As the rescue boat drew near a third log, McFarland was surprised to see that the occupant was none other than the tall Tennessean, who had drunkenly staggered aboard the *Sultana* at bayonet point. The crew of the yawl attempted to convince the trooper to get on board, but the Tennessean yelled in return: "Go to hell with your boat; if you couldn't come to help me before now you had better have stayed away." To the amazement of all, he slid from the log and swam downriver.[407]

In a snag 25 yards from the flooded western shore sat Chester Berry, enduring the intense pain of a fractured skull. With dawn came renewed hope, but also swarms of biting mosquitoes. Berry spent several hours perched in the snag, fighting the pesky insects while the river flowed beneath him. Finally rescued by the *Pocohontas*, Berry was taken to Memphis and placed in Washington Hospital.[408]

With the passing hours, the Memphis riverfront grew ever more chaotic. Nathan S. Williams of the 5th Indiana Cavalry later wrote that "the bodies of the dying, wounded, and scalded were to be seen on every hand."[409] At the foot of Beale Street, for example, a woman was discovered floating on a plank; in her arms was a dead infant.[410] Throughout the morning hours, steamers and small boats continued to unload their cargo of survivors, but by 11:30 A.M. the last boat carrying survivors from the *Sultana* put ashore.[411]

Wilson A. Fast provided a description of the riverfront at this time, Fast being among the final passengers to reach the city:

> Black with smoke, and burned and bruised and scarred, we walked down the gangplank, and as we stepped on shore the ladies of the Sanitary Commission (The Lord bless those noble women!) met us, took us aside one by one to the brink of the river, washed us, assisted those of us who still had remnants of clothing on to remove them (many were naked or supplied only with a blanket, worn Indian style), then clothed each of us with a red shirt and drawers of the common sanitary kind, placed us in an ambulance or other vehicle, and sent us uptown to a hospital.[412]

Another soldier, Manly C. White, described the scene in similar terms:

> We soon landed in Memphis. The excitement was intense. It seemed that everyone in the city was down to the wharf, and nearly every hack in the city was in charge of a soldier, backed down to the wharf-boat ready to take us to the hospital as fast as we were ready. As we stepped from the gangplank into the wharf-boat, to greet us were ladies of the Sanitary Commission and sisters of Charity (God bless them), who handed to each of us a red flannel shirt and drawers. As fast as we donned our red suits we stepped into a carriage and were driven rapidly to the hospital, where all was done for us that could be to make us comfortable. Many died after reaching the hospital.[413]

William A. McFarland disembarked from the *Silver Spray* in time to see the tall Tennessean stepping out of the river. The latter, who still appeared to be drunk, refused all commands to board the ambulance. A group of guards attempted to force the rebellious soldier into a carriage, but a fight erupted and three of the guards were knocked to the ground. The man was eventually subdued and a detail of guards escorted him toward Overton Hospital. On the way, the rowdy soldier stopped to collect various items of clothing from several store windows, and by the time the guards and their charge reached the hospital a mob of angry merchants trailed behind.[414]

Teams of mules and horses pulled the ambulances and wagons loaded with the wounded up the steep bank toward the hospitals in

Sgt. Henry C. Hamilton, Company F, 3rd Tennessee Cavalry. Died. (Courtesy of K. R. Hamilton)

Pvt. Robert N. Hamilton, Company F, 3rd Tennessee Cavalry. Survived. (Courtesy of K. R. Hamilton)

Pvt. John B. Hamilton, Company F, 3rd Tennessee Cavalry. Survived. (Courtesy of K. R. Hamilton)

Memphis. But many of those filling the hospitals would never survive to enjoy the freedom they had newly won. William Fies, describing the grim sights in one of the hospital wards, wrote:

> I was placed in a ward with quite a number who were severely scalded, or otherwise badly injured, and such misery and intense suffering as I witnessed while there is beyond my power to describe. The agonizing cries and groans of the burned and scalded were heartrending and almost unendurable, but in most cases the suffering was of short duration as the most of them were relieved by death in a few hours.[415]

Dr. Irwin estimated that 530 survivors were placed in hospitals and another 260 in the Soldier's Home. (Dr. Irwin's estimate included a few civilian passengers.)[416] According to published accounts in the Memphis newspapers, the Gayoso Hospital received 139 patients, the Adams, 139; the Washington, 143; the Overton, 90; the Officers', 6; and the Webster and the Soldier's Home, a few more. Jesse Hawes, in his book on the Cahaba prison camp, estimated that of the 757 people rescued following the *Sultana* disaster, nearly 300 died once they reached the hospitals.[417]

Those survivors who were not hospitalized searched, often in vain, for loved ones or fellow troops. Seth Hardin frantically looked for his bride along the Memphis riverfront, but exhausted and grieving, the man finally gave up his futile search and went to a "third rate hotel" on Adams Avenue for lodging. The Chicago banker, who had lost his wife and his belongings (including several thousand dollars), and dressed in borrowed clothing, was told by the desk clerk that he "could not board a person who had no baggage and looked as (Hardin) did." Hardin later found a room in another hotel.[418]

Ann Annis lay in a bed at the Gayoso Hospital suffering from exhaustion, but no doctor could treat the pain of the loss of her husband and child.[419] This woman would doubtless relive the tragic events of this morning for the rest of her life.

Robert Hamilton of the 3rd Tennessee Cavalry sought the whereabouts of his two brothers when he landed in Memphis. He found his brother John, but Henry was lost. Moreover, 20 members of Hamilton's company were missing.[420]

Samuel Pickens, also of the 3rd Tennessee Cavalry, tried to locate his brother William. The following day, Pickens wrote his mother

Pvt. William C. Pickens, Company B, 3rd Tennessee Cavalry. On April 28, his brother wrote to their mother the sad news that William was among the lost. (Courtesy of Helen Kerr)

and sister-in-law to give them the grim news of the disaster: "I must confess that to the best of my knowledge brother William is among the lost. I have not heard of him since the explosion took place and I have no hope of ever hearing of him any more."[421]

Another survivor, Arthur A. Jones, in a letter to his brother following the disaster wrote:

> Yesterday I was busy all day visiting Soldiers Home and different hospitals in search of the survivors of Co. C. Of those I could find but 17 out of the 42 who were on board at the time of the explosion. . . . We are still in hopes that more of our boys will yet be found, but it is very doubtful. Those of us who are left can only mourn their loss, and deeply sympathize with their friends and relatives. It will indeed be a great blow to those who were daily expecting their boys, fathers, and husbands home, many of them having been absent for years, others for months. After all their suffering in Southern prisons, getting safely within our lines, on our route homeward, congratulating ourselves on the good news and the time we were to have at home, all this, and to have this terrible calamity, hurling so many into eternity, it makes me shudder as I write. No tongue can tell or pen describe the suffering that was on the boat on the morning of the 27th.[422]

CHAPTER EIGHT

The Aftermath

THE CITIZENS OF Memphis, appalled by the explosion on board
the *Sultana*, responded quickly to the needs of the survivors. The
mayor invited six civilian passengers into his own home, and a Mrs.
Carlisle took the bodies of three drowned women to her house on
Dunlap Street to prepare them for burial.[423] One of the dead wom-
en was Sallie B. Woolfolk of Kentucky. Her body was decently prepared for burial and placed in a vault at Elmwood Cemetery,
awaiting the arrival of her family.[424] The officers and crew of the
Essex collected $1,000 for Ann Annis, while several women gath-
ered clothing for her.[425] A. J. Jones, owner of the Dramatic Saloon
located on Jefferson Street, established a fund for the benefit of the
victims to provide clothing and cover hotel bills.[426]

Benefits were staged by the Chicago Opera Troupe and the
Memphis New Theatre, which together brought in over $400. The
money, along with $200 collected by the Second Presbyterian
Church and Calvary Episcopal Church, was added to a sum of
$1,183 raised by the military and turned over to a committee com-
posed of Brig. Gen. A. L. Chetlain, Col. R. E. Clay, and Dr. Irwin.
Since these funds were not enough to distribute among all the victims, the committee decided to reserve them for those most in
need. The following individuals were selected to receive portions
of the money:

John E. Norton, 5th Michigan Cavalry, $100; De Witt Clinton
Spikes, $200; the widow of Sgt. Russell W. Thompson, Com-
pany K, 3rd Tennessee Cavalry, $100; Daniel McLeod,

$100; Wm. Witherspoon, $50; Robert McKinney, 6th Kentucky Cavalry, $25; Nathaniel Pendergast, 3rd Tennessee Cavalry, $25; Thomas H. Burnes, 1st Ohio Cavalry, $30; Silas W. Wade, 3rd Tennessee Cavalry, $50; Thomas Smith, 18th Michigan Infantry, $25; William D. Wade, 3rd Tennessee Cavalry, $100; Wm. Phillips, 2nd Indiana Cavalry, $25; John Archa, 95th Ohio Infantry, $25; Benjamin F. Learner, 57th Indiana Infantry, $50; James T. Ragan, 3rd Tennessee Cavalry, $50; Wm. Dailey, 3rd Tennessee Cavalry, $75; Seth J. Green, 9th Indiana Cavalry, $10; Lewis Bean, 6th Kentucky Cavalry, $50; Margaret Hickox, wife of Sgt. John E. Hickox, 3rd Tennessee Cavalry, $100; John W. Norcott, 18th Michigan Infantry, $10; Adolphus Russell, 2nd Ohio Cavalry, $10; and James White, 11th Tennessee Infantry, $15.[427]

The fortunate soldiers who had survived the nightmare were later placed on steamers to continue their journey to Camp Chase, Ohio. Many of these men were understandably filled with fear as they boarded the steamers, afraid that death might overtake them before they reached their destination. After boarding the steamer *St. Patrick* at Memphis, William McFarland searched for the safest place for the upriver journey and finally crawled into the yawl hanging over the stern, where he remained for the entire trip. Even here though McFarland jumped at the sound of steam escaping from the *St. Patrick*'s boilers.[428]

As Wilson A. Fast stood on the deck of the steamer that was to finally carry him home, he gazed out across the flooded Arkansas bottomland. When the boat passed Fogelman's Landing, Fast viewed a sight which filled him with sorrow. Rising above the muddy water was the *Sultana*'s charred jackstaff, a sentinel keeping vigil over the sunken vessel and the dead that lay with her.[429]

The recovery of bodies out of the Mississippi continued for several weeks after the *Sultana* disaster. The *Pocohontas* discovered six bodies below Helena, Arkansas, days after the incident, and William B. Floyd on board the *Grossbeak* reported that the gunboat's crew had come across victims as far south as Vicksburg.[430] Lt. P. W. Brown, traveling upriver to Memphis two weeks after the tragedy, sighted several corpses floating with the current. Crows were also observed feeding on many of the bloated bodies.[431] The Memphis *Argus* on May 12, 1865, reported "bodies of victims floating in the river and lying on the banks and in the driftwood on both sides of the river as far down as the White River. Dogs, hogs, and other animals preying on the bodies." The following grim story appeared in the same edition of the *Argus*:

> Fifteen miles below the city on the east bank of the Mississippi near the head of Cow Island, the nude and putrified body of a lady was seen. Hogs were eating the body: Many of the bodies have been picked up in the river by the gunboats, wrapped in canvas and thrown overboard.[432]

One week later, the *Argus* reported that the crew of the *Pauline Carroll* had sighted the body of a woman with a child in her arms floating in the Mississippi.[433]

The sailors aboard the U.S. gunboat *Exchange* viewed a similar sight as their vessel steamed upriver toward Memphis. The steerman of the *Exchange* later wrote:

> When coming up the Mississippi River, and when within 25 or 30 miles of Memphis, I saw what I supposed to be a large amount of driftwood floating in the river, but my attention was directed to a large number of birds of prey in company. On getting closer I discovered it to be human bodies at Cow Island bar. I was obliged to steer the vessel over the bar to avoid running over the bodies. This was the most heart-rending sight I ever beheld in all my life.[434]

The crew of the U.S.S. *Vindicator* also witnessed the gruesome aftermath of this disaster. Each day the sailors had to clear driftwood lodged in the steamer's wheels. This routine task in the days and weeks following the loss of the *Sultana* became a ghastly chore. Phineas D. Parker, the *Vindicator*'s engineer, wrote:

> I wish to say that the most horrible sight I saw during my whole service was immediately after that calamity. When clearing the wheels after the *Sultana* disaster we would find them clogged with dead bodies from the *Sultana*. The crew of the *Vindicator* were mostly old soldiers, and there came very near being a revolt because we were not allowed to bury the bodies which lodged in our wheels.[435]

The dead that had washed ashore were also prey to human scavengers. Inslee Deaderick, a Confederate soldier, observed several men at the river's edge stripping bodies and making off with piles of clothes. Deaderick later learned that the bodies were victims of the *Sultana*.[436]

An article in the Memphis *Daily Bulletin* on May 27, 1865, announced that a total of 197 bodies had so far been recovered. But the remaining victims of the *Sultana* were forever lost in the deep river or in the ashes of the destroyed steamer:

> The *Sultana* is in 26 feet of water, and settling. On her decks can be seen bones burned to cinders, knives, buttons, spoons, fragments of boots and blankets, and spots on the deck may be seen where the bodies of some victims kept the wood from burning. In a burned and cindered shoe was seen the bones of a foot, and skulls, and blackened limbs were thickly strewn all over. It is a sickening, horrible sight. At low water, the wreck will be high and dry.[437]

A few of the bodies recovered were positively identified. William Cruddis's body was marked with a label he had carefully attached to his uniform, and James W. Eadie carried a pass given to him by Capt. Lewis F. Hake of the 115th Ohio Volunteer Infantry. Also discovered in Eadie's uniform was a lottery ticket with his name on it.[438] The body of J. D. Fontaine of Dallas City, Illinois, was identified by the name printed on his shirt. A tattoo marked the identity of William A. Baker of the 3rd Tennessee Cavalry.[439]

Several of the dead were placed in two long trenches at the head of Chicken's Island, near the site of the wreckage of the *Sultana*. A small pine board had been placed on one of the trenches, which bore the following epitaph: "Lieutenant Briscoe, 4th Minnesota Cavalry, taken up by E.G. Thompson."[440] Most of the bodies, however, were buried in Elmwood Cemetery in Memphis. In 1867, the National Military Cemetery was established at Memphis, and most of the military dead were moved there from Elmwood. Unfortunately, only a few headstones bear the names of individuals; the majority simply read "Unknown U.S. Soldier."[441]

Esther and Susan Spikes were buried on April 28, 1865, at Elmwood Cemetery. Esther was 42 years old and Susan was 17.[442] The body of George Slater, second steward of the *Sultana*, was picked up north of Memphis and identified by papers found in his clothing. The Stewards' Association at Memphis raised money to finance a coffin, a lot at Elmwood Cemetery, and carriages for the funeral. The *Argus* reported that the funeral was "very well attended by all the stewards now in this city. The whole affair was

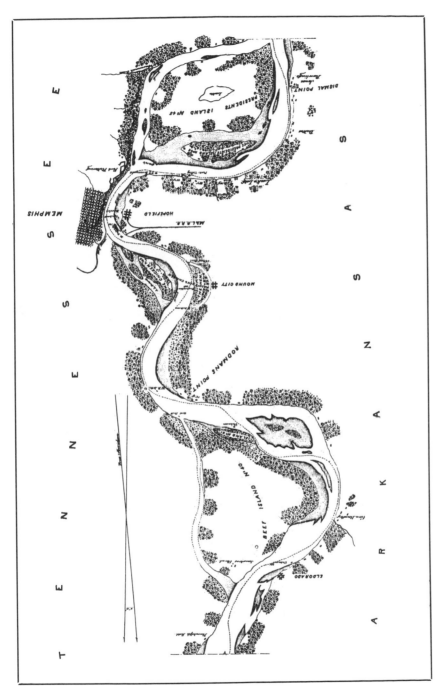

Col. Charles Suter's map of the lower Mississippi River showing the wreckage of the Sultana lodged at the head of Paddy's Hen and Chickens Island near Mound City, Arkansas. (U.S. Corps of Engineers)

handsomely done, and reflects great credit upon the participants."
Slater, from Steubenville, Ohio, was 28 years old and was survived
by his mother, sister, and brother.[443]

A vast majority of the military dead, however, were not buried
with the ceremony that Slater's body received. The Memphis *Argus*,
on May 6, 1865, reported the following solemn sight:

> A Funeral of Eleven. Yes, a funeral of eleven noble dead, was
> to be seen yesterday on their way to their last earthly abiding
> place. Not drawn in eleven different hearses followed by a
> great many carriages filled with mourning and sobbing
> friends, enclosed in finely trimmed and beautiful coffins, but
> in rude coffins piled on one another in a rough government
> wagon drawn by four horses through the busy streets, nobody
> taking any notice whatever. Such was the scene we witnessed
> yesterday as eleven dead soldiers were being hauled away to be
> buried. Such is one of the horrible features of this sad war;
> these noble men who died in the service of their country, have
> friends who love them like ourselves, but the fortunes of war
> have brought them to their death while far, far away from their
> loved ones. This is but a drop to the vast ocean of suffering that
> this "cruel war" has caused, and by far not the worst.[444]

Over the course of several weeks, Memphis newspapers carried
notices from people searching for the bodies of friends and rela-
tives. A Memphis woman contacted the Memphis *Argus* seeking
news of her brother, James O'Hara, a barkeeper on the steamer.[445]
Capt. James M. Fidler offered a reward for the recovery of the
body of his brother, Maj. W. H. Fidler.[446] On May 12, 1865, the
Argus carried a notice offering a $200 reward for the recovery of
the bodies of Norman Bercaw and Matthew T. Van Eman of the
175th Ohio Infantry.[447] Seth W. Hardin, Jr., after making several
futile trips up and down the river searching for his bride, placed a
reward notice in the Memphis *Daily Bulletin* offering $100 for the
recovery of his wife's body.[448]

The St. Louis *Daily Missouri Democrat* on May 1, 1865, reported
that Capt. J. Cass Mason was alive and recuperating at a house on
the Arkansas shore below Memphis. The article further reported
that Captain Curtis of the quartermaster department and Captain
Postal of the Memphis and St. Louis Packet Company had
procured the steamer *Jenny Lind* to make a diligent search for

The headstone of Pvt. William Cruddis at the National Cemetery at Memphis.

The majority of the soldiers who died in this disaster were never identified.

The rows of headstones at the National Cemetery at Memphis.

IN MEMORY OF THOSE WHO DIED
ON THE ILL-FATED PASSENGER STEAMER
SULTANA

ON APRIL 27, 1865, JUST NORTH OF MEMPHIS, THE
LUXURY STEAMER SULTANA'S MASSIVE BOILERS EXPLODED.
THE DISASTER CLAIMED OVER 1800 LIVES—A DEATH TOLL
EXCEEDING THAT OF THE TITANIC.

THE SOLDIER WAS RETURNING HOME AND LONGED TO SEE
LOVED ONES. THE BRIDE AND THE BRIDEGROOM TALKED OF
FUTURE PLANS, AND THE MOTHER EMBRACED HER BABE IN SLEEP.
WE SALUTE THEIR MEMORY, AND FOR THE AGONY AND TERROR OF
THAT NIGHT, WE BID THEM GOD'S MERCY.

PLACED BY
DR. ROBERT KAPLAN
DR. CHRISTINE MROZ
JIM AND BARBARA TAYLOR

HISTORIANS
HUGH E. BERRYMAN, PH.D. — JERRY O. POTTER, J.D.

MAY 1989

*This monument, erected in 1989 at the Elmwood Cemetery in Memphis,
stands near the unmarked graves of three of the Sultana's victims.*

Mason. Traveling as far as the foot of President's Island, below Memphis, they, however, found no sign of Mason.[449] Four days later, the *Daily Bulletin* printed the following reward notice: "Captain Thornburg, one of the owners of the *Sultana* and Captain Oier (*sic*), a brother-in-law of Captain Mason, have offered an additional $200 for the recovery of Captain Mason's body."[450] But Mason's body was never found. The remains of William Gambrel, William Straton, and Henry Ingraham were likewise never discovered.

As with the number of people eventually loaded on the *Sultana*, the number of deaths will never be known with any accuracy. An early report on May 19, 1865, by Brig. Gen. William Hoffman, the commissary general of prisoners, estimated the death toll at 1,238. This figure included 1,101 soldiers, and 137 civilians and crewmen. Hoffman based his count on an estimated 2,021 as the total number of people on the steamer traveling out of Memphis (1,866 soldiers, 70 civilian passengers, and 85 crewman.) As far as records show, however, the actual number of soldiers on board was over 2,300, with 100 civilians and 85 crewmen.[451] The total number of people on the *Sultana* could run then as high as 2,500. The Customs Department at Memphis estimated the death toll at 1,547.[452] It is this estimate that most authorities consider as the official death toll.

Hoffman reported the survival of 783 people: 765 troops and 18 civilians and crew members.[453] If the total number of people on the steamer was in fact 2,500, and if 783 survived, then the death toll comes to over 1,700. But even this number is probably too low.

As previously noted, Dr. Irwin, the army medical director at Memphis, claimed that 530 survivors had been taken to various hospitals in Memphis and that 260 more had been placed at the Soldier's Home. His estimate of approximately 800 survivors is roughly the same as Hoffman's. Neither estimate, though, takes into account those who died shortly after rescue. Jesse Hawes believed that approximately 300 of those who were hospitalized died soon after.[454] If this number of 300 is added to the official death toll of 1,547, then the total number of dead could run as high as 1,800.

Gen. Cadwallader C. Washburn. The Commander of the District of West Tennessee convened a military commission within hours of the disaster to investigate the tragedy. (Library of Congress)

CHAPTER NINE

The Investigations

On April 30, 1865, Secretary of War Edwin Stanton telegraphed Maj. Gen. Cadwallader C. Washburn, the commander of the District of West Tennessee, and ordered a board of inquiry to be commissioned to investigate the loss of the *Sultana*. Washburn, anticipating such an order from Washington, had already established a board at Memphis within hours of the tragedy. Heading his commission were Lt. Col. Thomas M. Brown, 7th Indiana Cavalry; Maj. R. G. Rombauer, 1st Illinois Light Artillery; and Capt. A. R. Eddy, assistant quartermaster.[455]

At 11:30 on the morning of April 27, George Kayton, the *Sultana*'s pilot, appeared before the board as its first witness. Kayton testified that following the explosion he had tried to keep the passengers on the steamer for as long as possible. Kayton expressed the opinion that the flames could have been contained and extinguished if the steamer's fire buckets had not been blown overboard by the blast. He also indicated that the steamer was fully supplied with life preservers (a total of 76). Kayton's testimony also contained the puzzling statement that while the *Sultana* was overcrowded at the time of the explosion, she was not overloaded.[456]

Another witness, William Snow, the senator-elect from Arkansas, testified that shortly after boarding the *Sultana* at Memphis, he had been told by the steamer's clerk that the boat was carrying the largest number of passengers ever brought up the Mississippi River on a single vessel. According to Snow, the clerk's records indicated a total of 2,175 people on board: 1,966 soldiers, 124 civilians, and 85 crewmen. Snow recalled that the clerk had voiced concerns about the consequences of a fire on board the boat.[457] Capt. J. O. Lewis of the Atlantic and Mississippi Steamboat Line (the *Sultana's* competing line) stated in his testimony that the *Sultana* should not have been carrying more than 1,300 passengers.[458]

The steamer's second engineer, Samuel Clemens, dying from severe burns, offered the following statement from his hospital bed:

> Left Memphis at 2 o'clock a.m. 27 inst. carrying about one hundred thirty five (135) pounds of steam. Considered the boilers safe after the repairs at Vicksburg. Though the work was apparently well done think it very probable the explosion was caused by defective repairs. The boat rolled considerably owing to her being very light.[459]

William Gaud, a passenger aboard the *Pauline Carroll*, testified that during the stopover in Vicksburg, he had talked with the *Sultana's* second clerk, William Straton. According to Gaud, Straton was growing concerned over the number of passengers being placed on the boat and had commented "what a terrible thing it would be if the *Sultana* should burn up with so many persons aboard." Gaud, chief clerk to the transportation quartermaster at Memphis during the war, told the board of inquiry that the *Sultana* should not have taken on more than 1,200 passengers.[460]

The military commission adjourned its proceedings on April 27 and reconvened on May 2 at army headquarters in Memphis. William Postal, agent for the St. Louis and Memphis Packet Company, was the first witness brought before the reopened commission. Postal testified that on April 30 he discovered that a portion of the steamer had floated to the surface of the river and that the rest of the hull was covered by as much as 12 feet of water. Visible among the debris lay a fragment of an artillery shell, which appeared to have been exposed to intense heat. Postal then raised the question of sabotage, since it was his opinion that the shell had once been inside the *Sultana's* furnace.[461] John Curtis, agent for the quartermaster department at Memphis, had accompanied Postal to the site of the disaster and later testified to the appearance of an exploded piece of artillery shell among the wreckage.[462]

The next witness, Pvt. Jacob Rush of the 3rd Ohio Cavalry, informed the commission that when the *Sultana* left Memphis it was rumored to be carrying 2,300 persons. He also testified that following the explosion the crew were themselves too panic-stricken to save the passengers.[463]

George R. Denton, Hatch's chief clerk, was the first witness to appear before the commission to raise the issue of bribery. Denton testified that prior to the shipment of prisoners from Vicksburg, Captain Kerns's chief clerk had informed him of the intense competition between the two steamboat lines to transport the paroled prisoners. The companies were offering 50 cents per head for the army's contract. Denton further reported that subsequent to his conference with Kerns's clerk, a runner for one of the steamboat lines had entered his office and demanded to know if there were any prisoners to be shipped. The runner, according to Denton, added that "if it takes money to get them, we have as much as anybody."[464]

The testimony of Lt. William Tillinghast implicated Frederic Speed in these bribery schemes. Tillinghast informed the commission that about a week prior to the arrival of the *Sultana* in Vicksburg, he had asked Speed on which steamer the prisoners would be placed. Speed had replied the *Sultana* and "that he should wait for the boat at all hazards." Tillinghast also testified that after the *Olive Branch* left Vicksburg, he had again asked Speed if any men were to be shipped on the *Sultana*. According to Tillinghast, Speed said the *Sultana* was a contract boat and, therefore, should get the men.[465]

Tillinghast also informed the board that on April 24, while aboard the *Sultana*, he had met William Jones, agent for the Atlantic and Mississippi line at Vicksburg, who offered him 15 cents for every man he could secure for the *Pauline Carroll*. Tillinghast told Jones, "All right, I would see him (Jones) again." Tillinghast never refused Jones's bribe and never informed anyone of it until after the disaster. Furthermore, Tillinghast failed to inform the commission that Captain Mason of the *Sultana* had offered him a similar deal as well.[466]

The next witness to testify was William Jones. Jones insisted that he never spoke with Captain Speed regarding the procurement of passengers for his company's boat, the *Pauline Carroll*. He did state that prior to the arrival of the *Pauline Carroll*, he had talked with Hatch and informed him that he had heard there were 2,000 to 2,500 prisoners waiting to be sent north. He asked Hatch if some of the men could not be put on the *Pauline Carroll*. According to Jones, Hatch stated that if the *Sultana* was not able to carry all the soldiers, 1,000 would be placed on the *Pauline Carroll*. Evidently, Jones, who had nothing to do with the transfer of prisoners, had been informed of the true number of prisoners to be loaded onto the *Sultana*, while Speed and Williams, officers in charge of the transfer, believed there were to be only 1,400. Furthermore, Hatch, after being told by Jones that there were 2,000 to 2,500 troops waiting to be shipped on the *Sultana*, took no steps to investigate if this number was more than the one steamer could safely carry. This is especially interesting in light of the fact that Hatch would later testify that he would not place more than 1,500 men on the *Sultana*. The transcript of Jones's testimony before the commission does not include his answer to the board's final question—whether he had "ever offered money or other consideration directly or indirectly." This of course was a critical question and one must wonder if the failure to record Jones's answer was intentional or a mere oversight.[467]

R. G. Taylor, who repaired the *Sultana*'s boiler at Vicksburg, was the next witness summoned before the Washburn Commission. Taylor informed the board that on April 23 Nathan Wintringer requested that he check one of the steamer's boilers. Taylor stated that upon inspection, he discovered a bulge and evidence of leakage on a riveted seam of the middle larboard boiler. Taylor asked Wintringer why this defect had not been repaired while the *Sultana* was docked in New Orleans, and Wintringer informed him that the boiler was not leaking at that time. Taylor then testified that Wintringer asked him if he could repair the boiler in a manner that would allow the *Sultana* to reach St. Louis. The boilermaker refused to touch the boiler unless he could make the repairs he felt were needed. Taylor walked off the boat with the intention of having nothing more to do with the steamer. According to Taylor, the engineer called him back and again asked him to do the best he could to get the *Sultana* out on the river as quickly as possible. Taylor informed the commission that he finally agreed to repair the leaking boiler but was prevented by Wintringer from hammering out the bulge before patching it. Taylor testified that more extensive repairs were needed to ensure the boiler's soundness. Taylor described his own work as only temporary, but Mason had promised him that the boiler would be thoroughly reworked when the steamer reached St. Louis. Taylor expressed the opinion that the boilers appeared burnt and that an inadequate supply of water was probably to blame. The boilermaker concluded his testimony by informing the board of inquiry that the boiler was not safe after his repairs in Vicksburg.[468]

Capt. George Williams claimed before the commission that he had nothing to do with the selection of the *Sultana* in the transport of prisoners and insisted that his only duty was the supervision and delivery of the men to the riverfront. It was Captain Kerns, quartermaster in charge of river transportation, who chose the *Sultana*, according to Williams. Williams further testified that on April 24 he had counted two trainloads of prisoners, the first containing approximately 570 men and the second about 800. He also stated that it was only later that he learned an additional 650 men had been placed aboard the *Sultana*. Williams tallied the total number of prisoners loaded on the steamer at 1,966. Williams evidently never realized that three trains, not two, had delivered prisoners to the *Sultana* from the parole camp.[469] Williams's estimate of the total number of soldiers placed on the *Sultana* is at best confusing. In addition to 570 soldiers from the first train and 800 on the last, Williams testified that an army officer told him that he had placed 650 soldiers on the *Sultana*. This would come to 2,020 men on board the steamer at Vicksburg.[470]

Williams went on to describe his initial suspicion that Speed had been bribed to keep men off the *Sultana* after Tillinghast told him that Speed was receiving 50 cents per man from the agent of the *Pauline Carroll*. Williams stated that he had reported his suspicions to General Dana but later decided that the allegations were not true. Williams concluded his testimony by claiming he had cautioned the prisoners about the risk of fire.[471]

For Williams to deny any involvement regarding the selection of the *Sultana* remains a puzzling feature of his testimony. Evidence overwhelmingly points to Williams's major role in the decision. It was Williams who refused to place any of the prisoners aboard the *Pauline Carroll*, because he believed that the agent of this boat had bribed Speed. In addition, the fact that Williams testified that it was Tillinghast who had informed him that Speed was receiving bribes raises interesting questions, for it was Tillinghast himself who later admitted to have been offered a bribe.

Reuben Hatch was the next witness sworn in before the commission. Hatch began by making it very clear to the board of inquiry that he had played no part in boarding the prisoners on the *Sultana*. Hatch believed that the men had been directed by Captain Speed. Hatch further testified that he had objected to the number of soldiers being loaded onto the one steamer, which he felt should not have carried more than 1,500 men. In fact, Hatch stated that had he been in charge of the prisoner transfer, he would have placed 1,000 on the *Sultana* and given the balance to either the *Lady Gay* or the *Pauline Carroll*. Hatch's testimony contradicts the version supplied by Captain Kerns, who, on at least two occasions, asked Hatch to divide the prisoners. As previously noted, Hatch refused to do so. Hatch did admit that at one point he started to board the *Sultana* to ascertain whether or not there was sufficient room for all the troops but decided not to because he felt the business of the transfer had been taken out of his hands. This decision not to board the *Sultana* was made despite Hatch's learning from Speed that there were, all told, 300 more prisoners loaded on the boat than had been expected.[472]

The Washburn Commission then called on Capt. Frederic Speed. Speed began by describing his initial concerns about Kerns, who he believed was being bribed to prevent a portion of the prisoners from being loaded onto the *Olive Branch*. Speed testified that the source of these allegations was Hatch, Kerns's superior. He further stated that after the *Sultana*'s arrival at Vicksburg, he met with Mason, who was upset to learn that no prisoners would be loaded onto his boat because the rolls for the men were not prepared. Speed also testified that after his initial meeting with Mason, he met with Mason and Capt. George Williams, who had just returned to Vicksburg. According to Speed, Williams inquired if it were not possible to get the men on the *Sultana* because he was anxious to have the matter closed. Speed recounted that it was at the conclusion of this meeting that the suggestion was made that prisoners' names be checked off as the soldiers walked onto the steamer. Rolls could be completed later.[473]

On the morning of April 24, Speed and Williams went to the parole camp to supervise the prisoner transfer. According to Speed, Williams went into Vicksburg with the first trainload and supervised the boarding of the prisoners. Speed remained at the camp. It is apparent from reviewing Speed's testimony that he, like George Williams (and for some still unexplained reason), believed that only two trains of soldiers left for Vicksburg that day. Speed further indicated to the commission that he believed the number of prisoners totaled 1,400 men and for this reason felt that all could safely be fitted aboard the *Sultana*. Speed informed the board of inquiry that when he arrived at the riverfront with the final load of prisoners, he was met by Captain Kerns, who asked if some of the men should not be put on the *Pauline Carroll*. Unsure of what to do, Speed testified that he approached Captain Williams, who was counting the men from the last train, and informed him of the concerns expressed by Kerns. Speed reported that Williams insisted the men could all go comfortably on the one steamer. Speed proceeded to order the balance of the men to board the *Sultana*. In his statement, Speed testified that he was "greatly surprised" when informed of the exact number of men aboard the steamer because it "largely exceeded" his expectation of 1,400.[474]

Speed flatly denied that he had chosen the *Sultana* and maintained that the decision belonged to Reuben Hatch. He also testified that at no time did Hatch tell him too many soldiers were being loaded onto the steamer. If Hatch had wanted to give up some of the men to the *Lady Gay* or the *Pauline Carroll*, Speed said he would have complied. Speed concluded his testimony by denying that anyone approached him with offers of money in exchange for prisoners.[475]

Capt. J. S. Nauson, in his testimony before the commission, described Captain Mason as a straightforward and honorable man. According to Nauson, Mason maintained a one-eighth interest in the *Sultana* (worth about $10,000), which was all Mason owned in the world. Nauson further reported that Mason had originally bought a quarter interest in the steamer but had sold half this share to his first clerk, William Gambrel. At the time of the explosion, Gambrel had yet to pay Mason. Captain Nauson indicated to the commission that the *Sultana* was not insured and that his company lost $15,000, which was stored in the *Sultana*'s safe.[476]

Following Nauson before the commission was Capt. J. S. Neal, a steamboat captain with 25 years experience. In his opinion, boilers never exploded except when they contained an insufficient supply of water.[477]

Capt. George Williams reappeared before the commission to clear up part of his earlier testimony concerning the number of troops on the *Sultana*. Since his last appearance, Williams had discovered an error in his addition and wished to be on record as stating that the true number of men loaded on the steamer at Vicksburg was actually 1,866, not 1,966. Williams also informed the board that before the first load of troops had arrived from the parole camp, 398 hospitalized soldiers had been placed on the *Sultana*. Williams concluded his testimony by asserting that Speed, and Speed alone, had total command of the prisoner exchange.[478]

Gen. Morgan Smith testified before the commission that on April 24, Captain Kerns feared too many men were being placed on the *Sultana* and asked if some of the troops might not be shared with another boat. Smith reported that he set out to investigate, but met at the parole camp an individual connected with the quartermaster department (probably Tillinghast), who stated that there were only 300 men left to board the *Sultana*. Smith concluded that all the prisoners could indeed fit very comfortably on the *Sultana* and immediately returned to his office. Smith further informed the commission that prior to the war he had headed a half-dozen steamers during 15 years as a riverboat captain, and in his opinion the number of passengers aboard the *Sultana* did not pose any danger to them or to the steamer. He did admit, however, that an imperfectly repaired boiler could lead to an explosion. Finally, Smith testified that it was Speed who commanded the shipment of prisoners aboard the *Sultana*. In Smith's opinion, failure to share the troops with another boat lay with the quartermaster department, which did not protest strongly enough the use of a single vessel.[479]

J. J. Witzig, the supervising inspector of steamboats for the fourth district, which included St. Louis and Memphis, testified before the Washburn Commission that he believed the explosion was a result of excess steam in the *Sultana*'s boilers.[480]

With the testimony of Witzig, the Washburn Commission concluded its investigation and on May 21, 1865, the Memphis *Daily Bulletin* made public the findings. According to the story, the committee concluded that the repairs performed on the middle larboard boiler at Vicksburg had been inadequate, and though this did not necessarily pose a direct threat to the *Sultana*'s safe operation, it should have alerted those in charge to the danger of carrying a high pressure of steam. The article further stated that a total of 1,866 paroled prisoners had been placed on the *Sultana* at Vicksburg, along with 70 cabin passengers and 85 crewmen. In the eyes of the commission, the *Sultana* left Vicksburg carrying 2,021 persons. (The article indicated that only 800 of these survived the explosion.) The commission's report further read:

> The safety of the boat was not particularly endangered by the number of men on board, but as there was no military necessity for placing them all upon one boat, the *Pauline Carroll*, being at the same time at Vicksburg with the *Sultana*, the men should have been divided.[181]

After examining the testimony, the commission also held that:

> The quartermaster's department at Vicksburg is censurable for not insisting on its rights, and for permitting others, without urgent protest to the general commanding, to perform its duties; and the adjutant general of the department of Mississippi is censurable for taking upon himself duties not properly belonging to him. There was no intention, however, on the part of the officers referred to, to do any injustice to the soldiers on board the *Sultana* or the government.[182]

The board concluded that insufficient water in the boilers caused the explosion. And with regard to the number of passengers loaded on the *Sultana*, "The evidence fully shows that the government has transferred as many or more troops on boats of no greater capacity than the *Sultana* frequently and with safety."[183]

On May 23, 1865, General Washburn sent a copy of the testimony taken before the commission to the secretary of war. In his letter accompanying the transcript, Washburn reiterated that the apparent cause of the explosion was lack of water in the boilers. He also stressed that the boilers were defective and known to be so, that the steamer had been detained at Vicksburg for 33 hours for repairs, and that these repairs were only partially carried out. Washburn disagreed with the commission's finding that the quartermaster's department was censurable for not effectively protesting against the placement of so many prisoners on the one steamer. Washburn reasoned that Hatch and Kerns had done everything possible to have a portion of the troops placed on the *Pauline Carroll*. Hatch and Kerns, according to Washburn, had been falsely accused of taking bribes from agents of the *Pauline Carroll* simply because of their efforts to divide the troops. General Washburn also believed that the business of shipping the troops had been taken away from Kerns and Hatch by Captain Speed. Washburn ended his letter by pointing out, "All the parties belonging to the boat who were in any wise responsible for the disaster lost their lives at the time of the explosion or have since died."[484]

Major General Dana also ordered a military commission to investigate the facts surrounding the loss of the *Sultana*. Among the witnesses to testify before this second commission were: Captain Kerns; G. G. Adams, chief clerk for Kerns; James P. McGuire, a steamboat passenger agent at Vicksburg; and Miles Sells, the agent for the *Sultana*.[485]

Kerns, appearing before the commission on May 5, 1865, testified that on the morning of April 24, Captain Mason came to his office and informed him that the *Sultana* was going to take "a lot of paroled prisoners" north. Mason further told Kerns that he was having a boiler on the *Sultana* patched and that he expected to have the repairs completed by the time the prisoners were loaded. Later that morning, Kerns heard from an unidentified person that all the prisoners remaining at the parole camp were to go on the *Sultana*. Kerns indicated to the commission that he believed that there were more soldiers at the camp than could be carried with comfort on one steamer.[486]

Upon learning of the *Lady Gay's* arrival in Vicksburg, Kerns went to Hatch and inquired if the *Lady Gay* should not be detained in order to receive a portion of the men. According to Kerns, Hatch commented that he did not have anything to do with the prisoner transfer but would telegraph Speed at the parole camp to determine if the steamer should be detained. Speed replied that all the troops could go on the *Sultana*.[487]

Kerns informed the board that it was not until he boarded the *Sultana* during the early afternoon of April 24 that he learned the number of men expected to be placed on the steamboat. The *Sultana's* clerk told Kerns that there were already 1,000 soldiers on board and he expected an additional 500. Kerns asked if this would not be a very large load for one boat, and the clerk replied that "he thought they could take them."[488]

Kerns reported that the steamer *Pauline Carroll* arrived in

Vicksburg between three and four on the afternoon of the 24th. By this time, Kerns had "thought the matter over" and concluded that "so large a number of men should not go on the *Sultana*." He again informed Hatch of his concerns and asked if the *Pauline Carroll* should not be detained to take part of the soldiers. Hatch told Kerns that he could not detain the steamer.[489]

Captain Kerns then testified that he went to General Smith and protested against so many men being placed on the *Sultana*. He requested Smith to use his influence to engage two boats.[490]

Kerns also stated that he had persuaded the captain of the *Pauline Carroll* not to leave until all the troops had arrived in Vicksburg from the parole camp. When the last trainload of men entered the city, Kerns reported that he asked Speed to place some of the soldiers on the *Pauline Carroll*. Speed replied that "he could not do it, that he had made all the arrangements for the men to go on the *Sultana*." Kerns disagreed with Speed and stated that since there were two majors with the prisoners, the men could be divided between the two boats with a major in charge of each group. Speed insisted the men could not be divided.[491]

Kerns testified that after getting no help from Speed, he approached George Williams and this time demanded that the prisoners be divided. Williams refused and stated, "The *Pauline Carroll* had offered 20 per cent a head for the men if they went on that boat and that she could not have a man."[492]

Kerns told the commission that by this time he had given up all hopes of getting any men placed on the *Pauline Carroll* but again boarded the steamer and asked her captain not to leave until all the men had boarded the *Sultana*.[493]

Kerns, after asking Williams and Speed if they thought all the men could go on the one boat, was assured by both officers that the soldiers "could all go without any trouble." Mason and Gambrel also told Kerns that the boat had carried as many men in the past.[494]

Kerns then met with William Jones, agent for the *Pauline Carroll* and the *Olive Branch*. Kerns told the agent that it was a "no go" because all the prisoners would have to go on the *Sultana*. At approximately 8 P.M., Kerns watched as the *Pauline Carroll* steamed away from Vicksburg.[495]

Kerns told the commission that in his opinion the maximum number of soldiers the *Sultana* should have carried was 1,200.

Kerns indicated that he would have hesitated to travel on the boat, because he did not believe that so many passengers could go in comfort.[496] William Kerns concluded his testimony by denying that he had anything to do with the actual loading of troops on the *Sultana*.[497]

G. G. Adams, Kerns's clerk, testified that William Jones was under the impression that a premium was being offered for the prisoners and that Jones was willing to pay as much as anyone.[498]

James McGuire, a passenger's agent at Vicksburg, told Morgan Smith (the Dana commission's highest ranking officer) and other members of the board that he was offered 10 cents per man by William Jones for all the prisoners he could obtain for Jones's steamboat line. McGuire stated that he then approached Tillinghast to learn how he should go about winning some of the prisoners. Tillinghast told McGuire that he was the man to see since he was in charge of shipping the prisoners. McGuire admitted to the commission that he told Tillinghast, "If I got them through his (Tillinghast's) efforts he should lose nothing by it." Later, McGuire discovered that Tillinghast had in fact nothing to do with the prisoner transfer, and he stopped trying to secure prisoners for Jones's steamers. McGuire also testified to the following facts:

> Lieut. Tillinghast told me that he tried to get the last eight hundred prisoners on the *Pauline Carroll*, that Jennings and Jones had offered from 10 to 25 cts a head for the prisoners, but that Capt. Speed had told him (Lt. Tillinghast) that as they had all come together they had better all go together. Lieut. Tillinghast said to me that he expected to go to Memphis to be before a Commission, and then in speaking of Capt. Mason, he said that the Captain of the *Sultana* was a gentleman, and although he had tried to keep the prisoners off of that boat (the *Sultana*) Captain Mason had said to him that if he had his measure, it should cost him nothing for clothing for a whole year and that not having his measure, he had made it all right anyhow.[499]

Miles Sells testified that shortly after the steamer reached Vicksburg, he and Mason called upon Hatch. Mason told Hatch that he wanted "all the men he could ship on his boat." According to Sells, Hatch informed Mason that Speed had indicated that only 300 to 500 men were ready for shipment. Mason said it would

Gen. William Hoffman, the officer standing to the right in the picture, was the Commissary General of Prisoners. He investigated the loss of the Sultana. (United States Army Military History Institute)

hardly pay him to wait until the next day for that number of men and claimed that if the men were ready he was entitled to them, the *Sultana* being one of the boats contracted to carry government freight. Sells concluded his testimony before the commission by denying that Mason offered bribes to anyone.[500]

On May 8, 1865, General Dana sent a report to Brig. Gen. William Hoffman, the U.S. Army commissary general of prisoners. Dana informed Hoffman that Capt. George Williams had originally been placed in charge of the prisoner transfer, but when Williams was forced to travel to Cairo, Illinois (to communicate with General Grant regarding problems surrounding the exchange), Captain Speed volunteered to assume Williams's duties at Vicksburg. During this time, Confederate officials began paroling prisoners and Dana ordered Speed "to prepare their rolls as rapidly as possible and send them North as rapidly as the rolls could be prepared, calculating, as near as circumstances would permit, about 1,000 at a load for the regular packets as they passed." In his report, Dana described his "great interest in expediting the departure of these brave fellows to their homes" and stated that he had watched the first load of 1,300 men board the *Henry Ames*. The *Olive Branch*, according to Dana, arrived shortly after and departed with 800 prisoners. Dana then reported to Hoffman that after the *Olive Branch* had set off upriver, Speed entered his office and demanded that Dana arrest Captain Kerns. According to Speed, Kerns had been bribed by the Merchants' and People's line to detain the *Olive Branch* until one of its own steamers could arrive to take on prisoners. Dana wrote that he refused to arrest Kerns until a full investigation was conducted.[501]

Dana then told Hoffman that the next steamer to reach Vicksburg was the *Sultana*, but since it arrived so soon after the departure of the *Olive Branch*, Speed had decided not to give it any soldiers. A short time later, again according to Dana, Speed informed him that, having consulted with George Williams (who had just returned to Vicksburg), a decision had been made to ship all the remaining prisoners on the *Sultana*. Williams had determined that the soldiers could be counted as they boarded and the rolls drawn up later. Dana wrote that this proposal met with his approval after Speed informed him that only 1,300 to 1,400 prisoners remained at Vicksburg.[502]

Dana further reported that on April 24, Captain Williams had sent word that the captain of the *Sultana* was eager to depart Vicksburg and would allow the authorities only limited time (roughly two hours) to decide the shipment of the remaining troops. Williams accused Speed of being bribed to keep prisoners off the *Sultana* so that they could be placed on a steamer belonging to the competing line. Dana stated that he had informed Williams about the allegations Speed had earlier made against Kerns and told Williams that he thought the rumors surrounding Speed were untrue. Williams later informed Dana that he had investigated these allegations, which revealed that Speed was innocent. Dana did order a telegram sent to Speed informing him that the *Sultana* would be leaving in an hour or two and inquiring if any more men would go by her.[503]

Dana also stated in his report that on the evening of April 24, Speed announced that all the prisoners were in from the camp. Dana indicated he had felt that evening that Speed had performed his difficult task with "great satisfaction and efficiency." Dana admitted to Hoffman that on the morning following the departure of the *Sultana*, he had been shocked when Speed informed him that 1,900 men were on the steamer. Having never seen the *Sultana*, Dana questioned both Speed and Williams on the *Sultana*'s carrying capacity and the condition of the men. He was assured by them that the load was not too large for the steamer. In fact, Dana wrote that both Speed and Williams told him that "the men were comfortable and not overcrowded, and that there were very few boats which had so much room for troops as the *Sultana*."[504] In an endorsement to his report, dated the same day, Dana wrote:

> Captain Speed was intrusted with the transfer and shipment of the prisoners, and assumed full and active management and control of it, and I therefore considered him fully responsible therefor. The quartermaster's department was ordered to provide the transportation, and I consider Captain Kerns, quartermaster in charge of transportation, responsible for the character of it.[505]

On April 30, 1865, the secretary of war ordered Brigadier General Hoffman to proceed to Memphis and Vicksburg to carry out his own investigation of the *Sultana* tragedy. After reviewing the transcripts from the Washburn and Dana investigations, Hoffman began a series of interviews with witnesses in Vicksburg. The first to be questioned was William Butler, the cotton merchant from Springfield, Illinois, who had witnessed conditions on board the *Sultana*.[506]

Captain Kerns, next to come before Hoffman, centered his testimony on the lack of provisions aboard the *Sultana*. No special arrangements for cooking had been devised, for example, considering the number aboard the boat. The assumption had been made that the *Sultana* was equipped with the same facilities as were to be found on all steamboats carrying soldiers. (In fact, the *Sultana* had only one stove.) Kerns also stated that no additional restroom facilities had been engineered for use by the soldiers before the boat pulled out of Vicksburg.[507]

Edward D. Butler, superintendent of military railroads at Vicksburg, confirmed that on April 24 three trainloads of prisoners had been shipped from the parole camp; the first left the camp about noon, the second around 1 P.M., and the third between 4 and 5 P.M. Butler testified that the first and third trains carried a combined total of 1,500 men, while the second moved approximately 400.[508]

Lewis Bean, with the 6th Kentucky Cavalry and among the last group of prisoners placed on the *Sultana*, remembered that there was much talk among the troops concerning the obvious overloading of the steamer. Bean informed Hoffman that the men could not understand why some of them were not placed on the steamer that lay alongside the *Sultana*. As he boarded the *Sultana*, Bean recalled hearing Major Fidler, the officer in charge of all the prisoners, tell Captain Mason that there were indeed too many men on board. Mason replied that he could not help it, the men were ready to go, and that he thought he could carry them through.[509]

Another witness to testify during Hoffman's investigation was Nathan Wintringer. Wintringer reported that the boilers had worked perfectly until the steamer was ten hours below Vicksburg. At this point, a small leak on the larboard boiler was discovered, and repairs made to it at Vicksburg were properly done. The engineer was confident that the boiler was as sound as it had been on leaving New Orleans. Wintringer further testified that the man who patched the boiler had informed him that "the repairing was a perfect job, and that the boiler was perfectly safe." No caution was voiced about carrying steam. Wintringer claimed that he knew nothing about recommended further repairs to be performed in St. Louis.[510]

The most critical passage in Wintringer's testimony deals with a conversation he had with Samuel Clemens shortly before the latter died from burns suffered in the explosion. Clemens, according to Wintringer, insisted that at the time of the explosion the boilers had plenty of water and did not carry an excess of pressure. As for the cause of the explosion, Wintringer theorized:

> . . .[T]he boat was top heavy and was consequently inclined to careen over from side to side, and in this way the water had been thrown from the upper boilers to the lower ones, exposing some parts of the upper ones to be heated, which parts gave way, when the water was suddenly brought back to its proper level.[511]

Hoffman's next witness, Captain Speed, told him that it was Hatch who selected the *Sultana* to carry the prisoners. Speed admitted that at no time did he personally inspect the *Sultana* to ascertain the number of troops it could hold safely and in reasonable comfort, though he did casually observe that the steamer appeared "roomy." He further testified that he was unaware of the repairs made to one of the *Sultana*'s boilers.[512]

Captain Williams was asked by Hoffman if at any time before or after the shipment of paroled prisoners to Vicksburg had he inspected the boat to determine her fitness to carry the numbers placed on her. Williams replied, "I did not inspect the boat with that view, but when I cautioned the men about fire, I asked them if they were comfortable, they replied that they were and I so judged them."[513]

Isaac West, an engineer and boilermaker from Cincinnati, informed Hoffman that in his opinion the probable cause of the explosion was lack of water in the boilers. Furthermore, he expressed the conviction that if the patch had indeed failed, this alone would not have resulted in an explosion.[514]

Cpl. Jeremiah Mahoney, 2nd Michigan Cavalry, testified that he was among the last to board the *Sultana* and after making his way to the hurricane deck found it so crowded with men that he could not get through. "The steamer was too much crowded and the men were anxious that some should go on board the *Pauline Carroll*.

Some of them did attempt to go on her, but they were told she had the smallpox aboard and to keep them off."[515]

General Hoffman opened his report (May 19, 1865) to Secretary of War Stanton with the following:

> Upon a careful consideration of all the facts as presented in the testimony herewith submitted, I am of the opinion that the shipment of so large a number of troops (1,866) on one boat was, under the circumstances, unnecessary, unjustifiable, and a great outrage on the troops. A proper order was issued by the general commanding the department for the embarkation of the paroled prisoners, and there were four officers of his staff who were responsible that this order was properly carried out, to wit; Col. R.B. Hatch, captain in the quartermaster's department, chief quartermaster; Capt. Frederic Speed, assistant adjutant-general, U.S. Volunteers, adjutant-general Department of Mississippi; Capt. George A. Williams, First U.S. Infantry, commissary of musters and in charge of paroled prisoners; and Capt. W.F. Kerns, assistant quartermaster, U.S. Volunteers, and master of transportation. If there was anything deficient or unsuitable in the character of the transportation furnished, one or more of these officers should be held accountable for the neglect.[516]

Hoffman positively established that on April 24, three trainloads of prisoners were placed aboard the *Sultana*; both Speed and Williams, who were in charge of the prisoner transfer, were mistaken in believing there were only two. At no time, according to Hoffman, did these officers adequately inspect the *Sultana* to determine her capacity or condition. Hoffman asserted that Williams and Speed, convinced that approximately 1,400 men were to be shipped aboard the *Sultana*, had refused to grant any troops to the *Pauline Carroll* because they believed that the agent for this steamer had bribed officials for a share of the prisoners. It was not until after all the men were aboard the *Sultana* that the two officers became aware of the "fearful load" that was on the boat. By this time, they seemed to think it was too late to divide the troops. Hoffman again pointed to the fact that neither Speed nor Williams inspected the boat to determine if there was enough room for all the men.[517]

General Hoffman also wrote that as the men were loaded on the *Sultana*, Captain Kerns grew ever more convinced that a division of the troops was in order. Hoffman noted Kerns's expression of concern to Hatch, who agreed with Kerns but failed to intervene on behalf of the soldiers. This, according to Hoffman, constituted a dereliction of duty on Hatch's part. (Hatch's failure to act was explained by prior difficulties Hatch had had with Captain Speed over the shipment of prisoners.) Hoffman pointed out to the secretary of war that two other steamers at Vicksburg could have taken part of the men, and "there was therefore no necessity for crowding them all on one boat." A single order from Hatch or a report of the facts to General Dana would have been, according to Hoffman, the only actions required to divide the men.[518]

In his discussion of conditions aboard the *Sultana*, Hoffman wrote:

> The testimony shows, and by a calculation of the area of the three decks, I am satisfied that there was scant sleeping room for all the men when every part of the boat, from the roof of the "texas" to the main deck, was fully occupied. At night it was impossible to move about, and it was only with much difficulty that it could be done during the daytime. . . . Before the troops embarked there were on the boat about sixty horses and mules and some hogs, 100 or more. The great weight on the upper deck made it necessary to set up stanchions in many places, in spite of which the deck perceptibly sagged.[519]

Hoffman indicated that conclusive evidence for the cause of the explosion could not be determined. What evidence there was, however, pointed to an insufficient supply of water in the boilers, rather than any repair work done at Vicksburg.[520]

General Hoffman expressed the opinion that Hatch, Kerns, Speed, and Williams were together responsible for the inordinate number of troops loaded on the *Sultana*, with Colonel Hatch and Captain Speed being the most censurable. In deciding the culpability of Captain Kerns, Hoffman reiterated that, while this officer had failed to make an inspection of the *Sultana*, he had alerted Smith and Hatch to the conditions on board, and that they should have acted upon his concerns. Hoffman was critical of Kerns for not reporting the repairs aboard the *Sultana* to his superiors.[521]

Lt. William Tillinghast, according to Hoffman, had by his own testimony been offered a bribe by agents of the *Pauline Carroll*, which he showed a willingness to accept, and which he had failed to report until after the loss of the *Sultana*.[522]

Hoffman also pointed a finger of guilt at Brig. Gen. Morgan Smith:

> Brig. Gen. M.L. Smith, U.S. Volunteers, had command of the District of Vicksburg at the time, but he had nothing officially to do with the shipment of the troops; yet as it was officially reported to him by Captain Kerns that too many men were being put on the *Sultana*, it was proper that he should have satisfied himself from good authority whether there was sufficient grounds for the report, and if he found it so he should have interfered to have the evil remedied. Had he done so the lives of many men would have been saved.[523]

Hoffman concluded his report to the secretary of war by calculating that at the time of the disaster 1,866 soldiers were on board the *Sultana* and of that number only 765 were saved. Of the 70 cabin passengers and 85 crewmen, a maximum of 18 survived. Hoffman placed the death toll at 1,238.[524]

CHAPTER TEN

The Guilty Go Unpunished

IN THE WAKE of the government inquiries, several theories were advanced to explain the exact cause of the explosion of the *Sultana*'s boilers. Blame for the disaster had first been put on sabotage. William Rowberry, the first mate, contended that some "infernal machine" had been placed in the boat's coal supply. Only sabotage, according to Rowberry, could account for any malfunction in the *Sultana*'s operation, because the boat was running very steady and carried little steam.[525]

As we have seen, the testimonies of William Postal and John Curtis before the Washburn Commission also pointed to the possibility of sabotage. Both men reported coming across a fragment of an artillery shell weighing almost a pound among some bricks in the wreckage. The piece of shell was blistered and appeared to have been recently exploded.[526] Moreover, a story appearing in the Memphis *Daily Bulletin* on May 2, 1865, quoted a witness before this commission who stated he had seen the doors of the furnace blow open just prior to the explosion.[527]

An article in the Cincinnati *Gazette* on May 1, 1865, voiced the opinion of many Northerners:

> The destruction of passenger steamers is an organized system of Southern warfare. We need not recall the examples of it. It has been openly declared in the South and frequently carried into execution on the Mississippi. So also the secret obstruction of railroads to precipitate passenger trains to destruction. Arson was organized to fire Northern cities.

Assassination . . . is brought into play to restore or avenge a de-
feated cause. Is it not in accordance with all this . . . that these
insurgents should conspire to sink, explode and fire the vessels
conveying our returning soldiers?[528]

Strongest support for the sabotage theory appeared in an article
published in the Memphis *Daily Appeal* on May 8, 1888, 23 years after the disaster. William C. Streeter, a resident of St. Louis, claimed
at a reunion of the survivors of the *Sultana* that a noted Confederate blockade runner and mail carrier named Robert Lowden
(known during the war as Charles Dale) was the author of the terrible disaster. Streeter alleged that Lowden told him after the close of
the war that while the steamer lay at Memphis, he had smuggled on
board the *Sultana* a large lump of coal that contained a torpedo.
This he deposited on the fuel pile in front of the boilers for the express purpose of destroying the steamer.[529]

Shortly after the disaster, Captain Thornburg, one of the owners
of the *Sultana*, stated he thought the explosion was caused by some
external source, but he did not believe this source to be a shell
placed among the coal. Thornburg said he intended to have every
boiler fragment removed from the wreckage for examination.[530]
During late June 1865, salvagers did remove one boiler; the other
three had been "blown to atoms."[531] There is no evidence, however,
that a detailed examination of the remaining boiler was ever performed.

Neither of the military's investigations into the loss of the
steamer gave any credence to the sabotage theory. The board of
inquiry commissioned by General Washburn concluded that the
cause of the explosion was insufficiency of water in the boilers, despite the testimony of the engineer on duty at the time of the blast,
who insisted the boilers held plenty of water. The inquiry conducted by General Hoffman closed without determining the root
cause of the *Sultana* disaster.[532]

Nathan Wintringer proposed that the explosion owed to the
boilers' experimental design. A type newly introduced to the lower
Mississippi, the flues on the *Sultana*'s boilers were arranged in a zig-
zag configuration, which made them very difficult to clean. The
rapid accumulation of sediment rendered them subject to overheating or burning. Wintringer pointed out that after the *Sultana*

and two other steamers, the *Walker R. Carter* and the *Missouri*, exploded, use of this type of boiler on the lower Mississippi was discontinued.[533]

J. J. Witzig, supervising inspector of steamboats for the St. Louis district, provided the most enlightening comments on the source of the *Sultana* explosion. Declaring the *Sultana*'s sinking as "perhaps the most frightful disaster ever recorded in the annals of steam navigation," Witzig concentrated his attention on the repairs made at Vicksburg. It was Witzig who pointed out that the small patch placed on the middle larboard boiler was made of iron a quarter of an inch thick, while the boiler itself was of iron seventeen/forty-eights of an inch in thickness. This variation in thickness was critical. It was Witzig's opinion that the patched boiler could only withstand pressure up to 100.43 pounds per square inch. Since the *Sultana*'s boilers carried the normal working pressure of 145 pounds from Vicksburg to Memphis, Witzig concluded that the pressure within the boiler was too great for the patch, which finally gave way.[534]

While concluding that improper repairs were directly linked to the disaster, Witzig also agreed with Wintringer that the boilers of the *Sultana* were not suited for travel along the lower Mississippi and that the possibility of overheating (due to accumulated sediment within the flues) was a great risk.[535] Witzig placed the blame for the explosion squarely on the shoulders of Wintringer. In his report Witzig wrote: "The boilers were imperfectly repaired at Vicksburg, which the engineer alone can be held responsible." He further stated: "When a boat leaves port, with machinery or engines in a bad condition, the law holds the engineer responsible. He is licensed for that purpose, and the master is not supposed to know anything about it. The law licenses Pilots and Engineers."[536]

Witzig emphasized that a master who allowed too many passengers on his boat violated the law, and he set the blame for the gross overcrowding of the *Sultana* on Captain Mason. The inspector further pointed out that the law restricted the number of passengers steamers could carry, but that the military had been forced to disregard these limitations during the war out of necessity. According to Witzig, "This war was already ended when this inhuman shipment was made and nobody pretended that there was a necessity."[537]

Following his investigation, Witzig notified Wintringer that his engineer's license would be revoked. The Board of Steamboat Inspectors in Washington issued its own order revoking Wintringer's license a short time later.[538]

Wintringer responded to the actions taken against him by submitting a letter to the *Daily Missouri Democrat*, which published it on June 19, 1865. The letter reads as follows:

> I wish to make the following statement of facts in regard to the *Sultana* disaster, as there are all kinds of reports in circulation, to the effect that the boilers were in bad condition when the boat left Vicksburg. There is no foundation for such reports, and they cannot be substantiated at all. The steamer *Sultana* left New Orleans on the evening of the 21st of April; we did not have many passengers, but had two hundred and twenty-five or fifty hogs-heads of sugar and some hogs as freight. Some twelve hours before arriving at Vicksburg, I discovered a leak on a side seam on the larboard boiler. We carried low steam and worked along moderately until we came to Vicksburg. We there cooled down and let the water out of the boilers, and procured the services of regular boiler repairers, and had the boiler repaired thoroughly; and to all appearance it was a very good job, and did not leak a drop after leaving there. We then took aboard some two thousand troops at Vicksburg, and left there about twelve o'clock on the night of the 24th of April, and arrived at Memphis on the evening of the 26th, about eight o'clock. We there discharged the sugar which was in the hold; also the hogs, which were on the after guards. We left Memphis about eleven o'clock the same evening, and went up to the coal yard, which is about a mile above the city wharf, and took aboard one thousand bushels of coal. I went off watch at the above place at twelve o'clock, and there was nothing wrong, nor was there any sign of a leak or a defect about the boilers up to that time. I knew nothing after that until I was awakened by the explosion, which was about three o'clock, seven miles above Memphis. I was not injured by the explosion. My partner, who was on duty at the time, was badly scalded, and died fourteen hours after the accident. I took his remains home to his family. On my arrival home I sent a statement to the local inspectors at St. Louis and requested Mr. Schaffer, one of the local Board of Inspectors, to have it published. I heard nothing from it until I received a note from Mr. Witzig, stating the local Board had

turned my letter over to him, which I suppose was their duty to do; also stating he had been to Memphis and Vicksburg, and from inquiries made (not upon sworn testimony), he thought it was his duty to revoke my license. Now, I think Witzig is entirely too fast. I think I am entitled to a trial and investigation before a proper court of justice; also the privilege of defending myself, which he has given me no chance to do.[539]

Wintringer concluded by slandering Witzig:

I am tried, condemned and executed without any hearing, by a man whose only qualification is to drink beer, and when he is on official duties is drunk half his time, and on his trip to Memphis fell into the river and came near drowning. I want only right and justice. I want the local Board of Inspectors to investigate my case, and on their decision I am willing to stand. What it may be I do not know. I know they are practical men and know the law.[540]

John Macquire and John Schaffer, on the board of inspectors at St. Louis under Witzig, received their superior's report condemning Wintringer and a copy of Wintringer's letter. After reviewing the documents, Macquire and Schaffer felt that blame lay either with Wintringer, a well-respected engineer who survived the disaster, or with Samuel Clemens, a subordinate, who perished soon after the explosion. The two inspectors, mindful that the dead could raise no defense, found Clemens to be the responsible party in the disaster and completely ignored the directions of their superior, J. J. Witzig, by refusing to revoke Wintringer's license. Macquire and Schaffer went so far as to publish a notice in the St. Louis *Republican* stating that Wintringer was in no way to blame for the accident inasmuch as he was off watch when the explosion occurred and had been off watch for three hours. Guilt lay solely with the man on duty at the moment the boiler blew—Samuel Clemens.[541]

If doubts still remain regarding the mechanics of the *Sultana*'s operation during her final voyage upriver in April 1865, can we at least ascertain the individual or individuals chiefly responsible for her overcrowding? The Washburn Commission censured William Kerns, Reuben Hatch, and Frederic Speed.[542] But Major General

Washburn in a letter to Secretary of War Stanton expressed disagreement with his own commission's censure of Kerns and Hatch. According to Washburn, both of these officers had done all they could to get a portion of the prisoners placed on the *Pauline Carroll*. He did, however, support the condemnation of Captain Speed.[543]

Maj. Gen. Napoleon J. T. Dana, in a letter to General William Hoffman dated May 8, 1865, also held Speed directly responsible for the *Sultana*'s overcrowding, since Speed had assumed full control of the prisoner transfer and shipment. But Dana added that Captain Kerns was responsible for the "character" of the transportation.[544]

The report of the Washburn Commission was forwarded to General Meigs, quartermaster general of the army, for his review. And on June 16, 1865, Meigs submitted a letter to the adjutant general of the army containing the following recommendation:

> As the Court finds that "the Quartermaster's Department at Vicksburg is censurable for not insisting on its rights, and for permitting others without urgent protest to the General Commanding to perform its duties; and the Adjutant General of the Department of the Mississippi is censurable for taking upon himself duties not properly belonging to him," I respectfully recommend that the officers of the Quartermaster's Department, as well as any others who are shown by the Report to have been concerned in this matter, be ordered before a Court Martial for trial.[545]

Meigs further specified that Hatch and Kerns were the quartermasters to be court-martialed. Later, Secretary of War Stanton ordered Hatch to be brought to trial.[546]

On June 3, 1865, Reuben Hatch was relieved of his duties as chief quartermaster for the Department of Mississippi. It was also on this date that the quartermaster general of the army approved the findings that the military examining board had reached four months earlier in New Orleans. Included in these findings was the board's assessment that Hatch was mentally unqualified to be a quartermaster.[547]

Controversy surrounding Hatch, meanwhile, continued, but with regard to a matter other than the *Sultana*. When Hatch boarded the steamer *Atlantic* on June 26 at New Orleans, he carried

$14,490 in government funds. The funds were to be turned over to Col. William Myers, the chief quartermaster at St. Louis, because, according to Hatch, no quartermaster at Vicksburg was authorized to receive the money. On the morning of June 30, the safe aboard the *Atlantic* was discovered robbed of its contents. The thief was caught later the same day and all the money belonging to the steamer and her passengers was returned—all, that is, except the government funds placed in the safe by Hatch. When the boat reached St. Louis, the package entrusted to Hatch was at last found, but it contained only $5,948: $8,542 belonging to the military was unaccounted for.[548]

In early July, a board of survey convened at St. Louis to investigate the loss. The military board concluded that Hatch, by removing the money from the Department of Mississippi and failing to turn the funds over to Captain Kerns or Captain Van Patton (bonded quartermasters on duty at Vicksburg at the time, who were in fact authorized to accept the money), had violated army regulations, thus rendering him personally liable for the missing funds. This money was later recovered from the Atlantic and Mississippi Steamboat Company.[549] Reuben Hatch was honorably mustered out of the army on July 28, 1865, but his military career ended as it had begun—in controversy.[550]

On November 1, 1865, a court was appointed to try Frederic Speed, and the case was set for the first Monday in December. The trial was continued on November 17 until January 8, 1866, at the request of Lt. Col. N. S. Gibson, the judge advocate, because he had been unable to obtain the necessary witnesses.[551] In a letter dated December 13, 1865, Speed wrote to Col. Adam Badeau (an officer on General Grant's staff, who had investigated the *Sultana* tragedy) and expressed concerns about his ability to defend himself successfully since several key witnesses would probably be unavailable:

> Dana is in Nevada and it is doubtful if he will come, even if the summons reaches him. One important witness—Dodge, late an officer of the Signal Corps—has stolen from Adams Express Co. and will not be likely to "report"—Tillinghast the fellow who started all the stories about the bribery, and as it proved, was the only one who was offered a bribe is now in jail,

at Chicago, charged with forgery. You can judge of the likelihood of his coming.[552]

Speed was correct about Tillinghast because this officer would
not testify at Speed's court-martial. William Tillinghast, the assistant quartermaster who had been at the center of the bribery allegations at Vicksburg, effectively ended his own military career on
August 20, 1865, when he deserted from the army. On September
23, 1865, R. J. Osterbrary, an officer at Vicksburg, sent the following telegram to the commanding general for the district of Illinois:
"Please send here under guard Lt. W.H. Tillinghast 66th U.S.C.
Inf. A deserter and a forger."[553]

Captain Speed further indicated to Colonel Badeau that at last
he could clear up the confusion surrounding the 300 prisoners
who boarded the steamer while George Williams was away from
the waterfront. If these men, patients from the military hospital in
Vicksburg removed by Dr. Kemble, were deducted from Williams's
total of 1,866, 1,566 was left as the actual number of prisoners
placed on the steamboat on April 24, thus proving that Speed's estimate of 1,400 to 1,500 passengers was a reasonable one.[554] But
Speed was in error. The doctor stated in his deposition taken on
November 22, 1865, that these 300 men were not counted by anyone because he never turned their rolls over to the authorities.
Kemble further testified that these men never boarded the *Sultana*.[555]

At 10 A.M., on January 9, Capt. Frederic Speed stood before the
court at Vicksburg and was arraigned on the following charges and
specifications:

> Neglect of duty to the prejudice of good order and military
> discipline.
> *Specification 1*: In this that he Captain Frederic Speed, Assis-
> tant Adjutant General United States Volunteers and senior of-
> ficer of the Adjutant General's Department, on duty at Head
> Quarters Department of the Mississippi, being charged by his
> Commanding Officer Major General N.J.T. Dana, then com-
> manding Department of Mississippi with the duty of receiving
> of certain officers and enlisted men in the military service of
> the United States, paroled as prisoners of war, by the authority
> of the so called, "Confederate States of America," and being
> charged by his commanding officer with the duty of superin-

tending the transfer of said paroled prisoners, from the place of parole at "Four Mile Bridge," near Vicksburg, Mississippi, to the Parole Camps established at Jefferson Barracks, Missouri, and at Camp Chase, near Columbus, Ohio, he the said Captain Speed did neglect to avail himself of the services of Captain Reuben B. Hatch, Assistant Quartermaster of Volunteers, and Chief Quartermaster Department of Mississippi, and Captain W.F. Kerns, Assistant Quartermaster of Volunteers, in charge of Water Transportation at the Post and Port of Vicksburg, Mississippi, in procuring the necessary and safe transportation for the aforesaid paroled prisoners up the Mississippi River, but the said Captain Speed did himself assume to discharge the duties properly belonging to the aforesaid Officers of the Quartermasters Department by deciding and directing that a large detachment of the paroled prisoners aforesaid, about eighteen hundred and eighty six (1886) in number should be transported northward from Vicksburg, Mississippi on one steamer, the *Sultana*, against the advice and remonstrances of the aforesaid officers of the Quartermasters Department, and the said Captain Speed did by placing between eighteen hundred and eighty six (1886) or thereabouts, paroled prisoners on board, greatly overload the said steamer *Sultana*, whose legal carrying capacity was three hundred and seventy six (376) passengers, which said steamer *Sultana* while making her trip with the eighteen hundred and eighty six (1886) paroled prisoners aforesaid on board, at a point on the Mississippi River, about seven (7) miles above Memphis, Tennessee, was destroyed by an explosion of her boiler, or boilers, and by fire, and thereupon a large number, to wit, eleven hundred and ten (1110) or thereabouts, of the paroled prisoners on board, whose names are unknown, lost their lives by drowning, scalding, and burning, and that the eleven hundred and ten (1110) paroled prisoners, would not have so lost their lives but for the misconduct of the said Captain Speed, in overloading said steamer *Sultana* as aforesaid.

All this at or near Vicksburg, Miss., and on the Mississippi River between Vicksburg, Mississippi, and Cairo, Illinois, on or about the 23rd, 24th, 25th, 26th, and 27th days of April, 1865.

Specification 2: In this that he Captain Frederic Speed, Assistant Adjutant General United States Volunteers, on duty at Head Quarters Department of Mississippi, did assume unwarrantable authority, in directing the arrangements for the transportation of a large number of paroled prisoners, officers and men belonging to the armies of the United States then at Vicksburg, Mississippi, awaiting transportation up the Mississippi River, and did without authority load and cause to be loaded, a large number, to-wit, eighteen hundred and eighty six (1886) or thereabouts paroled prisoners, on one boat the steamer *Sultana*, which said eighteen hundred and eighty six (1886) paroled prisoners, were largely in excess of the number which the steamer *Sultana* could carry with safety, and when at the same time, other and better conditioned steamboats, to-wit, *Pauline Carroll* and *Lady Gay*, were at the Port of Vicksburg aforesaid, and whose officers were ready and anxious to take a portion of the said paroled prisoners on board the boats aforesaid, he the said Captain Speed, knowing full that the aforesaid steamers *Pauline Carroll* and *Lady Gay* would if permitted take a portion of the said large number of paroled prisoners, Captain W.F. Kerns, Assistant Quartermaster United States Volunteers, in charge of River Transportation at Vicksburg, having informed the said Captain Speed of the desire of the Officers of the *Pauline Carroll* aforesaid, to take a portion of the paroled prisoners aforesaid, and that he the said Captain Speed against the remonstrances of the said Captain W.F. Kerns, A.Q.M., against crowding so many men on one boat, did with criminal neglect and carelessness, cause the whole number, to-wit, eighteen hundred and eighty six (1886) or thereabouts paroled prisoners aforesaid, to be placed upon the said steamer *Sultana*, and afterwards, from the effects of which a large load of paroled prisoners while said steamer *Sultana* was carrying the paroled prisoners aforesaid up the Mississippi River, the boiler or boilers of the boat aforesaid did explode, from the effects of which explosion, eleven hundred and ten (1110) or thereabouts of the said paroled prisoners, whose names are unknown, were scalded, burned, and drowned, until they were dead.

This at or near Vicksburg, Mississippi, and on the Mississippi River between Vicksburg, Mississippi, and Cairo, Illinois, on or about the 23rd, 24th, 25th, 26th, and 27th days of April, 1865.[556]

Speed, represented by L. W. Perce, entered a plea of not guilty to all the above charges.[557]

The prosecution opened its proof by calling George Williams to the stand. Williams testified that he had no personal knowledge of Speed's involvement in the placement of any soldiers aboard the *Sultana* and further stated that he did not know who directed that the prisoners be placed on this one steamer. When Williams returned to Vicksburg on April 23, he was informed by General Dana that Speed had assumed Williams's duties during his absence. Williams then sought to collect Speed's records in order to complete the prisoner transfer himself. According to Williams, however, Speed had suggested to him that, since there were only 1,300 to 1,400 soldiers remaining, Williams should allow him to continue supervising the shipment of troops.[558]

It was Williams who had agreed to count the soldiers as they came off the trains and boarded the *Sultana*. He testified to having counted two trainloads of men, totaling between 1,300 and 1,400 soldiers. Williams further stated that someone had told him that an additional 300 to 400 men from the army hospital in Vicksburg had been placed on the boat, bringing the total to 1,866.[559]

Williams informed Speed at the time that the Merchants' and People's line intended to file a complaint in Washington against the exchange office at Vicksburg because it had awarded a portion of the troops to the Atlantic and Mississippi Steamboat Company (the opposition line). Williams told Speed he did not intend to get mixed up in any quarrels of this sort, however, since it was the quartermaster department's duty to select the steamboats.[560]

Williams did admit that Speed had initially objected to shipping the prisoners aboard the *Sultana* on April 24 if it meant that the passenger rolls could not be properly prepared prior to the placement of men aboard this steamer.[561]

While he was counting the men from the last train, Williams met with Kerns, who brought up the matter of troop shipments. But Williams disavowed any involvement in the terms of the shipment by saying, "I have nothing to do with it. I am informed that there are officers receiving 50 cents per head for sending these men."[562]

Williams then stated in court that he believed the soldiers were comfortable aboard the *Sultana* and that he had in fact been assured by several of them that conditions were satisfactory. He further testified that he would not have hesitated to travel on the steamer himself.[563]

Portions of Williams's testimony are clearly inconsistent. For example, he first claimed to have had no knowledge concerning the selection of the *Sultana*. Despite his meeting with Mason and Speed on the evening of April 23, and a later meeting with Hatch and Speed, he nonetheless denied that any mention was ever made of the boat to be hired to carry the soldiers. He did admit, however, that after these meetings, it was understood by the three men that the *Sultana* would be the boat to get the prisoners.[654] Throughout his cross-examination, Williams maintained that Speed had played no part in the selection of the *Sultana*, since the decision rested solely with authorities in the quartermaster department.[565]

The next witness to testify, William Kerns, insisted before the court that he too had played no role in the selection of the *Sultana* and only learned of the decision on the morning of April 24 from Captain Mason. Kerns also testified that he had taken no part in the previous selection of the *Henry Ames* or the *Olive Branch* to carry prisoners.[566] Informed that hundreds of prisoners were to be shipped that day, Kerns tried, repeatedly, to convince the authorities that a second boat (either the *Lady Gay* or the *Pauline Carroll*) should be engaged.[567] From a financial standpoint, Kerns testified that it made no difference to the government whether the soldiers were boarded onto one boat or two.[568]

The next witness to be sworn in before the court was William Jones, the agent for the *Pauline Carroll*. Jones estimated that approximately 2,000 soldiers were loaded on the *Sultana* on April 24 and admitted to overhearing some of them objecting to being forced to board. He also indicated that the *Pauline Carroll* was about one-fourth larger in room and a quarter heavier than the *Sultana*.[569]

Jones was also the agent for the *Olive Branch*, which left Vicksburg on April 23 carrying 700 prisoners. Speed had accused Kerns of taking a bribe to detain the *Olive Branch*. The source of these allegations was Reuben Hatch, Kerns's superior, but it was Jones who informed the court that Hatch himself had made arrangements with the captain of the *Olive Branch* for the shipment of prisoners.[570]

It was Jones who allegedly offered Speed bribes, yet neither the prosecution nor the defense interrogated Jones on this matter. This was the second time Jones had been brought before a board of inquiry, and on neither occasion was Jones forced to reveal whether he made any illegal payments. Jones did testify that he never approached Speed in an effort to get passengers for his boats.[571]

Miles Sells, the agent for the *Sultana*, also appeared as a witness at the court-martial. Sells emphasized that Mason sought all the prisoners his boat could carry. Sells was present at Mason's first meeting with Speed on April 23, when Mason demanded passengers for his steamer. Mason, again according to Sells, was outraged when informed by Speed that only about 500 men could be readied for shipment.[572]

Sells was also present at the key meeting between Mason and George Williams in General Smith's office when the decision was made merely to check off the soldiers as they boarded the *Sultana* and to postpone the preparation of the rolls until the steamer pulled out of Vicksburg. At the conclusion of this meeting, Mason told Sells "there would be no trouble about getting all the men he wanted."[573]

Sells further testified that he met George Williams again, this time on board the *Sultana*, on the evening of April 23. Williams confirmed that the decision had been reached to ship all the prisoners the following day and that the rolls would be drawn up later.[574]

This suggestion by Williams was the main reason the majority of the paroled prisoners remaining at Vicksburg were placed on the *Sultana*. It was significant because Speed had earlier informed Hatch that the rolls of the soldiers would not be ready until April 27.[575] If time had been taken to draw up the rolls prior to the soldiers being loaded onto the *Sultana*, perhaps as few as 500 prisoners could have been readied for shipment.

The next witness to take the stand was J. J. Witzig, the supervising inspector of steamboats for the St. Louis district. Witzig, in answer to questions by the prosecution, stated that the *Sultana* was legally allowed to carry only 76 cabin and 300 deck passengers—a total of 376 passengers. The inspector further pointed out that by law a steamboat was allowed one passenger to every 16 feet of deck surface. Eyewitness accounts agree that there was standing room only when the *Sultana* left Vicksburg.[576] Witzig reported to the court that the placement of 1,800 to 2,000 soldiers on the *Sultana* could cause the boat to career, which would pose a real danger of explosion of the boilers.[577]

The court next heard from Captain Kerns's clerk, Elias Shull, who testified that on April 24, he issued a transportation pass for 1,966 paroled prisoners; 22 military guards; Thomas McEvan and four quartermaster department employees; Lt. Harvey Annis; and Pvt. George Smith, 87th Illinois Infantry. According to Shull's records, then, the military placed a total of 1,995 army personnel aboard the *Sultana*.[578]

E. B. Butler, the superintendent of railroads for the army at Vicksburg in April 1865, confirmed that three trains carried prisoners from the parole camp to Vicksburg throughout the afternoon of April 24, and he identified Speed as the officer in charge of the loading and running of these trains. At one point during the prisoner shipments, Butler warned Speed that one train was full, but Speed ordered onto it an additional 200 soldiers.[579]

Butler completed his testimony on January 22, 1866. The prosecutor, Lieutenant Colonel Gibson, at this point requested a continuance until March 3 because of the absence of Reuben Hatch, a material witness. Gibson informed the court that he had been unsuccessful so far in procuring the attendance of Hatch at the trial but believed he could order Hatch to appear by March 3.[580]

L. W. Perce, the civilian attorney representing Speed, objected vehemently to the continuance and reminded the court that the prosecution had had five months to prepare its case. He further argued that Speed had already notified the prosecution that Hatch would not voluntarily appear and that Speed had urged the government to compel Hatch's attendance. Perce also informed the court that Hatch himself had been ordered by the secretary of war to be brought to trial on charges similar to those filed against his client. Despite Perce's arguments, the court, after some deliberation, saw fit to grant the continuance until March 3.[581]

Nathan Wintringer took the stand on March 5, as the first witness following the long continuance. Wintringer described the repairs to the *Sultana*'s middle larboard boiler as performed by R. G. Taylor at Vicksburg and indicated that both he and Taylor deemed the repairs adequate for the boat's safe trip upriver.[582]

John L. McHarg, a farmer from Davenport, Iowa, followed Wintringer to the stand. In April 1865, McHarg had served as a first lieutenant with the 47th Colored Regiment and acted as assistant quartermaster of the parole camp near Vicksburg. On April 24, he advised Speed that one boat could not accommodate all the interned soldiers. According to McHarg, Speed upbraided him for that remark and warned him, "Officers sometimes get dismissed from the service for meddling with that which is none of their business."[583] McHarg also stated that Lieutenant Tillinghast had informed him that "other boats" were offering a premium to get some of the prisoners.[584]

With McHarg's testimony completed, the prosecutor announced that he had no further witnesses that day and requested a continuance until the following day. In support of his motion, Gibson told the court that Hatch still had not reported to Vicksburg to testify and had refused to obey several subpoenas compelling his appearance. The prosecutor reported that General Wood, the commander of the Department of Mississippi, had by this time requested that the secretary of war arrest Hatch and bring him to Vicksburg. The court continued the case over the objections of the defense.[585]

On March 8, Gibson again requested a continuance for an additional day due to the fact that no witnesses were available. Speed's attorney in turn demanded that the court refuse the continuance, arguing that the proceeding had already been delayed 40 days waiting on the appearance of Reuben Hatch. Perce told the court that during the long and needless delay, an important witness whose testimony would have gone far toward establishing his client's innocence had died. The attorney requested that the court force the prosecution to complete its proof. The court, again, granted another continuance.[586]

Additional witnesses were called on March 9. W. H. H. Emmon, Speed's former roommate, had served as an assistant adjutant general at Vicksburg. Emmon testified that Hatch met with Speed in their room early on the morning of April 24 to discuss details of the prisoner transfer. At the conclusion of the 20-minute meeting, Emmon confirmed that Speed and Hatch had agreed that the prisoners would be sent on the *Sultana*.[587]

J. Warren Miller, who acted as a captain and assistant adjutant general at Vicksburg at the time of the disaster, informed the court that on April 24, at approximately 4 P.M., George Williams rushed into his office "very much excited" to report that Speed had been induced, for a consideration, to detain prisoners at the parole camp that evening so that they could be sent on a steamer other than the *Sultana*.[588] According to Miller, Williams demanded that he order Speed to send the remaining prisoners into Vicksburg immediately. Miller told the court that he cautioned Williams about making any allegations unless he could prove them. Miller then testified that he telegrammed Speed the following message:

> Will all the troops now at the camp be sent on the *Sultana*? How soon will they be in? Captain of the *Sultana* has been here and says he will be able to leave in two hours. The General wishes to go to the boat to see them off.[589]

Dana, the general referred to in the above telegram, never went to the wharf to see the troops. Nor did Speed respond to Miller's telegram.[590]

The court adjourned after Miller's testimony. On March 13, Gibson informed the court that Hatch still had not arrived at Vicksburg and requested yet another continuance. The court, over repeated objections by the defense, agreed to resume the trial on March 27. But by this date, the prosecution had yet to compel the attendance of Hatch and the case was reset for May 7. When the court reconvened, however, Speed was away from Vicksburg. When the case was finally reopened on May 27, the prosecutor announced that he had yet to hear whether the secretary of war had taken any action to arrest Hatch. (There is no evidence to suggest Secretary of War Stanton did, in fact, force authorities to apprehend Hatch.) Gibson then informed the court that since everything possible had been done to compel the attendance of Hatch, he would close the prosecution's proof without him.[591]

Immediately after the close of the government's proof, Frederic Speed presented his first witness—exactly one year and one month after the *Sultana* disaster. H. A. Henderson, a former Confederate colonel and the Confederate assistant commissioner of exchange at the parole camp, told the court that prior to May 1, 1865, the Confederacy had delivered to the Union authorities at Vicksburg approximately 5,350 prisoners. He also testified he understood George Williams to be the Union officer in charge of the prisoner exchange.[592]

E. L. Davenport, Speed's next witness, served as the acting assistant commissioner of exchange at the parole camp in April 1865. Davenport described meeting George Williams on the afternoon of

April 23, at which time Williams ordered Davenport back to the camp to prepare the prisoners for immediate shipment.[593] Davenport further testified that on the afternoon of April 24 he received a telegram from Williams that read, "Lieutenant Davenport hurry up the men as fast as possible. The *Sultana* is waiting for them."[594] Davenport also told the court that Speed had not been assigned any particular duties at the camp on April 24 since Williams, before his departure on the first train to Vicksburg, had charged Davenport with conducting the prisoner exchange. Williams instructed Davenport to contact him personally if any problems arose.[595]

On May 28, the defense opened its proof by reading the depositions of Dr. George Kemble and Frank Miller. Kemble stated that on April 24 he placed 23 soldiers, confined to cots, on the *Sultana*; he also directed 278 hospitalized solders to report to the steamboat. Kemble reported that he boarded the *Sultana* for the first time on April 24 shortly before 1 P.M. and observed that the steamer's decks were not crowded. Informed that an additional 700 men were coming from the parole camp, though, he concluded the boat would be too great a health risk for the recovering soldiers. Kemble immediately told General Dana of his concerns and requested permission to remove all the sick men from the *Sultana*. After receiving Dana's consent, Kemble boarded the boat again and encountered George Williams, who objected to the removal of the sick because he had already entered their names in his records. Kemble removed the men after informing Williams that no one had counted them. Kemble further testified that as he was leaving the *Sultana*, he instructed the soldiers from the hospital to turn back. Kemble testified that these 278 men never actually boarded the *Sultana* and were not part of anyone's passenger count. These soldiers were taken north the following day aboard a hospital boat.[596]

Frank Miller was a major with the 66th U.S. Colored Infantry in command of the parole camp. In his deposition, Miller stated that at 2 P.M. on April 24, he had joined Captain Williams and Colonel Henderson at a saloon in Vicksburg. Miller testified that Williams later took him outside the saloon, where the following conversation took place:

> He asked me if I was a Mason. I told him I was not. He replied—"It makes no difference, I take you to be a gentleman." He stated that there were two lines of boats. One

of which was in the employ of the government. And the other not. And it was the wish of certain parties to place the prisoners on a different boat from that which it was intended that they should go. He requested that I should tell Lt. Davenport to hurry up the work at Camp Fisk. He said, "He had telegraphed to him, but lest he might not get the dispatch he wanted to send word by me also."[597]

On May 29, 1866, the attorney for Frederic Speed announced to the court that due to the absence of Dana, Miles Sells, and E. D. Butler, the accused was forced to rest his case. The defense closed its proof without Frederic Speed ever taking the stand.[598]

On June 1, the defense made final argument to the court; Lieutenant Colonel Gibson presented his argument three days later. At 11:30 A.M., on June 4, the case was submitted to the court. The following morning, at nine o'clock, the verdict was announced. Brig. Gen. Charles A. Gilchrist, president of the court, declared that Frederic Speed had been found guilty on all charges. The court sentenced Frederic Speed to dismissal from the service. General Wood approved the verdict and forwarded it to the secretary of war for final action.[599]

Sec. E. M. Stanton referred Speed's file to Brig. Gen. Joseph Holt, the judge advocate general of the army, for review. In a surprising reversal of the court's decision, Holt saw fit to clear Speed of all charges made against him. Holt wrote to Stanton:

> Capt. Speed took no such part in the transportation of the prisoners in question as should render him amendable to punishment; . . . his connection with the events which preceded the disaster to the *Sultana* was a wholly subordinate one; and . . . the facts developed in the evidence point out with distinctness other officers, whose indifference to the comfort of those placed temporarily in their charge resulted in, though without causing, the death of over 1,100 of their numbers.[600]

In exonerating Speed, Holt maintained that Capt. George Williams, upon his return to Vicksburg on April 23, had formally assumed control of the prisoner transfer. Moreover, Holt indicated that it was Williams who declared that the prisoners were comfortable after making his count. Finally, the judge advocate general

*Gen. Joseph Holt. The Judge Advocate General of the Army saved
Frederic Speed from disgrace.* (Library of Congress)

reiterated that it was Captain Williams, and not Speed, who had angrily refused to divide the soldiers after being advised by Kerns against placing all the men on the one steamer.[601]

But Holt made it clear it was not his intent "to cast censure upon the conduct of Captain Williams." In fact, in his report to Stanton, Holt included several reasons justifying Williams's conduct. Holt reasoned that since Williams had only returned to Vicksburg on April 23, he could not be held responsible for arrangements made prior to his arrival. Second, Williams had refused to divide the prisoners because he believed that agents for another steamer had offered illegal bribes to Speed and others for a portion of solders. Holt indicated that Williams had indeed resisted efforts to divide the prisoners but only because of the confusion over the number of men to be shipped. When he ascertained the number, Williams genuinely believed it was too late to divide the troops.[602]

General Holt was not as understanding with regard to Hatch's role in these events. According to Holt, it was Hatch who had promised Mason a load of prisoners and selected the *Sultana* to transport them:

> That Captain Hatch felt a consciousness of some responsibility for the disaster is believed to be shown by the fact that though three times subpoenaed to give testimony at the trial, and though the trial was prolonged three months that his presence might be secured, he refused to obey the summons; and that, notwithstanding every effort was made to compel his presence, the Secretary of War being finally appealed to order his arrest as guilty of contempt, it was found necessary to finish the trial without his evidence.[603]

Joseph Holt echoed the findings of the Washburn Commission when he reported that it was shown "by abundant evidence, that the boat, though overcrowded, was not overloaded; that in shipments of troops by steamer no attention was ever paid, throughout the war, to the legal carrying capacity of the ship."[604]

Holt in attempting to place blame for the *Sultana* disaster wrote:

> Terrible as was the disaster to the *Sultana*, there is no evidence that it was caused by the overcrowding of her decks, and it is therefore difficult to say upon whom the responsibility for the loss of 1,100 lives should rest. The engineer testifies that he considered the boilers well and sufficiently repaired, but his

criminality in risking the lives of so many men, knowing, as he did, the condition of his boat, was great and without palliation. Whoever should be regarded as meriting punishment for his connection with this event, it is believed that it is not Captain Speed.[605]

Holt recommended to Stanton that the guilty verdict not be approved and that "Captain Speed be publicly exonerated from the charges which have been made against his character as an officer." The secretary of war followed the judge advocate general's recommendation and refused to approve Speed's sentence. Capt. Frederic Speed was honorably mustered out of the army on September 1, 1866.[606]

CHAPTER ELEVEN

Sultana Incident Closed

WITH THE EXONERATION of Speed, the government officially closed its files on the *Sultana*. The army absolved itself of any wrongdoing in the sacrifice of so many lives. The Washburn Commission, which conducted the principal military inquiry of the disaster, had concluded: "The evidence fully shows that the government has transferred as many or more troops on boats of no greater capacity than the *Sultana* frequently and with safety."[607] And Brig. Gen. Joseph Holt reported to the secretary of war that ". . . the boat, though overcrowded, was not overloaded; that in shipments of troops by steamer no attention was ever paid, throughout the war, to the legal carrying capacity of the ship."[608]

During the war, necessity may have dictated that large numbers of troops be quickly transported to battle. Moreover, it may have been true that at such times scant attention was paid to the legal carrying capacities of the steamers used to move the troops. But no military urgency required so many soldiers to be placed on the *Sultana*.

Certain members of the military evidently recognized that, with the surrender of the Confederacy, operations must be conducted on a peacetime basis. Col. Lewis Parsons, the chief quartermaster for river transportation for the army on May 2, 1865, issued the following circular:

> As it is probable a large number of troops will soon be returning to their homes the strictest attention should be given to prevent the use of any but perfectly safe transports under

experienced and careful masters provided with everything
necessary for the safety and comfort of troops. Especial care
should be taken to see that they are thoroughly clean and that
they are not overloaded. The late calamity to the Steamer
Sultana shows the need of extreme caution which will be expected from all officers in the management of River
Transportation.[609]

Even Secretary of War Stanton in his annual report for 1865,
admitted that the *Sultana* had been dangerously overloaded at the
time of the explosion:

> The destruction of the steamer *Sultana* on the Mississippi
> River, near Memphis, on the 27th of April last, also occasioned
> by the explosion of her boilers and burning of the boat, and
> resulting loss of over 1200 officers and soldiers—a loss greatly
> increased, I think, by an improper and unnecessary overload-
> ing of the boat.[610]

Maj. Gen. Napoleon Jackson Tecumseh Dana was very aware of
the problems surrounding the prisoner transfer, yet he took no
action to prevent the overcrowding of troops aboard the *Sultana*.
But no criticism was ever leveled against Dana for his role in the
events of April 1865. Dana resigned from the army exactly one
month after the loss of the *Sultana*. Dana was hired as general agent
for the American-Russian Commercial Company of Alaska and
thereafter as an executive officer for several railroads, notably the
Chicago, Burlington and Quincy. He died on July 17, 1905, at the
age of 83 in Portsmouth, N.H.[611]

As with Dana, the strongest indictment against Gen. Morgan L.
Smith was his failure to act. Told on two occasions by Kerns that too
many men were being put on the *Sultana*, Smith never once visited
the steamer to investigate conditions on board even though he had
promised Kerns he would. In the words of General Washburn,
"Had he done so the lives of many men would have been saved."[612]
Following his resignation from the army in June 1865, Smith
remained in Vicksburg. On December 18, 1866, Smith then 46
years old, married Louise Gennella, age 20.[613] Smith briefly served
as consul to the Sandwich Islands (later known as Hawaii), and on
his return from the Pacific, Smith was tendered the governorship
of the Colorado Territory, which he declined.[614] During the administration of President Grant, Smith was appointed the second assis-

tant postmaster general. He soon resigned this position, however, and contracted with the government to carry mail on routes to the West, the Northwest, and the South.[615]

On December 29, 1874, Smith's life ended mysteriously. *The New York Times* on the following day printed the following:

> Yesterday morning Gen. M.L. Smith was found dead in his bed at Taylor's Hotel. He arrived at the hotel on Saturday night and registered himself "M.L. Smith, Washington, D.C." On Sunday he remained in his room all day and refused to see two gentlemen who called upon him. The names on their cards were E.M. Tomlinson and J.M. Currie, and one of the cards was addressed to "Gen. M.L. Smith."[616]

An article appearing in the St. Louis *Post Dispatch* on January 2, 1875, questioned the circumstances of Smith's death:

> It is said that he (Smith) has been very much excited for some time past, in consequence of his name having been connected with some expositions in relations to mail contracts, and it is even intimated that he may have committed suicide.[617]

The "expositions" were a series of stories appearing in the latter part of December 1874 in papers across the nation regarding the ongoing investigation of the Pacific Mail Steamship Company by the Ways and Means Committee of the U.S. House of Representatives. This company had been awarded a contract on August 27, 1872, by the postmaster general to carry mail to the Far East. Pursuant to this contract, the company received approximately $500,000 per year from the government.[618] In the latter part of 1874 and early 1875, investigators were alleging that the steamship company had made fraudulent payments to several government officials. On January 9, 1875, the St. Louis *Post Dispatch* announced in a headline: "Today's Abortive Efforts To Find The Bribe-takers—An Unidentified Gen. Smith Comes Upon The Scene." The article stated that John Schumaker, an attorney for the Pacific Mail Steamship Company, paid $50,000 in cash to a man introduced to him as General Smith. The story also reported that Schumaker took no receipt for the money.[619] A *New York Times* article on January 12 further identified this General Smith as Morgan L. Smith. The report went on to say that Lyman Elmore, an attorney in New York, testified before the Ways and Means Committee that in May 1872 Morgan Smith told him an attorney for the Pacific

Mail Steamship Company was going to pay him some money. He then asked if Elmore could help him in the transaction. The story further read that Elmore was later approached by John Schumaker, who informed him that he had a $50,000 check he had been instructed to give Elmore or someone Elmore would indicate. Elmore told Schumaker that it was Smith he was to pay but advised against paying Smith with a check. The article reported that Schumaker cashed the check and turned the cash over to Smith in Elmore's office.[620]

The testimony taken before the House committee established that Smith, as assistant postmaster general, had accepted a bribe offered him by an attorney for the Pacific Mail Steamship Company in May 1872. In August of the same year, the postmaster general awarded the company a contract worth $500,000 per year.[621]

Political influence may have saved Reuben Hatch from prosecution in the *Sultana* case, as it had in the previous allegations of criminal misconduct leveled against him. The allegations directed against Hatch at Cairo in 1862 and those at Vicksburg were very similar. As quartermaster at Cairo, Hatch had, among other things, been accused of chartering the steamer *Keystone* for $1,200 per month and preparing false documents reflecting a payment of $1,800 per month.[622] Chester Berry, in describing later events at Vicksburg, wrote:

> (T)here were a number of boats at Vicksburg at the time we (the exchanged prisoners) were to be sent north, but all demanded the $5 per man and would take but 1,000 men. Finally the quartermaster succeeded in persuading the captain of the "*Sultana*" to take the entire 2,000 at $3 per head, that would give him $6,000 for the trip, whereas, if he only took 1,000 at $5 he would only make $5,000. The report said that the captain of the "*Sultana*" signed the papers for $10,000 and that the quartermaster cashed them on the spot for $6,000.[623]

Unfortunately, Berry did not specify the quartermaster he was referring to, nor did he disclose the source of these allegations. But there can be little doubt that Berry was referring to Hatch. Under the above scheme, Hatch would stand to earn $4,000 in illegal profits were all the prisoners shipped on the one steamer.

Reuben Hatch was mustered out of the army on July 28, 1865,

but his quartermaster's accounts were not settled until 1870. In July 1871, Hatch died at the age of 53. His wife wrote the secretary of war the following year:

> To the government my Husband gave the best years of his life; at the Battle of Pleasant Hill and in the Red River Campaign, he lost his health, and was a sufferer in consequence until his *death*, in July last; he was harassed, I might say *persecuted*, from the day he entered the Service (and he was not alone in that) by the Enemies of the Government at home, and abroad.[624]

Capt. George Williams's actions surrounding the placement of the soldiers aboard the *Sultana*, while never the subject of a court-martial, cannot be dismissed. His influence in postponing the preparation of prisoner rolls clearly paved the way for the adoption of only one steamer to carry the Union troops.

By failing to make a proper count on April 24 (a responsibility he had agreed to take on), Williams seriously underestimated the number of men on the *Sultana*, and thus jeopardized any remaining possibility that the sheer size of the passenger load would convince the authorities that another steamer should be enlisted to transport a share of the troops.

Despite his role in magnifying the loss of life in the *Sultana* disaster, George Williams's military future was untarnished by the events at Vicksburg. He continued his army career after the war and was eventually promoted to the rank of major. In the years following the end of the war, he served at Charleston, Raleigh, Savannah, Fort Gibson (Indian Territory), and Fort Totten (Dakota Territory). During his tour of duty at Fort Totten, Major Williams suffered from an aggravated hernia, a condition he had incurred during the war. Forced to retire from the service on October 8, 1870, Williams moved to Newburgh, New York, where he served four terms as a member of the board of education. He died on April 2, 1889.[625]

While Frederic Speed was the only officer connected with the *Sultana* tragedy to be court-martialed, reconstruction of the case points up the fact that it was Dana's statement that chiefly served to implicate Speed in any major wrongdoing. Contrary to the findings of the court-martial tribunal, it was Hatch and Williams who insisted on the use of the *Sultana* and Williams who commanded the prisoners onto the boat. Speed was not entirely free of criticism, because it was he who maintained the impression on April 23 and 24 that 1,400 prisoners remained at Vicksburg to be shipped north. It is simply incredible that Speed, or for that matter the entire military authority at Vicksburg, did not realize the number of prisoners housed at the parole camp. These men had been at Camp Fisk for weeks and Speed had himself already supervised the loading of 2,000 men on the *Henry Ames* and the *Olive Branch*. And by underestimating the number of prisoners to be loaded on the *Sultana*, Speed not only mislead himself but also George Williams into believing that there would be no problem in placing all the remaining soldiers on one steamer. Negligence in performance of duty, and not the bribery schemes he was charged with by others, implicates Speed in the events leading up to the *Sultana* disaster.

Following his discharge from the army in September 1866, Speed entered into a lumber business in Vicksburg. In 1867 and 1868, he served as the circuit and chancery court clerk for Warren County, Mississippi. Speed also read law during these years and was admitted to practice law in 1868. The following year, Speed was appointed the criminal court judge for Warren County. Later, as editor of the Vicksburg *Weekly Times and Republican*, Speed grew to be a powerful voice in Mississippi politics.[626] In 1871, Speed married Adele Hillyer, daughter of Col. Giles M. Hillyer, a successful newspaper man from Natchez.[627] It was later said of Speed:

> Leading an active and useful life, he has endeavored by an honorable and upright career to impress upon the young men of his acquaintance the importance of qualifying themselves for the duties and responsibilities of life, and it was but natural to find him unanimously chosen as the president of the Young Men's Christian Association, an organization which is exerting a beneficial influence in the community and in whose behalf he is an untiring worker.[628]

Speed died on March 10, 1911, in Vicksburg, which honored him with a street named to commemorate one of its leading citizens.[629]

The conduct of Nathan Wintringer, the *Sultana*'s chief engineer, should have resulted in criminal prosecution for manslaughter, but he was never brought before any court. Licensed by law to see to the safe operation of the steamer's machinery, Wintringer abandoned his years of steamboat experience, with tragic consequences

Frederic Speed. Following his discharge from the army, Speed became a judge, a newspaper editor, and a powerful voice in Mississippi politics. (Old Courthouse Museum, Vicksburg, Mississippi)

for the *Sultana*'s passengers. From the testimony of R. G. Taylor, the boilermaker who was unable to perform the full repairs he deemed necessary, it is clear that both Wintringer and Mason sacrificed safety for a lucrative contract transporting troops. Taylor's recommendations went unheeded, despite the chances Wintringer must have been aware he was taking with the boat's damaged boiler.

Following the *Sultana* disaster, Wintringer gained prominence as a steamboat operator engaged in the Pittsburgh/Wheeling trade. He owned the first and second *Abner O'Neal* and the *C.W. Batchelor*.[630] But memories of the *Sultana* may have haunted him toward the end of his life. A few months before his death, Wintringer wrote Chester Berry the following message regarding a planned reunion of *Sultana* survivors:

> I would like to attend the reunion if I could make it suit at the time to do so, and hear the experiences that will be given there. Hoping you may have a pleasant meeting of old friends to talk over the perils of that terrible night, and that not one of you may ever experience such another is the wish of N. Wintringer.[631]

Wintringer did not attend the reunion. Did knowledge of his own culpability keep him away? The remorse in his letter to Berry would lead one to believe Wintringer recognized, to some extent, the role he played in sacrificing so many. Nathan Wintringer died on October 11, 1886, at Steubenville, Ohio.[632]

Capt. J. Cass Mason perhaps paid the greatest price among those responsible for the scale of the *Sultana* disaster. In 1884, Mason's widow, Rowena Mason, sought redress for the loss of her husband and executed a power of attorney granting M. A. McDonald, a Denver lawyer, the power to prosecute a suit in the Court of Claims in Washington for the value of the *Sultana*.[633] On March 11, 1884, McDonald requested the secretary of war to furnish him with copies of all the reports and papers the government had in its possession regarding the loss of the *Sultana*. The quartermaster general of the army in a letter to the secretary of war recommended that these records not be turned over to the attorney because ". . . Mr. McDonald's main purpose appears to be the preparation of some kind of a claim upon the Government. . . ."[634] On March 20, 1884, the secretary of war wrote a letter to McDonald refusing him access to the *Sultana*'s records.[635] Rowena Mason subsequently dropped any claim she may have sought from the government.

McDonald was not the first attorney to investigate the loss of the *Sultana*. On February 12, 1867, R. J. Atkinson, a lawyer acting on behalf of the surviving owners of the steamboat, made application to the army for copies of the records relating to the government's inquiry into the disaster. The lawyer indicated in his request that if the government could not furnish the records, then he wished to be informed if any presumption of blame attached to the owners or management of the boat. The army never furnished Atkinson with any records, claiming that none could be located.[636]

CHAPTER TWELVE

". . . To Be So Soon Forgotten . . ."

WHY THE STORY of the steamboat *Sultana* should have passed almost unnoticed into the pages of American history can be partially explained if one recalls the turbulence of events that shook the nation at this time. The long Civil War had ended only a few weeks before the ill-fated *Sultana* steamed beyond the lights of Memphis for the last time. Newspapers were still devoting pages to the cessation of hostilities and the surrendering Confederate armies. President Lincoln's death only a few days before the loss of the *Sultana* filled the papers with stories of the assassination, a possible conspiracy, and the funeral rites. John Wilkes Booth had been killed the day the *Sultana* reached Memphis. Those few editors who granted more than passing comment concerning the *Sultana* and her victims were likely to relegate the disaster to back pages.

Jesse Hawes, whose comrades had been passengers aboard the *Sultana*, wrote of this tragedy:

> In the long list embracing every engagement of the Rebellion, the Union killed on the field have exceeded the loss of lives by this explosion in only four great battles: the Wilderness, Gettysburg, Spottsylvania and Antietam. There have been more lives lost by this explosion than were killed from the Union ranks in the combined battles of Fredericksburg, Franklin, and Five Forks; more than were killed from the Union ranks on the fields of battle at Pea Ridge, Perryville, and Pleasant Hill combined; more than the Union loss in killed at Chancellorsville, or Chickamauga, or Shiloh. Only the fact that

185

it occurred just at the close of the great war, just when the
country was bowed in grief at the murder of its beloved first
citizen, gave it relatively a minor place in the history of that
time.[637]

But there are more subtle reasons lying behind the scant coverage of the *Sultana* tragedy. In April 1865, America had just concluded a war that had lasted four long years and cost over 600,000
lives.[638] Newspapers chronicled the loss of life from the battlefields
during this bloody war. By the time Lee and Grant faced each other
at Appomattox, few families remained untouched by the death of a
loved one. Shortly after the *Sultana* disaster, a reporter for the
Memphis *Argus* mirrored the nation's near indifference to death by
writing:

> We have, as a people, become so accustomed to suffering of
> horrors during the past few years that they soon seem to lose
> their appalling features, and are forgotten. Only a few days
> ago 1500 lives were sacrificed to fire and water, almost within
> sight of the city. Yet, even now, the disaster is scarcely
> mentioned—some new excitement has taken its place.[639]

Moreover, this tragedy occurred in the West, far removed from
the large newspapers of the East. Such papers as *The New York Times*
gave little or no coverage to this horrible event. No doubt if the
Sultana had exploded on an Eastern river, the front pages of the
major newspapers of the nation would have been covered with stories outlining the disaster.

Another reason why this event passed almost without notice was
the fact that most of those aboard the *Sultana* on April 27, 1865,
were from the heartland of America. Had they been from Eastern
states, the nation in all likelihood would not have forgotten them. It
must also be remembered that the majority of the soldiers aboard
the steamer on her final trip were enlisted men—not colonels or
generals. They were farmers, clerks, and laborers. Men who had
made no mark in life. History memorializes the deaths of the
famous, but forgets those of common, ordinary men. Who remem-
bers the steerage passengers aboard the *Titanic*?

Thousands, though, did not forget the *Sultana* or her passengers:
parents whose sons would never return from war; wives who
mourned lost husbands; and children who would grow up with only
faint memories of their departed fathers. With the exception

Sgt. John Clark Ely, Company F, 115th Ohio Infantry. Died. A wife and four small children waited for the warrior who would never return. (Courtesy of Dorothy E. Bates)

Pvt. Samuel H. Raudebaugh, Company K, 65th Ohio Infantry. Survived. (Chester Berry, *Loss of the* Sultana *and Reminiscences of Survivors*)

of the carnage of battle, few single events in the history of America touched the lives of so many as did the tragedy of the *Sultana*. John Clark Ely, with the 115th Ohio Volunteer Infantry, died on April 27, 1865. In Ohio, his wife and four small children waited for the soldier who would never return.[640] Eli Finley Provines, a 19-year-old private attached to the McLaughlin's Squadron, Ohio Volunteer Cavalry, went down with the *Sultana*. And when, on July 15, 1865, an army representative broke the sad news to his parents, John S. Provines rose from the dinner table and suffered a fatal heart attack. Soon Louisa Finley Provines and her five young children stood at the grave of John, mourning not only the loss of her husband but also her son. At the Wesley Chapel Cemetery near Sumner, Illinois, lies the grave of John A. Provines and nearby stands a marker over the empty grave of his son, Eli.[641]

In Cincinnati, Katherine Schneider waited with her three small daughters for the return of her husband, Adam Schneider, a private with the 183rd Ohio Infantry, but the reunion would never take place. Adam Schneider died on April 27, 1865. The passing years failed to diminish the grief felt by this family for their departed husband and father. On April 24, 1901, Hannah Braunwart, one of Schneider's daughters, wrote the following to a group of *Sultana* survivors:

> With sorrow in my heart, I will write a few lines to you, and gratefully do I thank you all, to remember this terrible catastrophe where, at the time our poor father, and husband lost his life and so many faithful soldiers. He, promising to be at home to his dear ones, never returned, but a friend, (who) died some time ago, lived to tell about it. This man (Michael Conrad) being a very careless disposition, could not for any reason be wakened on any other night, but April 27th always brought him to our house, and cry, cry like a baby. It certainly was terrible. I am with you in your reunion in spirit and I hope to be with them as long as they live.[642]

The survivors of the *Sultana* were never to forget that dark, spring morning in April 1865. Many would never recover from the hours spent in the cold river. Michael Daly, a 42-year-old private with the 18th Michigan Infantry, for example, suffered from failing health for several months, until his death in January 1866.[643] William M. Morrow, who contracted a severe cold from the exposure suffered in the flooded river, died shortly after his discharge from the army.[644]

Fortunate to be alive, some would nevertheless suffer physically and mentally for the rest of their lives. George H. Young, for example, would write:

> As a memento of that terrible night I still suffer from bronchitis and asthma, which has compelled me to reside in Colorado, and, strive as I may, I cannot repress an involuntary fright on hearing in the stillness of the night any unusual noise.[645]

On April 27, 1865, Joseph Hines was two days short of his 19th birthday. He would escape the *Sultana*'s flames, but the hours he spent in the Mississippi River eventually took their toll. In 1884, Hines submitted a declaration for an invalid pension in which he described his rheumatism and chronic diarrhea. Hines listed the source of his disabilities as exposure resulting from an event nearly 20 years passed—the explosion of the *Sultana*.[646]

The shared suffering of the soldiers on board the *Sultana* naturally created a strong bond among the survivors, and a group of these men formed the *Sultana* Association. At its first meeting on December 30, 1885, held at Fostoria, Ohio, a committee was appointed to prepare a memorial. A petition to Congress requesting a pension for each of the survivors was also drawn up.[647] Several years later, in 1918, James H. Kimberlin, a member of the association, expressed disappointment in the failure of Congress to recognize the group's petition:

> Our association twenty-five years ago appointed a monument committee to go before Congress and ask that an appropriation be made for the erection of a suitable monument to those dead martyrs, and every congress has been appealed to, but the committee has as often met with the same cold indifference.[648]

Samuel H. Raudebaugh, another survivor and a member of the *Sultana* Association, likewise expressed bitter resentment over the government's indifference when he wrote:

> About 1,500 as noble heroes and as great sufferers as this Nation ever had went down, and did not so much as have their poor emaciated bodies buried. Let me ask, should they not have as good a monument as any General? And, second, because so many of the survivors cannot furnish the evidence

the Government requires to get a pension for injuries received in the disaster. The government asks the sworn statement of a commissioned officer or two comrades who were eyewitnesses to the injury.

I was blown off the boat when sound asleep and injured in my breast and groin, and am from it every day I live, but I cannot tell how it was done, nor what did it, much less can anyone else. When the explosion occurred we were sound asleep, and were blown up into the air among one another along with pieces of the wreck, and scarcely two of us were taken out at the same place; hence we cannot help one another as we could had we been injured in battle, in camp, or on the march. I am voicing the sentiment of many loyal hearts when I say this Government will never do its duty to its suffering defenders until a respectable monument is erected in memory of the *Sultana* dead and a special pension is given to every survivor.[649]

Congress never did allocate funds for the erection of a monument in memory of the *Sultana* or those lost aboard her. But Congress was not wholly unwilling to recognize the *Sultana* tragedy, because on January 6, 1896, 31 years after the destruction of the steamer, Representative Henry R. Gibson of Tennessee introduced a bill (H.R. 3296) drafted "to do justice to the survivors of the shipwreck of the *Sultana*." This legislation read as follows:

Be it enacted by the Senate and House of Representatives of the United States of America in Congress assembled, That all the survivors of the shipwreck of the *Sultana* steamboat, on the Mississippi River, in April, eighteen hundred and sixty-five, who are now drawing or may be entitled to draw pensions, and all their widows, shall be entitled to arrears from the date of the filing of their original claim under the general law when they failed to obtain a pension thereunder, but have been or may be pensioned under the act approved June twenty-seventh, eighteen hundred and ninety, entitled "An Act granting pensions to soldiers and sailors who are incapacitated for the performance of manual labor, and providing for pensions to widows, minor children, and dependent parents;" and all claims filed under said Act shall relate to and entitle the claimant to draw a pension from the date his original claim was filed under the general law; and on application of any pensioner entitled under this Act, by letter or otherwise, a reissue pension certificate shall be granted him or her entitling him or her to the arrears provided by this Act; and no claim agent or other person shall be entitled to receive any compensation for services in making application for such arrears.[650]

In an expression of belated concern for the survivors and the families of the dead, the House of Representatives referred the bill to the Committee on Invalid Pension and ordered it to be printed. There is no evidence, though, that H.R. 3296 was ever returned to the House for further action.[651]

James H. Kimberlin died on April 28, 1924, 59 years and one day after the sinking of the _Sultana_. Toward the end of his life, his bitterness grew as he watched the roster of survivors shorten. By 1919, only 70 remained. That these living and those who had died should go still unacknowledged in American history was for Kimberlin a disheartening comment on the country's unfeeling attitude toward its veterans who had been aboard the _Sultana_. Shortly before his death, Kimberlin wrote:

> The men who had endured the torments of a hell on earth, starved, famished from thirst, eaten with vermin, having endured all the indignities, insults and abuses possible for an armed bully to bestow upon them, to be so soon forgotten does not speak well for our government or the American people.[652]

A group of survivors in East Tennessee formed a _Sultana_ survivor association, which met every April 27th for years following the tragedy. These men did not wait for the government to erect a monument. On July 4, 1916, the _Sultana_ monument was unveiled at the Mount Olive Cemetery, near Knoxville. The following words are chiseled into the stone face of the marker: "In memory of the men who were on the _Sultana_ that was destroyed April 27, 1865, by explosion on the Mississippi River near Memphis, Tennessee." On its sides and back are inscribed the names of the 365 Tennesseans who had been aboard the steamer.[653]

As years passed, the roster of the Tennessee survivors grew smaller and smaller. On April 27, 1930, the following article appeared in the _Knoxville Journal_ chronicling the 65th anniversary of the _Sultana_ tragedy:

> A stocky man, with white mustache and brown-gray hair, his shoulders stooped with cares of eighty-four years, will go today from his home in Knoxville to the "Rockford Presbyterian"

A badge of the Sultana *Association commemorating the reunion held on April 28, 1908, at Upper Sandusky, Ohio.* (Courtesy of David L. Hartline)

Members of the Tennessee Sultana *Survivors Association. The photograph was taken at Knoxville around the turn of the century.* (Courtesy of Edgar R. Keeble and Norman Shaw)

The dedication of the Sultana *monument on July 4, 1916, at the Mount Olive Cemetery near Knoxville.* (Courtesy of Edgar R. Keeble and Norman Shaw)

A group of East Tennessee survivors of the Sultana *at a reunion on April 27, 1894.* (Courtesy of Edgar R. Keeble and Norman Shaw)

church, and there elect himself to all the offices of the *Sultana* Survivors' association.

Alone, he will attend what would have been a reunion had another of his comrades lived. There will be speeches—and he will make them, dinner, and he will eat it; he will call a business session, answer the roll, close the meeting, and return to his home.

He is the last survivor of East Tennessee Federal soldiers who were saved when the *Sultana* sank near Memphis, with a death toll of 1328 on April 27, 1865. Sixty-five years ago today.

Pleasant Marion Keeble, . . . the lone survivor, will observe the memory of his comrades today and keep the pledge he made with them a half century ago.

Then, there were more than a hundred who met annually. Twenty years ago there were forty, ten years ago there were eleven. In 1928 four were living, at the reunion last year there were two—now there is only one.[654]

Pleasant Keeble died on March 4, 1931. With his death and the deaths of the few remaining survivors, the nation forgot the horrible tragedy that occurred in the predawn darkness of April 27, 1865. The *Sultana* and her passengers became a mere footnote lost in the pages of American history. James H. Kimberlin was right when he wrote ". . . to be so soon forgotten does not speak well for our government or the American people."[655]

> Some of them have left behind a name that is remembered to their praise; but of others there is no memory, for it perished when they perished, and they are as though they had never lived. . . . *The Holy Bible*, New Catholic Edition, Sirach 44:8,9

APPENDIX

Explanation and Guide to the Lists of Passengers and Crew of the *Sultana*

THE FOLLOWING PAGES contain the names of the crew members, the civilian passengers, and the soldiers who were aboard the *Sultana* on her final trip. The first two lists are those of the crew members and the civilian passengers. Unfortunately, the lists are very incomplete since there are no known records regarding the identity of these individuals. The names of the crew and civilian passengers contained on the following pages were obtained from articles appearing in newspapers in New Orleans, Memphis, and St. Louis. In all there were approximately 100 civilian passengers and 85 members of the crew. Of this number, only 18 survived.

The third list is that of the Union soldiers aboard the *Sultana* at the time she steamed from Vicksburg. Credit must again be given to Gene Salecker of Chicago, Illinois, who worked for many years compiling the names of the soldiers on the *Sultana*'s final tragic voyage. Gene was kind enough to give me the fruits of his research which I combined with my list to arrive at the one appearing on the following pages.

Many sources were used in the gathering of these names. Two of the primary ones were articles appearing shortly after the disaster in newspapers in Memphis and St. Louis, and Chester Berry's book, which contained an incomplete list. The Adjutant General's Reports for the states of Kentucky, Indiana, Ohio, and Michigan contained the names of many of the soldiers from these states. The best guide to the Tennessee soldiers is the work entitled *TENNESSEANS IN THE CIVIL WAR*, published in 1965 by the

195

Civil War Centennial Commission. Finally, the records from the National Cemetery in Memphis helped to identify the soldiers who were later buried there.

The list of soldiers contains the names of 2,317 soldiers. Below is a breakdown by state of this total number:

Alabama	1
Illinois	3
Indiana	459
Iowa	1
Kentucky	194
Michigan	310
Missouri	1
Ohio	791
Pennsylvania	1
Tennessee	514
Virginia	37
Unknown	5
	2,317

This list is by no means complete and, unfortunately, contains many inaccuracies. Gene and I faced two major problems in trying to compile an accurate list. First, we were greatly hampered by the fact that the record keeping by the Army at Vicksburg in April 1865 was almost nonexistent. Furthermore, many of the names appearing in the newspapers following the tragedy and in Chester Berry's book were misspelled. We attempted to correct the spelling by checking other sources, but this was not always possible.

Information about individual soldiers whose names appear on this list can be obtained through the National Archives in Washington, D.C., by requesting the military records and the pension records.

I apologize for any errors which may be found on this list, but Gene and I worked diligently for over ten years to make the list as complete and accurate as possible. Our purpose was to acknowledge a group of Americans that history has forgotten. I hope we have done this.

Jerry O. Potter
Memphis, Tennessee

List of Crew of the *Sultana**

LAST NAME	FIRST NAME	POSITION	
Butler	Thomas	Watchman	Died
Clemens	Samuel	Second Engineer	Died
Cross	Henry	Stewart	Died
Durkin	Thomas	Deckhand	Died
Gambrel	William J.	First Clerk	Died
Ingraham	Henry	Pilot	Died
Kayton	George	Pilot	
Maginty	Thomas	Barkeeper	Died
Mason	J. Cass	Captain	Died
O'Hara	James	Barkeeper	Died
Rowberry	William	First Mate	
Slater	George	Second Stewart	Died
Straton	William	Second Clerk	Died
Welch	J.	Deckhand	Died
Wintringer	Nathan	First Engineer	

*There were 85 members of the crew.

List of Civilian Passengers
Aboard the *Sultana**

LAST NAME	FIRST NAME	HOME	
Annis	(Infant)	Unknown	Died
Annis	Lt. Harvey	Unknown	Died
Annis	Ann	Unknown	
Fontaine	J. D.	Dallas City, IL	Died
Hardin	Mrs. S.H., Jr.	Chicago, IL	Died
Hardin	Seth H., Jr.	Chicago, IL	
Hoge	Mrs.	Unknown	Died
Long	William	Leavenworth, KS	
McEvan	Thomas	Unknown	
McLeod	Daniel	St. Louis, MO	Injured
Sheppard	Mr.	Indiana Sanitary Agent	
Snow	William	Arkansas	
Spikes	DeWitt Clinton	Son of Samuel Spikes	
Spikes	Elizabeth	Spikes Family Member	Died
Spikes	Esther	Wife of Samuel Spikes	Died
Spikes	(Female)	Child of Samuel Spikes	Died
Spikes	(Female)	Niece of Samuel Spikes	Died
Spikes	(Male)	Son of Samuel Spikes	Died
Spikes	(Male)	Son of Samuel Spikes	Died
Spikes	Samuel	Assumption Parish, LA	Died
Spikes	Susan	Spikes Family Member	Died
Spikes	Unknown	Spikes Family Member	
Spikes	Unknown	Spikes Family Member	
Spikes	Unknown	Spikes Family Member	
Witherspoon	William	Government Employee	
Woolfolk	Sallie B.	Hickman, KY	Died

---

*There were approximately 100 civilian passengers.

List of Soldiers Aboard the *Sultana*

	LAST NAME	FIRST NAME	RANK	CO.	REGIMENT	STATE
	ABBADUSKA	CHRISTIAN W.	PVT	F	18TH INF	MICHIGAN
*	ABELER	WILLIAM	PVT	C	37TH INF	OHIO
*	ABSHER	WILSON	PVT	I	3RD CAV	TENNESSEE
	ADAMS	JOHN	PVT	G	125TH INF	OHIO
	ADDINGTON	GEORGE W.	SGT	L	9TH CAV	INDIANA
*	AINSWORTH	JOHN L.	PVT	B	18TH INF	MICHIGAN
	ALBECK	FRED	PVT	A	2ND CAV	MICHIGAN
	ALDFANT	S.M.	PVT	D	30TH INF	INDIANA
	ALDRICH	HOSEA C.	SGT	G	18TH INF	MICHIGAN
*	ALDRICH	RANSOM D.	PVT	B	18TH INF	MICHIGAN
	ALEXANDER	JOHN T.	PVT	C	93RD INF	INDIANA
*	ALEXANDER	JOSEPH D.	PVT	M	9TH CAV	INDIANA
	ALEXANDER	PERRY H.	CPL	G	115TH INF	OHIO
	ALLEN	BENJAMIN F	PVT	K	95TH INF	OHIO
	ALLEN	DANIEL	PVT	K	3RD CAV	TENNESSEE
*	ALLEN	MORRIS	PVT	F	95TH INF	OHIO
*	ALLEN	ROBERT	PVT	A	6TH CAV	KENTUCKY
*	ALLEN	THOMAS J.	SGT	F	3RD CAV	TENNESSEE
	ALLISON	HIRAM	CPL	G	9TH CAV	INDIANA
	ALLISON	R.C.	PVT	D	6TH CAV	KENTUCKY
*	ALLMAN	JAMES	PVT	A	2ND CAV	OHIO
*	ALLTOP	GEORGE W.	PVT	F	51ST INF	OHIO
	ALNEY	JOHN	PVT	E	2ND CAV	MICHIGAN
	ALTON	ROBERT	PVT	F	93RD INF	INDIANA
	AMES	SANFORD P.	PVT	E	7TH CAV	INDIANA
	AMSBAUGH	DAVID R.	CPL	C	102ND INF	OHIO
	ANDERSON	GEORGE	PVT	F	102ND INF	OHIO
	ANDERSON	ISAAC F.	CPL	I	3RD CAV	TENNESSEE
	ANDERSON	JAMES	PVT	D	1ST CAV	OHIO

* DIED
** BURIED AT THE MEMPHIS NATIONAL CEMETERY

	ANDERSON	JAMES	CPL	E	3RD CAV	TENNESSEE
*	ANDERSON	JAMES C.	PVT	I	3RD	TENNESSEE
	ANDREWS	WILLIAM H.	SGT	A	75TH INF	OHIO
	APPLEGATE	JOHN S.	PVT	C	6TH CAV	INDIANA
	ARCHA	JOHN	PVT	F	90TH INF	OHIO
*	ARMSTRONG	JOHN M.	CPL	M	9TH CAV	INDIANA
	ARMSTRONG	ROBERT B.	PVT	I	7TH CAV	INDIANA
	ARNOLD	S.R.	PVT		6TH CAV	KENTUCKY
	ARNOLD	W.T.	PVT	B	1ST CAV	KENTUCKY
	ASHLEY	JAMES KING	PVT	L	1ST CAV	KENTUCKY
	ATCHLEY	PLEASANT S.	CPL	K	3RD CAV	TENNESSEE
	ATCHLEY	THOMAS	PVT	C	2ND CAV	TENNESSEE
*	AUBREY	MORRIS	PVT	H	72 INF	OHIO
*	AUBRY	FRANCIS	PVT	A	7TH CAV	OHIO
*	AUGENBACKE	GUSTAVE	PVT	C	37TH INF	OHIO
*	AUSTIN	DAVID B.	CPL	C	50TH INF	OHIO
	AUTRY	WILLIAM	PVT	H	7TH CAV	TENNESSEE
*	BAADA	PHILLIP	PVT	C	58TH INF	OHIO
	BABCOCK	JOHN	PVT	K	24TH INF	OHIO
	BACAN	NORNEAR	PVT	G	50TH INF	OHIO
	BADER	PHILLIP H.	SGT	B	10TH CAV	OHIO
	BADGET	B.	PVT	G	3RD CAV	TENNESSEE
*	BADGLEY	BENTON	PVT	G	175TH INF	OHIO
	BAGGART	M.	PVT	I	3RD CAV	TENNESSEE
	BAGGETT	JAMES D.	PVT	K	3RD CAV	TENNESSEE
*	BAHN	ADAM	PVT	B	102ND INF	OHIO
*	BAHN	JOHN	PVT	H	183RD INF	OHIO
*	BAILEY	HIRAM	PVT	K	9TH CAV	INDIANA
	BAILEY	RUFUS M.	SGT	F	3RD CAV	TENNESSEE
	BAILEY	WYATT	PVT	B	3RD CAV	TENNESSEE
	BAILEY	WILLIAM	PVT	B	3RD CAV	TENNESSEE
*	BAIRD	MARTIN V.B.	PVT	B	115TH INF	OHIO
	BAKER	CLEAVER	PVT	G	3RD CAV	TENNESSEE
	BAKER	GREG G.	PVT	M	9TH CAV	INDIANA
	BAKER	JACOB	PVT	G	3RD CAV	TENNESSEE
	BAKER	JAMES	PVT	G	3RD CAV	TENNESSEE
*	BAKER	JEROME D.	SGT	C	18TH INF	MICHIGAN
*	BAKER	JOHN	PVT	D	102ND INF	OHIO

---

* DIED
** BURIED AT THE MEMPHIS NATIONAL CEMETERY

	BAKER	JOHN	PVT	G	3RD CAV	TENNESSEE
*	BAKER	MADISON T.	PVT	B	13TH CAV	INDIANA
	BAKER	MURRY S.	CPL	D	4TH CAV	MICHIGAN
	BAKER	O.O.	PVT	M	9TH CAV	INDIANA
*	BAKER	WILLIAM	PVT	A	7TH CAV	OHIO
*	BAKER	WILLIAM A.	PVT	E	3RD CAV	TENNESSEE
*	BALDWIN	JONAS K.	CPL	A	7TH CAV	OHIO
	BALEY	WILLIAM	PVT	I	3RD CAV	TENNESSEE
	BALEY	WYATT	CPL	B	3RD CAV	TENNESSEE
*	BALL	HENRY	PVT	H	102ND INF	OHIO
	BALLARD	J.P.	PVT	F	3RD CAV	KENTUCKY
*	BALLENGER	FRANKLIN	PVT	H	9TH CAV	INDIANA
	BANEAN	THOMAS	PVT		3RD CAV	TENNESSEE
*	BANEY	JOHN	PVT	H	102ND INF	OHIO
	BANI	H.F.	PVT		38TH INF	INDIANA
	BANKHEAD	HENRY	PVT	A	6TH CAV	KENTUCKY
	BANKS	JACOB N.	PVT	A	3RD CAV	KENTUCKY
	BARDEN	W.H.	PVT		5TH CAV	INDIANA
	BARDON	OTTO	PVT	H	102ND INF	OHIO
	BARKER	FRANKLIN	PVT	K	2ND CAV	MICHIGAN
*	BARKLEY	NATHAN	SGT	L	5TH CAV	OHIO
	BARLEY	WILLIAM J.	PVT	G	3RD CAV	TENNESSEE
*	BARLOW	JEREMIAH	PVT	A	10TH CAV	INDIANA
*	BARNES	AUGUSTUS M.	PVT	D	6TH CAV	MICHIGAN
*	BARNES	EDWARD	MUSICIAN	F	175TH INF	OHIO
	BARNES	WILLIAM C.	PVT	F	23RD INF	OHIO
	BARNETT	ANDERSON F.	CPL	H	3RD CAV	TENNESSEE
	BARNETT	JAMES T.W.	LT		12TH CAV	KENTUCKY
*	BARNUM	JOHN P.	PVT	E	18TH INF	MICHIGAN
	BARR	GEORGE J.	PVT	G	11TH	MICHIGAN
	BARR	W.	PVT	B	64TH INF	OHIO
*	BARRACK	WILLIAM	PVT	I	7TH CAV	INDIANA
*	BARRER	WILLIAM	LT	G	175TH INF	OHIO
*	BARRETT	AUGUSTUS	PVT	K	7TH CAV	INDIANA
*	BARRETT	EDWARD P.	PVT	H	18TH INF	MICHIGAN
	BARRETT	HENRY	PVT	H	3RD CAV	TENNESSEE
	BARROW	G.E.	PVT	D	3RD CAV	KENTUCKY
	BARTLETT	CHARLES M.	PVT	C	6TH CAV	KENTUCKY

---

* DIED
** BURIED AT THE MEMPHIS NATIONAL CEMETERY

*	BATTLES	ISAAC	PVT	K	3RD CAV	TENNESSEE
	BATTLES	WILLIAM F.	PVT	K	3RD CAV	TENNESSEE
*	BAUMGARDINER	W.J.	PVT	K	183RD INF	OHIO
	BAXON	JOHN	PVT	B	5TH INF	KENTUCKY
	BAYLESS	WILLIAM	PVT	I	4TH CAV	TENNESSEE
*	BAYLESS	JAMES	PVT	D	3RD CAV	TENNESSEE
*	BAYNE	JAMES	PVT	D	175TH INF	OHIO
	BEACH	JAMES D.	PVT	D	102ND INF	OHIO
*	BEAL	AMOS	PVT	E	102ND INF	OHIO
	BEAL	W.	PVT	B	36TH INF	INDIANA
	BEAN	JAMES R.P.	PVT	I	3RD CAV	TENNESSEE
	BEAN	JAMES T.	SGT	A	7TH CAV	OHIO
	BEAN	LEWIS	PVT	A	6TH CAV	KENTUCKY
*	BEARD	JAMES O.	SGT	G	3RD CAV	TENNESSEE
*	BEARD	OTTERBINE G.	PVT	I	31ST INF	INDIANA
*	BEARDON	BARTON S.	CPL	C	124TH INF	INDIANA
	BEATTY	JAMES	SGT	A	93RD INF	OHIO
*	BECHTOLSHEIMER	ANTON	PVT	H	47TH INF	OHIO
	BECKNER	HOUSTON	PVT	C	3RD CAV	TENNESSEE
	BEDMAN	J.	CPL	A	10TH CAV	INDIANA
*	BEDWELL	CHARLES	PVT	F	3RD CAV	TENNESSEE
**	BEHLEN	GEORGE W.	PVT	C	57TH INF	INDIANA
*	BELKNAP	CHARLES M.	SGT	F	51ST INF	OHIO
*	BELL	FRANCES M.	CPL	A	3RD CAV	TENNESSEE
*	BELL	JAMES	PVT	H	9TH CAV	INDIANA
	BELL	JOHN K.	PVT	A	7TH CAV	OHIO
	BEMENT	GEORGE	SGT	F	25TH INF	MICHIGAN
	BENDER	NICHOLAS	PVT	B	4TH CAV	KENTUCKY
	BENSON	FELIX	PVT		64TH INF	INDIANA
*	BERCAW	NORMAN	PVT	G	175TH INF	OHIO
	BERRY	CHESTER D.	PVT	I	20TH INF	MICHIGAN
	BERRY	WILLARD N.	PVT	A	8TH CAV	INDIANA
	BEVINGTON	JOSIAH S.	PVT	A	102ND INF	OHIO
*	BICE	JOSEPH	PVT	G	14TH	OHIO
	BICUS	JAMES	PVT		2ND CAV	TENNESSEE
*	BIERLY	JACOB	CPL	E	102ND INF	OHIO
	BINDLE	ROMEO	PVT	H	10TH CAV	INDIANA
*	BIRD	JOHN E.	PVT	D	18TH INF	MICHIGAN

* DIED
** BURIED AT THE MEMPHIS NATIONAL CEMETERY

	BISHARD	CHARLES J.	PVT	B	97TH INF	OHIO
*	BISHLEN	JOHN	PVT	K	65TH INF	OHIO
*	BISHOP	JOHN	PVT	C	3RD CAV	TENNESSEE
*	BISHOP	WILLIAM	PVT	C	3RD CAV	TENNESSEE
**	BLACK	JOHN C.	PVT	K	70TH INF	OHIO
	BLACK	WILLIAM		K	9TH CAV	INDIANA
	BLACKBURN	JOSEPH	PVT	E	7TH CAV	INDIANA
	BLAIN	WILLIAM	PVT	K	3RD CAV	TENNESSEE
	BLAIR	THOMAS Q.	SGT	F	59TH INF	OHIO
*	BLAKE	GEORGE W.	PVT	H	9TH CAV	INDIANA
	BLAKELY	JACOB	PVT	E	4TH CAV	MICHIGAN
	BLAND	J.L.	SGT	B	97TH INF	OHIO
	BLANE	HENRY	PVT	M	7TH CAV	OHIO
*	BLESSINGER	FREDERICK	CPL	B	9TH CAV	INDIANA
	BLOCK	WILLIAM	PVT	H	9TH CAV	INDIANA
*	BOGART	CHARLES H.	PVT	F	3RD CAV	TENNESSEE
*	BOGART	LEVI M.	PVT	K	3RD CAV	TENNESSEE
	BOGART	SOLOMAN F.	PVT	F	3RD CAV	TENNESSEE
*	BOLENBAUGH	IRWIN M.	PVT	K	20TH INF	OHIO
*	BOLES	JAMES	PVT	D	3RD CAV	TENNESSEE
	BONEUR	MATTHEW	PVT	F	4TH CAV	KENTUCKY
	BONHAGE	HENRY	PVT	A	6TH CAV	KENTUCKY
*	BONNER	JOHN	SGT	F	9TH CAV	INDIANA
	BOODY	LEVI B.	SGT	C	115TH INF	OHIO
*	BOOKOUT	JESSE L.	PVT	F	3RD CAV	TENNESSEE
	BOON	WILLIAM S.	PVT	H	102ND INF	OHIO
	BOOR	WILLIAM	PVT	D	64TH INF	OHIO
	BORNS	E.	SGT	G	18TH INF	MICHIGAN
	BOTTON	C.S.	PVT		5TH CAV	TENNESSEE
*	BOTTS	THOMAS	PVT	A	7TH CAV	OHIO
*	BOWER	JOHN C.	PVT	C	58TH INF	OHIO
	BOWLAND	ABNER	PVT	C	4TH CAV	KENTUCKY
*	BOYCE	EDWARD	PVT	K	22ND INF	MICHIGAN
*	BOYD	GEORGE W.	PVT	G	175TH INF	OHIO
*	BRADDISH	JAMES W.	CPL	A	18TH INF	MICHIGAN
	BRADLEY	C.H.	PVT	M	3RD CAV	OHIO
	BRADLEY	FRANCIS M.	PVT	K	10TH CAV	INDIANA
	BRADLEY	G.	PVT	A	7TH CAV	VIRGINIA

* DIED
** BURIED AT THE MEMPHIS NATIONAL CEMETERY

	BRADY	JAMES K.	PVT	B	64TH INF	OHIO
*	BRAGG	JOHN M.	PVT	M	9TH CAV	INDIANA
	BRAITER	H.W.	SGT	G	65TH INF	OHIO
	BRAMMER	DAVID E.	PVT	K	2ND CAV	OHIO
*	BRANAGAN	PATRICK	PVT	E	18TH INF	MICHIGAN
*	BRANDT	JACOB	PVT	A	72ND INF	OHIO
*	BRANHAM	JOHN	PVT	C	3RD CAV	TENNESSEE
	BRANNON	BENJAMIN N.	PVT		2ND CAV	TENNESSEE
*	BRANUM	ELIJAH JOHN	PVT	C	3RD CAV	TENNESSEE
*	BRANUM	ROBERT	PVT	A	58TH INF	OHIO
*	BRATTON	HUGH W.	PVT	G	64TH INF	OHIO
*	BRAUGHTON	JAMES W.	PVT	B	6TH CAV	KENTUCKY
*	BRAUM	ADAM	PVT	A	37TH INF	OHIO
	BRECKETT	B.	PVT	B	4TH CAV	KENTUCKY
	BREMER	J.L.	SGT	L	1ST ENG	MICHIGAN
*	BRENZIER	AMOS	PVT	H	102ND INF	OHIO
*	BRENZIER	DAVID T.	PVT	H	102ND INF	OHIO
*	BRESAN	PETER	PVT	D	58TH INF	OHIO
*	BREWER	GEORGE H.	CPL	E	18TH INF	MICHIGAN
*	BRICKETT	JAMES	CPL	A	7TH CAV	OHIO
*	BRIDGEMAN	AUSTIN A.	PVT	F	63RD INF	OHIO
*	BRIGG	WILLIAM	CPL	M	9TH CAV	INDIANA
*	BRIGGS	SAMUEL C.	SGT	K	17TH	MICHIGAN
	BRINGMAN	JOSEPH D.	PVT	D	102ND INF	OHIO
*	BRINK	SAMUEL	PVT	A	64TH INF	OHIO
*	BRINK	THOMAS	PVT	A	64TH INF	OHIO
	BROADSHAW	D.	PVT	M	8TH CAV	MICHIGAN
	BROCK	JAMES J.	PVT	I	3RD CAV	TENNESSEE
	BROCKLON	J.	PVT	E	7TH CAV	INDIANA
	BROFFORD	JOHN	PVT	E	7TH CAV	OHIO
*	BROMBLEY	JASPER P.	PVT	A	2ND MTD INF	TENNESSEE
*	BROOKS	JAMES	PVT	G	3RD CAV	TENNESSEE
*	BROOKS	JOSEPH	PVT	G	3RD CAV	TENNESSEE
	BROOKS	LEMUEL E.	SGT	C	2ND CAV	MICHIGAN
*	BROTHERS	HIRAM	PVT	G	13TH CAV	INDIANA
	BROWN	A.	PVT	A	37TH INF	OHIO
	BROWN	ALEXANDER C.	SGT	I	2ND CAV	OHIO
	BROWN	BENJAMIN	PVT	L	4TH CAV	OHIO

* DIED
** BURIED AT THE MEMPHIS NATIONAL CEMETERY

*	BROWN	DANIEL V.	PVT	C	124TH INF	INDIANA
	BROWN	ISAAC	PVT	K	9TH CAV	OHIO
*	BROWN	ISAIAH	PVT	B	2ND CAV	INDIANA
	BROWN	J.	SGT	C	29TH INF	INDIANA
	BROWN	J.	PVT	G	2ND CAV	INDIANA
	BROWN	JAMES	PVT	C	124TH	INDIANA
	BROWN	JAMES	PVT	D	3RD CAV	TENNESSEE
	BROWN	JOHN	PVT	H	5TH CAV	MICHIGAN
	BROWN	JOHN	PVT	C	70TH INF	OHIO
*	BROWN	JOHN M.	PVT	B	3RD CAV	TENNESSEE
	BROWN	M.S	PVT	B	3RD CAV	TENNESSEE
*	BROWN	MILES E.	SGT	H	3RD CAV	TENNESSEE
	BROWN	PETER H.	CPL	C	3RD CAV	TENNESSEE
	BROWN	PHILLIP M.	PVT	G	6TH CAV	KENTUCKY
*	BROWN	WILLIAM	PVT	H	5TH CAV	MICHIGAN
*	BROWN	WILLIAM L.	PVT	B	3RD CAV	TENNESSEE
	BROWN	WILLIAM V.	PVT	H	9TH INF	INDIANA
	BROWNLEY	J.B.	PVT	A	2ND MTD INF	TENNESSEE
	BRUBAKER	JACOB	PVT	F	9TH CAV	OHIO
	BRUNNER	MICHAEL	PVT	C	59TH INF	OHIO
	BRYANT	CHARLES F.	PVT	C	124TH INF	INDIANA
	BUCHANAN	WILLIAM	SGT	D	93RD INF	INDIANA
	BUCKBEE	JAMES	PVT	K	9TH CAV	VIRGINIA
	BUCKLEY	JAMES	PVT	C	6TH CAV	KENTUCKY
*	BUHL	W.A.			114TH INF	OHIO
*	BUNN	JOB T.	SGT	L	1ST ENG	MICHIGAN
*	BURBRINK	AUGUST	PVT	A	7TH CAV	OHIO
	BURLEY	WILLIAM J.	CPL	E	3RD CAV	TENNESSEE
	BURLINGHAM	E.J.	PVT	I	0TH CAV	MICHIGAN
	BURNES	THOMAS N.	PVT	B	1ST CAV	OHIO
*	BURNETT	EDMUND M.	PVT	E	3RD CAV	TENNESSEE
	BURNETT	HUGH A.	CPL	E	3RD CAV	TENNESSEE
**	BURNETT	ISAAC	PVT	M	10TH CAV	OHIO
	BURNETT	WILLIAM B.	PVT	E	3RD CAV	TENNESSEE
	BURNS	E.	PVT	G	18TH INF	MICHIGAN
**	BURNS	MICHAEL	PVT	G	18TH INF	MICHIGAN
*	BURNS	PATRICK	PVT	K	6TH CAV	KENTUCKY
	BURNSIDE	ROBERT	PVT	K	102ND INF	OHIO

---

* DIED
** BURIED AT THE MEMPHIS NATIONAL CEMETERY

*	BURT	JOHN H.	PVT	D	102ND INF	OHIO
*	BUSLEY	LEVI	PVT	M	5TH CAV	MICHIGAN
	BUTLER	JOHN E.	PVT	A	15TH	MICHIGAN
	BYBEE	WESLEY	PVT	D	175ND INF	OHIO
	BYERLY	WILLIAM J.	PVT	E	3RD CAV	OHIO
	BYRON	JOHN H.	PVT	B	3RD CAV	TENNESSEE
	BYRON	JOSEPH	PVT	E	2ND CAV	MICHIGAN
	CADDY	CHARLES	PVT	E	183RD INF	OHIO
*	CALWELL	JAMES	PVT	G	18TH INF	MICHIGAN
	CAMERON	BENJAMIN B.	PVT	A	7TH CAV	OHIO
	CAMMACK	JAMES	PVT	F	6TH CAV	KENTUCKY
*	CAMPBELL	HIRAM	PVT	B	58TH INF	OHIO
*	CAMPBELL	HUGH S.	PVT	G	3RD CAV	TENNESSEE
*	CAMPBELL	JOHN H.	PVT	A	3RD CAV	TENNESSEE
*	CAMPBELL	NATHANIEL J.	PVT	G	3RD CAV	TENNESSEE
	CAMPBELL	WILLIAM T.	PVT	K	7TH CAV	TENNESSEE
	CANTRELL	JOHN	PVT	G	3RD CAV	TENNESSEE
	CARDEIRLLE	W.M.	PVT	A	7TH CAV	VIRGINIA
	CARELL	E. ABRAHAM	PVT	F	18TH INF	MICHIGAN
	CAREY	J.	SGT	C	4TH CAV	KENTUCKY
	CAREY	OLIVER	PVT	I	8TH CAV	MICHIGAN
	CARHART	JAMES E.	SGT	H	5TH CAV	MICHIGAN
*	CARLIN	JAMES W.	MAJOR		71ST INF	OHIO
	CARLIN	JOHN	PVT	C	2ND CAV	MICHIGAN
	CARMACK	THOMAS J.	CPL	A	64TH INF	OHIO
	CARNEY	GEORGE W.	PVT	K	3RD CAV	TENNESSEE
	CARNS	SAMUEL	PVT	C	1ST CAV	TENNESSEE
	CARR	J.M.	PVT	G	40TH INF	INDIANA
*	CARR	JOHN W.	PVT	E	50TH INF	OHIO
	CARR	RICHARD A.	PVT	B	7TH CAV	OHIO
*	CARROLL	WILLIAM	PVT	D	175TH INF	OHIO
*	CARTER	FRANCIS M.	PVT	D	15TH INF	OHIO
	CARTER	JAMES M.	PVT	C	3RD CAV	TENNESSEE
	CARTER	JOHN C.	PVT	L	3RD CAV	TENNESSEE
	CARTER	MORRIS J.	PVT	M	9TH CAV	OHIO
	CARTER	T.A.	PVT	A	17TH CAV	KENTUCKY
*	CARTWRIGHT	CHARLES	PVT	I	8TH CAV	MICHIGAN
*	CARVER	JAMES	PVT	B	3RD CAV	TENNESSEE

* DIED
** BURIED AT THE MEMPHIS NATIONAL CEMETERY

	CARVER	JESSE	PVT	B	3RD CAV	TENNESSEE
	CARVER	WILLIAM	SGT	B	3RD CAV	TENNESSEE
*	CASH	H.W.	CPL	K	3RD CAV	TENNESSEE
*	CASS	J.W.	PVT	B	99TH INF	INDIANA
	CASSEL	ABRAHAM	PVT	B	21ST INF	OHIO
*	CASSEL	JOHN, JR.	PVT	K	102ND INF	OHIO
	CASTICE	MYRON	PVT	M	1ST CAV	MICHIGAN
	CAUP	M.V.	PVT	H	20TH ART	INDIANA
*	CAVES	JAMES P.	CPL	K	3RD CAV	TENNESSEE
	CEHART	J.L.	SGT	H	5TH CAV	MICHIGAN
	CHAG	S.	PVT		5TH CAV	INDIANA
	CHANCE	WILLIAM M.	PVT	H	9TH CAV	INDIANA
*	CHANDLER	BENJAMIN	PVT	K	3RD CAV	TENNESSEE
*	CHAPPEL	ISAAC	PVT	C	79TH INF	INDIANA
	CHEATHAM	GEORGE H.	PVT	F	6TH CAV	KENTUCKY
	CHELF	SIMEON D.	CPL	G	6TH CAV	KENTUCKY
	CHRISTER	JACOB	PVT		40TH INF	INDIANA
*	CHRISTIAN	JAMES N.	PVT	L	9TH CAV	INDIANA
	CHRISTINE	HARMON A.	PVT	H	102ND INF	OHIO
	CHRISTINE	WILLIAM A.	PVT.	H	102ND INF	OHIO
	CHRISTOPHER	WILLIAM	PVT	H	64TH INF	OHIO
*	CHURCH	CHARLES C.	PVT	B	9TH CAV	INDIANA
	CISHARD	T.R.	PVT	B	97TH INF	OHIO
	CLANCHAM	J.M.	PVT	G	2ND CAV	TENNESSEE
*	CLANCY	WILLIAM F.	PVT		20TH	OHIO
	CLANSVILLE	G.	PVT	F	12TH CAV	INDIANA
	CLAPSADDLE	FRANKLIN A.	PVT	F	115TH INF	OHIO
*	CLARK	MILTON C.	SGT	B	28TH INF	KENTUCKY
	CLARKSON	GEORGE A.	PVT	II	5TH CAV	MICHIGAN
	CLARY	EDWARD D.	SGT	L	6TH CAV	INDIANA
*	CLARY	JAMES K.	PVT	F	41ST INF	OHIO
	CLAY	CHARLES		E	6TH CAV	KENTUCKY
	CLEVELAND	URIAH	PVT	A	38TH INF	INDIANA
*	CLEVENGER	CHARLES W.	PVT	G	9TH CAV	INDIANA
	CLINE	HENRY M.	SGT	B	45TH	OHIO
	CLINGER	GEORGE M.	CPL	E	16TH INF	KENTUCKY
*	CLIPNER	JOHN	PVT	H	78TH INF	OHIO
	CLUNEY	CHARLES	SGT	D	6TH CAV	KENTUCKY

---

* DIED
** BURIED AT THE MEMPHIS NATIONAL CEMETERY

*	CLUTTER	LORAN K.	PVT	K	46TH INF	OHIO
*	COCHRAN	HARVEY	PVT	F	3RD CAV	TENNESSEE
*	COCHRAN	HENRY	PVT	G	3RD CAV	TENNESSEE
	COCHRAN	HORACE H.	PVT	C	115TH INF	OHIO
*	CODY	THOMAS	PVT	C	115TH INF	OHIO
	COLE	ORLANDO M.	PVT	F	18TH INF	MICHIGAN
	COLE	DAVID	PVT	B	23RD INF	MICHIGAN
	COLEMAN	E.	PVT	C	6TH CAV	KENTUCKY
*	COLEMAN	WILLIAM L.	CAPTAIN	D	40TH INF	INDIANA
	COLLINS	JAMES R.	PVT	F	3RD CAV	TENNESSEE
*	COLLINS	JOSEPH H.	PVT	G	3RD CAV	TENNESSEE
	COLLINS	PATRICK	CPL	K	12TH CAV	OHIO
	COLLINS	W.J.	CPL	D	9TH CAV	INDIANA
	COLLINS	WILLIAM	PVT	L	4TH CAV	KENTUCKY
	COLVIN	JAMES	PVT	F	6TH CAV	KENTUCKY
	COLVIN	WINFIELD S.	PVT	F	6TH CAV	KENTUCKY
	COLWELL	H.C.	PVT	D	37TH INF	KENTUCKY
	COMMON	RICHARD	PVT		3RD CAV	TENNESSEE
*	CONDOR	STEPHEN	PVT	K	6TH CAV	KENTUCKY
	CONELLSON	J.B.	SGT	B	3RD CAV	TENNESSEE
	CONGERS	WILLIAM	PVT	D	3RD CAV	INDIANA
	CONLEY	BARNEY	PVT	C	115TH INF	OHIO
	CONNER	GEORGE W.	PVT	F	3RD CAV	TENNESSEE
	CONNER	WILLIAM	PVT	B	24TH INF	INDIANA
	CONOVER	GEORGE W.	PVT	B	175TH INF	OHIO
	CONRAD	MICHAEL	PVT	C	183RD INF	OHIO
	CONYERS	WILLIAM	PVT	B	3RD CAV	INDIANA
	COOK	J.	PVT	A	1ST ART	KENTUCKY
*	COOK	JAMES C.	PVT	C	115TH INF	OHIO
	COOK	JAMES S.	PVT	C	115TH INF	OHIO
	COOK	LOUIS	PVT	D	28TH INF	OHIO
	COOK	W.A.	PVT	H	40TH INF	INDIANA
*	COOK	W.H.H.	CPL	E	2ND CAV	KENTUCKY
	COOPER	JOHN	PVT	D	10TH CAV	INDIANA
	COOPER	JOSEPH	PVT	D	3RD CAV	TENNESSEE
	COOPER	ROBERT	PVT	I	3RD CAV	TENNESSEE
	COPELAND	JOSEPH	PVT	A	3RD CAV	TENNESSEE
*	CORBIN	WILLIAM S.	PVT	G	7TH CAV	INDIANA

* DIED
** BURIED AT THE MEMPHIS NATIONAL CEMETERY

*	CORLISS	JOHN S.	PVT	C	2ND CAV	MICHIGAN
	CORMSTEAD	CHARLES	PVT	K	2ND CAV	MICHIGAN
	CORNELL	ALBERT W.	CPL	B	18TH INF	MICHIGAN
*	CORNWELL	JOHN	SGT	A	100TH INF	OHIO
*	CORTS	JOSEPH B.	SGT	D	102ND INF	OHIO
*	CORY	OLIVER	PVT	I	8TH CAV	MICHIGAN
	COTTON	W.S.	PVT	G	50TH INF	OHIO
	COUNTRYMAN	GEORGE A.	MUSICIAN	K	18TH INF	MICHIGAN
*	COURTNEY	JOSEPH S.	SGT	C	3RD CAV	TENNESSEE
*	COURTNEY	WILLIAM S.	CPL	C	3RD CAV	TENNESSEE
*	COUTER	ELIAS	PVT	E	102ND INF	OHIO
	COVER	HENRY	SGT	C	115TH INF	OHIO
	COWAN	SAMUEL A.	SGT	A	3RD CAV	TENNESSEE
*	COWDEN	JOHN	SGT	B	3RD CAV	TENNESSEE
*	COX	JESSE	CPL	C	3RD CAV	TENNESSEE
*	COX	ROBERT	PVT	G	115TH INF	OHIO
	COX	W.H.	PVT	B	1ST CAV	KENTUCKY
	COYTON	W.A.	PVT	B	7TH CAV	KENTUCKY
*	CRABBS	JACOB	PVT	C	47TH INF	INDIANA
	CRAIG	ANTHONY	PVT	C	1ST CAV	VIRGINIA
	CRAMNER	ASAPH O.	SGT	B	64TH INF	OHIO
	CRANE	H.M.	SGT	H	45TH INF	OHIO
*	CRANE	IRA	PVT	F	72ND INF	OHIO
*	CRANMER	JERRY C.	PVT	G	115TH INF	OHIO
	CRAWFORD	EMERSON T.		H	10TH CAV	INDIANA
	CRAWFORD	EZRA	SGT	A	102ND INF	OHIO
	CRAWFORD	H.P.	PVT	I	3RD CAV	TENNESSEE
*	CRAWFORD	JOHN L.	PVT	A	MCLAUGHIN'S	OHIO
	CRAWFORD	WILLIAM P.	PVT	I	3RD CAV	TENNESSEE
	CRAWLER	JACOB	PVT	L	10TH CAV	INDIANA
*	CREW	BENJAMIN H.	CPL	F	115TH INF	OHIO
	CRISP	WILLIAM	PVT	D	18TH INF	MICHIGAN
*	CROSS	GEORGE F.	PVT	C	115TH INF	OHIO
*	CROW	WILLIAM	CPL	H	102ND INF	OHIO
*	CROWELL	GEORGE W.	PVT	C	78TH INF	OHIO
**	CRUDDIS	WILLIAM	PVT	I	1ST CAV	VIRGINIA
	CRUM	A.H.	PVT	G	35TH INF	INDIANA
*	CRUSE	WILLIAM R.	PVT	E	3RD CAV	TENNESSEE

* DIED
** BURIED AT THE MEMPHIS NATIONAL CEMETERY

	CSULTER	M.	PVT	K	4TH CAV	KENTUCKY
*	CULNON	JOHN	PVT	G	115TH INF	OHIO
	CULP	ANDREW J.	PVT	G	2ND MTD INF	TENNESSEE
	CULP	JACKSON	PVT	K	50TH INF	OHIO
	CUMMINGS	CHARLES A.	PVT	I	1ST CAV	KENTUCKY
	CUNNINGHAM	JAMES	PVT	H	3RD CAV	TENNESSEE
*	CURNUTT	ELISHA	PVT	G	14TH INF	KENTUCKY
	CURREY	M.	PVT	I	4TH CAV	KENTUCKY
*	CURTEN	RICHARD DAVID	PVT	G	3RD CAV	TENNESSEE
*	CURTIS	DANIEL	SGT	A	9TH CAV	INDIANA
	CURTIS	JAMES M.	PVT	A	3RD CAV	TENNESSEE
	CURTIS	WILLIAM	PVT	F	1ST CAV	VIRGINIA
*	CUSIC	DAVID	PVT	H	3RD CAV	TENNESSEE
*	D'ARMOND	THOMAS	PVT	E	3RD CAV	TENNESSEE
*	DADNY	GEORGE	PVT	I	6TH CAV	KENTUCKY
	DAGGY	GEORGE W.	PVT	L	9TH CAV	INDIANA
	DAILEY	JOHN	PVT	I	3RD CAV	TENNESSEE
	DALEY	WILLIAM M.	PVT	L	3RD CAV	TENNESSEE
	DALY	MICHAEL	PVT	C	18TH INF	MICHIGAN
	DANA	W.	PVT	G	115TH INF	OHIO
	DANIEL	CURTIS	SGT	A	9TH CAV	INDIANA
	DANIEL	ISAAC E.	PVT	A	7TH CAV	OHIO
	DANY	B.	PVT	E	7TH CAV	INDIANA
	DARISON	W.	PVT		3RD CAV	KENTUCKY
	DARLIN	JAMES	PVT	C	10TH CAV	TENNESSEE
	DARROW	JAMES M.	PVT	G	115TH INF	OHIO
	DARROW	MARVIN SAMUEL	PVT	B	18TH INF	MICHIGAN
	DAUGHERTY	JASON M.	PVT	K	3RD CAV	TENNESSEE
	DAUGHERTY	THOMAS	PVT	H	6TH CAV	KENTUCKY
	DAVENHAFF	J.C.	PVT	I	4TH CAV	MICHIGAN
	DAVENPORT	ISAAC NOAH	PVT	K	7TH CAV	TENNESSEE
	DAVENPORT	J.P.	PVT	C	7TH CAV	TENNESSEE
*	DAVENPORT	SETH H.	PVT	G	6TH CAV	KENTUCKY
	DAVIDSON	JOHN	PVT	A	22ND INF	OHIO
	DAVIDSON	JOHN	PVT	B	83RD INF	OHIO
	DAVIES	GEORGE C.	SGT	B	3RD CAV	TENNESSEE
	DAVIES	GEORGE W.	PVT	B	3RD CAV	TENNESSEE
	DAVIES	WILLIAM M.	PVT	B	3RD CAV	TENNESSEE

---

* DIED
** BURIED AT THE MEMPHIS NATIONAL CEMETERY

	DAVIS	BENJAMIN G.	PVT	L	7TH CAV	KENTUCKY
*	DAVIS	ELIJAH	PVT	F	3RD CAV	TENNESSEE
	DAVIS	J.F.	PVT		7TH CAV	MICHIGAN
	DAVIS	JAMES A.	SGT	B	3RD CAV	TENNESSEE
	DAVIS	JASPER N.	PVT	I	6TH CAV	INDIANA
	DAVIS	JOHN	PVT	D	100TH INF	OHIO
	DAVIS	JOHN C.	SGT	B	3RD CAV	TENNESSEE
	DAVIS	JOHN G.	PVT	K	65TH INF	OHIO
	DAVIS	JOHN L.	LT	B	71ST INF	OHIO
	DAVIS	M.P.W.	PVT		15TH INF	KENTUCKY
**	DAVIS	MILTON J.	SGT	D	9TH CAV	OHIO
	DAVIS	WILLIAM	PVT	K	3RD CAV	TENNESSEE
	DAVIS	WILLIAM, Jr.	PVT	G	115TH INF	OHIO
*	DAWSON	GEORGE W.	PVT	G	30TH INF	INDIANA
	DAY	ELIAS R.	CPL	A	9TH CAV	INDIANA
	DAY	JOHN P.	CPL	L	8TH CAV	MICHIGAN
*	DAY	PATRICK	PVT	A	9TH CAV	INDIANA
*	DEAN	JOSEPH F.	SGT		3RD CAV	KENTUCKY
**	DEAN	JOSEPH T.	SGT	C	7TH CAV	INDIANA
	DEARMOND	HENRY H.	SGT	I	3RD CAV	TENNESSEE
*	DECKER	JASPER	PVT	L	IST ENG.	MICHIGAN
	DECKER	JEFFERSON	PVT	E	80TH	INDIANA
	DEEKER	J.	SGT	C	3RD CAV	TENNESSEE
	DEERMAN	LEWIS A.	PVT	K	3RD CAV	TENNESSEE
*	DEERMAN	SOLOMON	PVT	K	3RD CAV	TENNESSEE
*	DEITRICK	CHARLES W.	CPL	F	115TH INF	OHIO
	DELAND	CHARLES	CPL	K	18TH INF	MICHIGAN
*	DELANO	GEORGE W.	PVT	H	9TH CAV	INDIANA
*	DELINE	ORVILLE	PVT	C	18TH INF	MICHIGAN
	DEMISE	THOMAS	PVT	I	8TH CAV	INDIANA
	DEMMAN	T.	PVT	D	3RD CAV	TENNESSEE
	DEMOSS	JOHN	PVT	D	51ST INF	OHIO
*	DEMOSS	THOMAS	PVT	I	8TH CAV	INDIANA
	DEPMER	AARON	PVT	A	103RD INF	OHIO
*	DERAMOND	THOMAS J.	PVT	D	3RD CAV	TENNESSEE
	DERRYBERRY	JOHN	PVT	A	7TH CAV	TENNESSEE
	DEVELIN	JAMES	PVT	C	4TH CAV	TENNESSEE
	DEVENDORF	JOHN C.	PVT	I	4TH CAV	MICHIGAN

---

* DIED
** BURIED AT THE MEMPHIS NATIONAL CEMETERY

	DIBBEY	M.	PVT	D	8TH INF	MICHIGAN
	DICKENS	L.F.	LT.	E	2ND CAV	MICHIGAN
	DICKENS	NEWTON	PVT	A	4TH CAV	TENNESSEE
*	DICKERSON	RILEY	PVT	C	115TH INF	OHIO
	DICKEY	J.K.	PVT	K	60TH INF	INDIANA
	DICKINSON	SIMEON F.	LT	E	2ND CAV	MICHIGAN
	DICUS	JAMES	PVT	D	2ND MTD INF	TENNESSEE
	DILLANDER	JOSEPH	PVT.	C	3RD CAV	INDIANA
	DILLARD	JAMES	PVT	C	2ND CAV	MICHIGAN
*	DILLING	ADAM	PVT	K	101ST INF	OHIO
	DINGMAN	MCKENZIE	PVT	E	4TH CAV	MICHIGAN
	DITMORE	AARON	SGT	B	44TH INF	OHIO
*	DIVELBISS	JOHN	CPL	E	102ND INF	OHIO
*	DIXON	ARCHIE C.	PVT	E	7TH CAV	OHIO
	DIXON	G.	PVT	C	80TH INF	INDIANA
*	DIXON	JOHN	PVT	C	3RD CAV	TENNESSEE
	DIXON	WILLIAM F.	LT.	A	10TH CAV	INDIANA
*	DLIFER	GEORGE	PVT	H	99TH INF	INDIANA
*	DOAN	THOMAS R.	PVT	B	17TH	MICHIGAN
	DODDARD	JAMES	PVT	C	2ND MTD INF	KENTUCKY
	DOGGY	GEORGE W.	PVT	L	9TH CAV	INDIANA
*	DOLAN	JAMES	PVT	C	115TH INF	OHIO
*	DONAHUE	LEVI	PVT	C	124TH INF	INDIANA
	DONALD	EDWARD O.	PVT	D	35TH INF	INDIANA
*	DONALD	HOSEA	PVT	B	MCLAUGHLIN'S	OHIO
	DONALDSON	DRYDEN D.	CPL	A	3RD CAV	TENNESSEE
*	DONER	DANIEL W.		E	7TH CAV	INDIANA
	DONEY	NAPOLEON	PVT	A	18TH	MICHIGAN
*	DONLEY	MARTIN	PVT	L	5TH CAV	OHIO
*	DONMIRE	JOHN	PVT	K	100TH INF	OHIO
*	DORMAN	HENRY	PVT	K	9TH CAV	INDIANA
	DORNA	JACOB	PVT	A	7TH CAV	OHIO
	DOSENBERRY	GEORGE A.	PVT	C	115TH INF	OHIO
*	DOTY	NATHAN	PVT	C	115TH INF	OHIO
	DOUGHERTY	MICHAEL	PVT	M	13TH CAV	PENNSYL-VANIA
**	DOUGLAS	DAVID H.	PVT	G	67TH INF	INDIANA
	DOUGLASS	JAMES E.	CPL	D	3RD CAV	TENNESSEE

---

* DIED
** BURIED AT THE MEMPHIS NATIONAL CEMETERY

*	DOWNING	GEORGE	PVT	G	9TH CAV	INDIANA
*	DOWNING	JONATHAN R.	PVT	G	9TH CAV	INDIANA
	DRAIMAN	MCKENZIE	PVT	E	2ND CAV	MICHIGAN
*	DRAINER	JACOB	PVT	A	7TH CAV	OHIO
	DRAPER	PRIOR L.	PVT	I	3RD INF	TENNESSEE
	DROMGOOLE	ROLLA M.	PVT	A	4TH MTD INF	TENNESSEE
*	DRUMM	CHARLES	PVT	A	7TH CAV	OHIO
	DUBAY	ANTONE	CPL	D	8TH CAV	MICHIGAN
	DUCET	DUFFY A.	CPL	E	15TH	MICHIGAN
	DUESLER	GEORGE W.	PVT	D	18TH INF	MICHIGAN
*	DUGAN	WILLIAM R.	PVT	A	7TH CAV	OHIO
	DUKE	WILLIAM W.	SGT	D	42ND INF	OHIO
*	DUNAFIN	ISAAC	SGT	E	21ST	OHIO
*	DUNHAM	ALONZO	PVT	H	9TH CAV	INDIANA
*	DUNLAP	HIRAM B.	PVT	A	3RD CAV	TENNESSEE
	DUNLAP	SAMUEL P.	PVT	A	3RD CAV	TENNESSEE
	DUNSMORE	JOHN W.	PVT	I	1ST ENG	MICHIGAN
*	DYER	SAMUEL A.	SGT	C	3RD CAV	TENNESSEE
*	EADIE	JAMES W.	CPL	C	115TH INF	OHIO
*	EADIE	JOHN JR.	LT	C	115TH INF	OHIO
*	EARICH	WILLIAM	PVT	D	102ND INF	OHIO
	EARL	JOHN E.	LT	L	1ST ENG	MICHIGAN
*	EASTICK	NEWMAN A.	PVT	G	4TH	MICHIGAN
*	EATINGER	GILLIS W.	PVT	C	115TH INF	OHIO
*	ECORD	AARON		F	90TH INF	OHIO
	EDDA	N.R.	PVT		3RD CAV	TENNESSEE
	EDDLEMAN	DAVID	CPL	I	64TH INF	OHIO
	EDDLEMAN	JACOB	PVT	I	64TH INF	OHIO
	EDDY	WILLIAM	PVT	D	18TH INF	MICHIGAN
*	EDWARDS	JACOB	PVT	I	40TH INF	OHIO
	EDWARDS	W.H.	PVT	K	4TH CAV	KENTUCKY
	EGRUNN			A	6TH CAV	KENTUCKY
*	ELDER	JOHN L.	SGT	K	6TH CAV	KENTUCKY
	ELDER	WILLIAM H.	PVT	H	58TH INF	OHIO
	ELDRIDGE	CHARLES M.	PVT	G	3RD CAV	TENNESSEE
	ELHIM	JAMES	PVT		4TH CAV	KENTUCKY
*	ELICK	JOHN	PVT	A	58TH INF	OHIO
	ELKIN	JAMES	PVT	A	2ND CAV	KENTUCKY

---

* DIED
** BURIED AT THE MEMPHIS NATIONAL CEMETERY

*	ELKINS	FRANCIS M.	PVT	K	7TH CAV	INDIANA
*	ELLENBERGER	JOHN C.	PVT	I	40TH INF	INDIANA
*	ELLENBURG	JOSEPH	PVT	B	3RD CAV	TENNESSEE
	ELLIAS	R.D.		A	9TH CAV	INDIANA
*	ELLIOTT	DAVID E.	CAPTAIN	E	75 TH	INDIANA
	ELLIOTT	J. WALTER	CAPTAIN	F	44TH U.S.C.T.	INDIANA
	ELLIOTT	JAMES	PVT	C	124TH INF	INDIANA
**	ELLIOTT	JASON M.	PVT	F	3RD CAV	TENNESSEE
*	ELLIOTT	JASPER W.	PVT.	F	3RD CAV	TENNESSEE
*	ELLIOTT	JOHN C.	PVT	F	3RD CAV	TENNESSEE
	ELLIOTT	JOSEPH TAYLOR	LT.	C	124TH INF	INDIANA
	ELLIOTT	URIAH	CPL	C	6TH CAV	KENTUCKY
*	ELLIOTT	WILLIAM	PVT	A	6TH CAV	KENTUCKY
*	ELLIS	EDWARD	PVT	C	115TH INF	OHIO
	ELLISON	JAMES O.	PVT	I	3RD CAV	TENNESSEE
	ELLISON	JOSIAH S.	CPL.	I	3RD CAV	TENNESSEE
	ELLISON	THOMAS	PVT	I	3RD CAV	TENNESSEE
	ELMOR	R.	PVT	G	3RD CAV	KENTUCKY
*	ELY	JOHN CLARK	SGT	C	115TH INF	OHIO
	ELZA	ROBERT M.	CPL	E	3RD CAV	TENNESSEE
	EMENERY	W.	PVT	A	2ND CAV	TENNESSEE
	EMERICK	J.	PVT	L	18TH	KENTUCKY
	EMERINE	ELI	PVT	K	65TH INF	OHIO
	EMERSON	ALBERT G.	SGT	C	97TH INF	OHIO
*	EMMONS	JOHN W.	PVT	K	9TH CAV	INDIANA
	ENGLE	JOHN	PVT	D	21ST	OHIO
**	ENGLEHART	JOHN M.	PVT	C	9TH CAV	INDIANA
	ENGLISH	W.	PVT	C	7TH CAV	VIRGINIA
	ENLOW	RICHARD F.	PVT	L	3RD CAV	TENNESSEE
	ESLICH	N.A.	PVT	G	4TH CAV	MICHIGAN
*	ESPY	JOSEPH	CPL	C	124TH INF	INDIANA
*	ESTES	JAMES K.	CPL	F	3RD CAV	TENNESSEE
	ETZLE	MARTIN L.	PVT	F	15TH	OHIO
	EVANS	CHARLES	PVT	A	9TH CAV	INDIANA
*	EVANS	DAVID W.	PVT	L	5TH CAV	INDIANA
	EVANS	EDWARD W.	PVT	D	1ST CAV	OHIO
	EVANS	SAMUEL M.	PVT	H	3RD CAV	TENNESSEE
*	EVANS	THOMAS	CPL	G	115TH INF	OHIO

* DIED
** BURIED AT THE MEMPHIS NATIONAL CEMETERY

	EVANSBERRY	H.	PVT	E	6TH CAV	KENTUCKY
*	EVENS	GEORGE L.	PVT	G	17TH	INDIANA
*	EVERETT	JAMES	PVT	A	3RD CAV	TENNESSEE
	EVERETT	LUKE L.	PVT	A	8TH INF	TENNESSEE
*	EVERETT	THOMAS	PVT	G	3RD CAV	TENNESSEE
*	EVERETT	WILLIAM T.	SGT	H	3RD CAV	TENNESSEE
	EVERHART	JOHN	CPL	C	115TH INF	OHIO
	EVERMAN	NATHAN D.	PVT	F	40TH INF	INDIANA
*	EVITT	WILLIAM T.	SGT	H	3RD CAV	TENNESSEE
	FABER	J.H.	PVT	A	5TH CAV	KENTUCKY
*	FABRA	DAVID	PVT	A	102ND INF	OHIO
	FABROW	M.B.	PVT	K	4TH CAV	KENTUCKY
*	FAIRCHILD	AMOS W.	PVT	K	65TH INF	OHIO
	FALDERMAN	BENJAMIN	PVT	K	121ST INF	OHIO
	FALKNER	JOHN	PVT	A	7TH CAV	OHIO
*	FAN	GREENEBURG	PVT	H	3RD CAV	TENNESSE
*	FANNING	ALBERT	PVT	A	7TH CAV	OHIO
*	FANRAT	WILLIAM F.	CPL	G	18TH INF	MICHIGAN
	FANTINGER	J.H.	PVT	I	17TH	INDIANA
	FARL	JOHN	CPL	D	7TH CAV	INDIANA
*	FARMER	ADAM	PVT	A	3RD CAV	TENNESSEE
	FARMER	ELIAS	PVT	A	3RD CAV	TENNESSEE
	FARMER	ELISHA	PVT	H	3RD CAV	TENNESSEE
	FARMER	G.	PVT	H	3RD CAV	TENNESSEE
*	FARMER	JOHN A.	PVT	A	3RD CAV	TENNESSEE
*	FARMER	JOSEPH O.	PVT	H	3RD CAV	TENNESSEE
*	FARMER	JULIUS M.	PVT	K	8TH CAV	MICHIGAN
	FARRELL	JOHN	PVT	D	7TH CAV	INDIANA
	FARRELL	M.	SGT	D	10TH CAV	INDIANA
*	FARRELL	WILLIAM	PVT	L	124TH INF	INDIANA
	FARRELL	WILLIAM	PVT	H	3RD CAV	TENNESSEE
	FARRER	JOHN	PVT	K	8TH CAV	MICHIGAN
	FARROTT	G. WILLIAM	PVT	H	3RD CAV	TENNESSEE
	FAST	L.R.	PVT	B	8TH CAV	MICHIGAN
	FAST	WILLIAM N.	SGT	K	102ND INF	OHIO
	FAST	WILSON A.	SGT	K	102D INF	OHIO
	FAULKNER	JOHN	PVT	A	7TH CAV	OHIO
*	FAUROTE	WILLIAM L.	CPL	G	18TH INF	MICHIGAN

---

* DIED
** BURIED AT THE MEMPHIS NATIONAL CEMETERY

	FENCLEY	J.M.	PVT	B	49TH INF	OHIO
*	FERGERSON	JOHN HENRY	PVT	D	3RD CAV	TENNESSEE
*	FERGERSON	WILLIAM H.	PVT	F	3RD CAV	TENNESSEE
	FESLER	JOHN M.	PVT	B	49TH INF	OHIO
*	FIDLER	WILLIAM H.	MAJOR	S	6TH CAV	KENTUCKY
	FIELD	GILBERT W.	PVT	D	23RD INF	OHIO
	FIES	WILLIAM	SGT	B	64TH INF	OHIO
	FINCH	WILLIAM B.	PVT	D	5TH CAV	MICHIGAN
*	FINCH	WILLIAM H.	SGT	D	18TH INF	MICHIGAN
*	FINGER	FRANK	PVT	F	3RD CAV	TENNESSEE
*	FINGER	JACOB	PVT	B	3RD CAV	TENNESSEE
	FINKLE	BENJAMIN R.	PVT	M	7TH CAV	MICHIGAN
*	FINLEY	REESE N.	PVT	A	3RD CAV	TENNESSEE
	FIREY	J.	BUGLER	C	6TH CAV	KENTUCKY
	FISHER	AUSTIN T.	PVT	B	72ND INF	OHIO
*	FISHER	DANIEL, JR.	PVT	B	102ND INF	OHIO
*	FISHER	ELISHA	PVT	H	3RD CAV	TENNESSEE
*	FISHER	EMANUEL L.	PVT	F	3RD CAV	TENNESSEE
*	FISHER	GEORGE S.	PVT	K	9TH CAV	INDIANA
	FITZGERALD	WILLIAM	PVT	C	8TH CAV	MICHIGAN
*	FLEAGLE	JOHN	PVT	K	100TH INF	OHIO
*	FLEMING	JAMES ADGATE	PVT	D	100TH INF	OHIO
	FLETCHER	BENJAMIN	CPL	A	57TH INF	INDIANA
	FLICK	JACOB				UNKNOWN
*	FLINT	LYSANDER L.	PVT	C	102ND INF	OHIO
*	FLINT	THOMAS	PVT	F	52ND INF	OHIO
*	FLUKE	ARTHUR W.	SGT	C	6TH CAV	KENTUCKY
	FOGLE	JOHN	PVT	F	115TH INF	OHIO
	FOGLESONG	NATHANIEL M.	PVT	A	18TH INF	MICHIGAN
	FOLDERMAN	BARNETT	CPL	K	9TH CAV	INDIANA
	FOLEY	PATRICK W.	CPL	B	28TH	KENTUCKY
*	FOLEY	JAMES	PVT	A	6TH CAV	KENTUCKY
*	FOLTZ	PETER	PVT	A	7TH CAV	OHIO
	FOODS	A.	PVT	B	4TH CAV	KENTUCKY
**	FORD	EDWIN	CPL	D	18TH INF	MICHIGAN
	FORDEND	L.D.	PVT	I	4TH CAV	MICHIGAN
	FOREST	THOMAS	PVT	K	21ST	OHIO
*	FORT	LEWIS R.	PVT	E	8TH CAV	MICHIGAN

* DIED
** BURIED AT THE MEMPHIS NATIONAL CEMETERY

FORY	ALEXANDER	PVT	F	8TH CAV	INDIANA
FOSTER	HENRY C.	PVT	A	1ST CAV	VIRGINIA
* FOWLER	ANDREW E.	SGT	L	3RD CAV	TENNESSEE
FOX	JOHN, JR.	CPL	A	50TH INF	OHIO
FRANKLIN	B.	PVT	F	4TH CAV	INDIANA
* FRANKLIN	JAMES H.	SGT	A	3RD CAV	TENNESSEE
* FRANKLIN	MORGAN S.	PVT	C	93RD INF	INDIANA
FRANZ	DAVID	PVT	A	103RD INF	OHIO
FRAZEE	MARTIN	SGT	C	2ND CAV	INDIANA
* FRAZIER	JACOB	SGT	I	3RD CAV	TENNESSEE
FRAZIER	SQUIRE	CPL	G	102ND INF	OHIO
FREDERICK	GEORGE H.	PVT	D	7TH CAV	INDIANA
FREE	M.C.	PVT	M	1ST CAV	MICHIGAN
FRIESNER	WILLIAM S.	CAPTAIN	K	58TH INF	OHIO
* FRINK	MILES S.	PVT	H	18TH INF	MICHIGAN
FRITZ	PETER	PVT	A	7TH CAV	OHIO
FRITZ	SAMUEL	PVT	F	175TH INF	OHIO
FROELAND	GEORGE	PVT	E	23RD INF	MICHIGAN
FRY	ALEXANDER	PVT	F	8TH CAV	INDIANA
FRY	DANIEL B.	PVT	K	102ND INF	OHIO
* FRY	JOSEPH M.	SGT	C	3RD CAV	TENNESSEE
* FULLER	ALEXANDER	PVT	F	18TH	MICHIGAN
FULLER	JAMES	PVT	F	3RD CAV	TENNESSEE
FURNIA	S.D.	PVT		4TH CAV	MICHIGAN
GAFF	JOHN	PVT	H	98TH INF	OHIO
* GAFFNEY	MATTHEW	CAPTAIN	L	10TH CAV	INDIANA
GAGE	JOSEPH	PVT	I	2ND CAV	MICHIGAN
* GALBREATH	JOHN W.	PVT	C	124TH INF	INDIANA
* GALE	A. ORRIS	PVT	F	18TH	MICHIGAN
GALINER	JAMES	PVT	I	4TH CAV	KENTUCKY
GALLAGHER	J.	PVT	D	4TH CAV	KENTUCKY
GAMBER	JOHN	PVT	A	41ST	OHIO
GAMBILL	HENRY	PVT	B	14TH INF	KENTUCKY
* GAMBLE	MOSES	PVT	A	3RD CAV	TENNESSEE
* GAMER	CALAWAY	PVT	H	3RD CAV	TENNESSEE
GANZE	WILSON	PVT	C	47TH INF	INDIANA
GARBER	DANIEL	PVT	E	102ND INF	OHIO
GARDNER	DAVID	PVT		5TH ART	MICHIGAN

* DIED
** BURIED AT THE MEMPHIS NATIONAL CEMETERY

	GARDNER	JAMES W.	PVT	F	65TH INF	INDIANA
*	GARRETT	EDWIN W.	MUSICIAN	H	115TH INF	OHIO
*	GARRISON	JOHN J.	PVT	C	115TH INF	OHIO
	GARTHMAN	JOHN H.	PVT	C	7TH CAV	INDIANA
	GARVES	DANIEL	CPL	E	70TH INF	OHIO
	GASKILL	DAVID	SGT	M	9TH CAV	INDIANA
	GASS	JESSE M.	CPL	H	93RD INF	INDIANA
	GASS	NATHAN J.	SGT	H	93RD INF	INDIANA
	GASTIN	WILLIAM A.	PVT	K	3RD CAV	OHIO
	GASTON	G.M.	PVT	K	121ST INF	OHIO
	GASTON	STEPHEN M.	MUSICIAN	K	9TH CAV	INDIANA
	GATHMAN	JOHN H.	PVT	C	7TH CAV	INDIANA
*	GAUPH	LOUIS	PVT	A	6TH CAV	KENTUCKY
	GAURBER	J.	PVT	A	41ST INF	OHIO
*	GAY	ASA	PVT	A	97TH INF	OHIO
	GAY	JOSEPH H.	PVT	B	9TH CAV	INDIANA
*	GAYLORD	ROBERT	PVT	C	115TH INF	OHIO
	GEER	RYLAN	PVT	F	8TH CAV	MICHIGAN
*	GEESEMAN	DAVID	PVT	G	65TH INF	OHIO
	GEN	JAMES	PVT		93RD INF	INDIANA
	GERMAN	ANDREW	PVT	G	72ND INF	OHIO
	GESSLER	COARA	PVT	D	57TH INF	OHIO
*	GETTERMAN	JOHN	PVT	F	183RD INF	OHIO
*	GHEEN	T.P.	SGT	C	8TH CAV	MICHIGAN
	GIBSON	DAVID	PVT	I	3RD CAV	TENNESSEE
*	GIBSON	JOSEPH	PVT	I	3RD CAV	TENNESSEE
*	GILBA	FREDERICK	CPL	A	7TH CAV	OHIO
	GILBREATH	ROBERT W.	PVT	E	9TH CAV	INDIANA
	GILLMAN	H.	PVT	C	4TH CAV	KENTUCKY
*	GILMORE	JOHN	PVT	E	93RD INF	INDIANA
*	GILMORE	MICHAEL	PVT	H	50TH INF	OHIO
	GINN	THOMAS J.	PVT	F	57TH INF	INDIANA
	GITHENS	LAFAYETTE	PVT	F	56TH INF	OHIO
*	GIVINS	WILLIAM A.	PVT	L	3RD CAV	TENNESSEE
*	GLAZE	WILLIAM P.	PVT	L	9TH CAV	INDIANA
	GLEASON	GEORGE G.	PVT	D	2ND CAV	MICHIGAN
	GOFF	JOHN	PVT	H	98TH INF	OHIO
	GOLDEN	JAMES	PVT	C	3RD CAV	TENNESSEE

* DIED
** BURIED AT THE MEMPHIS NATIONAL CEMETERY

	GOLDSWOOD	CHARLES B.	MUSICIAN	G	115TH INF	OHIO
	GOODFLASHLER	G.W.	PVT	A	7TH CAV	VIRGINIA
	GOODRICH	WILLIAM N.	PVT	E	18TH INF	MICHIGAN
	GOTERMAN	JOHN	PVT	F	103RD INF	OHIO
	GOW	JAMES	PVT	D	93RD INF	INDIANA
	GRAHAM	JOHN	PVT	G	10TH CAV	INDIANA
	GRAHAM	JOHN W.	PVT	A	2ND CAV	OHIO
	GRAHAM	LANDON	PVT	C	3RD CAV	TENNESSEE
*	GRAVES	WILLIAM H.	SGT	G	9TH CAV	INDIANA
	GRAY	JOSEPH H.	PVT	B	9TH CAV	INDIANA
	GRAY	MORGAN L.	CPL	E	6TH CAV	TENNESSEE
	GRAY	S.	PVT	A	4TH CAV	KENTUCKY
*	GRAY	THOMAS J.	PVT	E	175TH INF	OHIO
	GRAY	WILLIAM	PVT	I	23RD INF	OHIO
	GREANT	JAQUES	PVT	C	93RD INF	INDIANA
	GREEN	ARNOLD	PVT	K	1ST S.S.	MICHIGAN
	GREEN	CHARLES	PVT	L	3RD CAV	OHIO
	GREEN	SETH J.	PVT	K	9TH CAV	INDIANA
*	GREEN	WILLIAM	SGT	G	50TH INF	OHIO
*	GREENFIELD	LEVI	SGT	C	18TH INF	MICHIGAN
	GREENFIELD	REUBEN	PVT	D	102ND INF	OHIO
	GREENOVER	JOHN G.	PVT	C	115TH INF	OHIO
	GREER	C.B.	PVT	F	8TH CAV	MICHIGAN
	GREER	JESSE A.	PVT	A	2ND MTD INF	TENNESSEE
	GREG	WILLIAM	SGT	G	65TH INF	OHIO
	GREGLAND	CHARLES	CPL	K	18TH INF	MICHIGAN
	GREGORY	MYRUM W.	CPL	C	55TH INF	OHIO
*	GREGORY	EDGAR W.	SGT	C	65TH INF	OHIO
*	GRICE	DAVID	PVT	D	102ND INF	OHIO
*	GRIFFIN	HOLSTON	CPL	E	3RD CAV	TENNESSEE
*	GRIFFIN	JAMES O.	PVT	I	50TH INF	OHIO
*	GRIM	WILLIAM	PVT	C	9TH CAV	OHIO
*	GROSS	ALEXANDER	PVT	G	3RD CAV	TENNESSEE
	GROVE	JAMES	PVT	D	93RD INF	INDIANA
*	GRUBAUGH	DAVID	PVT	G	65TH INF	OHIO
	GRUBBS	ISAAC	PVT	A	5TH CAV	INDIANA
*	GRUELL	NATHAN E.	CPL	M	9TH CAV	INDIANA
*	GUARD	JAMES WATT	PVT	A	102ND INF	OHIO

---

* DIED
** BURIED AT THE MEMPHIS NATIONAL CEMETERY

GUARD	JOHN W.	PVT	K	7TH CAV	INDIANA
GUATIN	W.A.	PVT	K	3RD CAV	OHIO
GUEAR	STEPHEN	PVT	F	40TH INF	INDIANA
* GUIB	JACOB	PVT	A	102ND INF	OHIO
* GUNTHER	JOHN	MUSICIAN	E	183RD INF	OHIO
* GUSTIN	WILLIAM	PVT	K	3RD CAV	OHIO
HAAS	JOHN	PVT	E	37TH INF	OHIO
HABBLER	H.	PVT	G	91ST INF	INDIANA
HACHSELL	J.L.	PVT	E	7TH CAV	INDIANA
* HACKENBURG	AUGUST	CPL	I	57TH INF	INDIANA
HACKNEY	RICE LEVI	PVT	I	3RD CAV	TENNESSEE
HAGART	W.	PVT	A	7TH CAV	KENTUCKY
* HAGUE	SAMUEL	PVT	F	72ND INF	OHIO
HAIGHT	GEORGE C.	MUSICIAN	H	18TH	MICHIGAN
HAILEY	CHRISTOPHER C.	PVT	K	2ND CAV	OHIO
HAINES	SAMUEL	PVT	G	40TH INF	INDIANA
HAKE	LEWIS F.	CAPTAIN	B	115TH INF	OHIO
HALE	ELWOOD	CPL	I	51ST INF	OHIO
HALE	N.H.	PVT		46TH INF	KENTUCKY
HALE	OLIVER P.	PVT	A	18TH	MICHIGAN
HALEY	JOHN	PVT	A	102ND INF	OHIO
* HALL	ANDERSON	PVT	K	40TH INF	INDIANA
* HALL	GEORGE L.	PVT	A	102ND INF	OHIO
* HALL	JAMES T.	SGT	I	6TH CAV	KENTUCKY
** HALL	JOHN F.	PVT	C	7TH CAV	INDIANA
HALL	R.T.	PVT	K	2ND CAV	KENTUCKY
* HALLOWAY	ENOS	PVT	M	9TH CAV	INDIANA
* HALNES	D.A.	PVT	L	3RD CAV	TENNESSEE
HAMBLIN	OGILVIE E.	PVT	E	2ND CAV	MICHIGAN
HAMBRICK	ANDREW J.	PVT	G	3RD CAV	TENNESSEE
* HAMILTON	HENRY C.	SGT	F	3RD CAV	TENNESSEE
HAMILTON	JAMES	PVT	G	3RD CAV	TENNESSEE
HAMILTON	JOHN B.	PVT	F	3RD CAV	TENNESSEE
HAMILTON	RICHARD	PVT		6TH CAV	KENTUCKY
HAMILTON	ROBERT N.	PVT	F	3RD CAV	TENNESSEE
HAMILTON	SIMON	CPL	H	15TH	OHIO
* HAMMEL	SAMUEL	PVT	H	95TH INF	OHIO
* HAMMONDS	JOHN	PVT	A	6TH CAV	KENTUCKY

---

* DIED
** BURIED AT THE MEMPHIS NATIONAL CEMETERY

*	HAMPTON	FRANK	PVT	I	18TH INF	MICHIGAN
*	HAMPTON	FRANK HENRY	PVT	G	18TH INF	MICHIGAN
	HAMPTON	JACOB	PVT	C	3RD CAV	TENNESSEE
	HANA	H.H.		G	121 INF	INDIANA
*	HANCOCK	WILLIAM B.	PVT	L	3RD CAV	TENNESSEE
*	HAND	JOHN F.	PVT	B	3RD CAV	TENNESSEE
	HANDOR	JOHN C.	CPL	F	7TH CAV	KENTUCKY
	HANNUM	THOMAS	SGT	A	7TH CAV	OHIO
	HANSON	SAMUEL	PVT	D	175TH INF	OHIO
	HANSON	THOMPSON	PVT	E	9TH CAV	OHIO
*	HARALD	JACOB	PVT	K	9TH CAV	INDIANA
	HARDIN	L.D.	PVT	D	2ND CAV	INDIANA
	HARDIN	WILLIAM H.	PVT	H	9TH CAV	INDIANA
*	HAREN	MICHIEL	SGT	B	3RD CAV	TENNESSEE
	HARGUARD	PHILLIP	PVT	B	21ST	OHIO
	HARIN	WILLIAM	SGT	D	3RD CAV	TENNESSEE
	HARMON	DANIEL	PVT	K	18TH INF	MICHIGAN
*	HARNLY	MANUEL	PVT	D	102ND INF	OHIO
	HAROVER	FRANCIS M.	CAPTAIN	D	175TH INF	OHIO
	HAROVER	JOHN	PVT	D	7TH CAV	TENNESSEE
	HARPER	EDWARD C.	PVT	G	4TH CAV	KENTUCKY
	HARREN	DAVID	PVT		2ND CAV	MICHIGAN
*	HARRINGTON	GIDEON	CPL	H	102ND INF	OHIO
*	HARRINGTON	PATRICK	PVT	C	124TH INF	INDIANA
	HARRIS	DAVID D.	PVT	F	3RD CAV	TENNESSEE
	HARRIS	DEWITT E.	PVT		3RD CAV	TENNESSEE
*	HARRIS	GEORGE	PVT	C	115TH INF	OHIO
	HARRIS	ISRAEL	PVT	H	24TH	MICHIGAN
	HARRIS	JOEL F.	PVT	F	18TH INF	MICHIGAN
	HARRIS	JOHN	PVT	C	115TH INF	OHIO
*	HARRIS	WILLIAM H.	PVT	F	18TH INF	MICHIGAN
*	HARRIS	WILLIAM B.	CPL	D	3RD CAV	TENNESSEE
*	HARRISON	LONGSHORE D.	PVT	B	7TH CAV	OHIO
	HART	JOHN	PVT	I	6TH CAV	MICHIGAN
*	HARTLEY	FRANK	CPL	K	9TH CAV	INDIANA
	HARTMAN	AMON	PVT	E	9TH CAV	OHIO
*	HARTMAN	JOHN F.	PVT	K	102ND INF	OHIO
	HARTMAN	LEMUAL	SGT	A	6TH CAV	KENTUCKY

* DIED
** BURIED AT THE MEMPHIS NATIONAL CEMETERY

*	HASHAW	ADAM R.	PVT	A	4TH MTD INF	TENNESSEE
	HASHAWE	A.	PVT	C	80TH INF	INDIANA
	HASKELL	B.M.	PVT	A	3RD CAV	INDIANA
*	HASKINS	PERRY	PVT	A	50TH INF	OHIO
	HASPILK	H.L.	PVT	K	40TH INF	INDIANA
	HASS	GEORGE	PVT	A	102ND INF	OHIO
	HATCH	ABSALOM W.	CPL	F	1ST ENG	MICHIGAN
	HAUGH	L.	PVT	E	9TH CAV	OHIO
*	HAUN	JOSHUA A.	PVT	E	3RD CAV	TENNESSEE
	HAUP	BENJAMIN	SGT	A	6TH CAV	KENTUCKY
	HAVEN	LYMAN	PVT	G	18TH	MICHIGAN
	HAWK	MARION	PVT	D	3RD CAV	OHIO
*	HAWKEN	JOHN	CPL	B	58TH INF	OHIO
*	HAWKINS	WARREN A.	PVT	C	9TH CAV	INDIANA
*	HAWN	MICHAEL	SGT	B	3RD CAV	TENNESSEE
	HAWTHORN	DARIUS F.	SGT	I	9TH CAV	INDIANA
*	HAYBOUR	GEORGE	PVT	M	13TH CAV	INDIANA
*	HAYDIMAN	THOMAS H.	PVT	D	6TH CAV	KENTUCKY
	HAYNER	ENOCH	PVT	A	12TH CAV	OHIO
*	HAYNES	DAVID A.	PVT	L	3RD CAV	TENNESSEE
*	HAZELRIGG	HENRY L.	CPL	K	40TH INF	INDIANA
	HEADRICK	DANIEL A.	PVT	A	3RD CAV	TENNESSEE
	HEAVEN	L.		G	18TH INF	MICHIGAN
*	HEBBLER	HENRY	PVT	G	91ST INF	INDIANA
	HECKNER	LEVI	PVT	I	3RD CAV	TENNESSEE
	HEDGES	GEORGE	SGT	K	9TH CAV	OHIO
	HEDGES	GEORGE	SGT	K	9TH CAV	OHIO
**	HELLER	RAHNEY	SGT	F	50TH INF	OHIO
	HELMINGER	JACOB	SGT	B	50TH INF	OHIO
*	HENDERSON	J.C.	PVT	E	3RD CAV	TENNESSEE
*	HENDERSON	WESLEY	PVT	A	102ND INF	OHIO
*	HENDRICKS	ADAM M.	PVT	F	115TH INF	OHIO
*	HENDRIXON	GEORGE W.	PVT	E	175TH INF	OHIO
	HENKS	T.W.	CAPTAIN		4TH CAV	MISSOURI
*	HENNICH	CHARLES	PVT	E	2ND CAV	MICHIGAN
*	HENRY	CHARLES	PVT	E	2ND CAV	MICHIGAN
*	HENRY	JOHN WESLEY	PVT	D	3RD CAV	TENNESSEE
*	HENSINGER	JOHN	PVT	D	37TH INF	OHIO

* DIED
** BURIED AT THE MEMPHIS NATIONAL CEMETERY

	HERNGER	J.	PVT	D	57TH INF	OHIO
	HERSHER	M.R.	PVT		35TH INF	INDIANA
	HERSHEY	MOSES B.	PVT	A	29TH INF	MICHIGAN
	HERTZ	JOHN	PVT	I	6TH CAV	MICHIGAN
*	HESS	ALEXANDER	PVT	D	97TH INF	OHIO
	HESS	JOHN	PVT	E	37TH INF	OHIO
*	HESSER	LOUIS	PVT	K	47TH INF	OHIO
	HESSINGER	H.P.	PVT	H	3RD CAV	TENNESSEE
*	HICKERSON	JAMES A.	CPL	C	124TH INF	INDIANA
	HICKEY	WILLIAM J.	CPL	E	3RD CAV	TENNESSEE
*	HICKMAN	PETER	PVT	E	3RD CAV	TENNESSEE
	HICKMAN	ROBERT L.	PVT	C	3RD CAV	TENNESSEE
**	HICKOX	JOHN E.	SGT	H	3RD CAV	TENNESSEE
*	HICKS	JAMES H.	PVT	F	3RD CAV	TENNESSEE
	HIGDON	CHARLES T.	PVT	C	4TH CAV	KENTUCKY
*	HIGGINS	EARL T.	PVT	I	93RD INF	INDIANA
*	HILL	DANIEL	PVT	D	2ND CAV	MICHIGAN
*	HILL	GEORGE	PVT	A	7TH CAV	OHIO
	HILL	GEORGE	PVT	D	100TH INF	OHIO
	HILL	WILLIAM S.	PVT	L	3RD CAV	TENNESSEE
*	HINCHEY	LARKIN E.	PVT	D	3RD CAV	TENNESSEE
	HINDES	ELIAS E.	PVT	A	18TH	MICHIGAN
*	HINDES	THOMAS J.	PVT	K	18TH INF	MICHIGAN
*	HINDES	WILLIAM H.	PVT	F	18TH INF	MICHIGAN
	HINERS	S.C.	CPL	G	40TH INF	INDIANA
	HINES	JAMES	PVT	K	58TH INF	OHIO
	HINES	JAMES	PVT	I	3RD CAV	TENNESSEE
	HINES	JOSEPH	PVT	I	3RD CAV	TENNESSEE
	HINES	O.E.	SGT	D	3RD CAV	TENNESSEE
	HINES	SAMUEL	PVT	B	5TH CAV	TENNESSEE
*	HINES	THEODORE N.	PVT	K	18TH INF	MICHIGAN
*	HINES	Y.F.	PVT	F	18TH INF	MICHIGAN
	HINKLEY	JOHN B.	SGT	A	9TH CAV	INDIANA
	HITES	DAVID	SGT	G	102ND INF	OHIO
*	HOBACK	GEORGE W.	PVT	C	3RD CAV	TENNESSEE
	HOBBS	LEVI A.	PVT	G	6TH CAV	KENTUCKY
	HOBI	A.P.	SGT	F	6TH CAV	INDIANA
	HODGES	WILEY J.	PVT	F	3RD CAV	TENNESSEE

* DIED
** BURIED AT THE MEMPHIS NATIONAL CEMETERY

	HOE	ALEX	PVT		18TH INF	MICHIGAN
	HOGAN	M.	PVT	H	4TH CAV	KENTUCKY
	HOGLYN	J.B.	PVT	H	6TH CAV	KENTUCKY
	HOGRLIN	JAMES	PVT	C	84TH INF	INDIANA
*	HOHNS	MORGAN	PVT	F	18TH INF	MICHIGAN
	HOLLER	R.	PVT	H	2ND CAV	MICHIGAN
	HOLLEY	J.N.	PVT	H	4TH CAV	KENTUCKY
*	HOLMES	MORGAN L.	PVT	F	18TH INF	MICHIGAN
*	HOLMES	SAMUEL A.	PVT	D	175TH INF	OHIO
*	HOLMES	WYMAN	PVT	G	13TH CAV	INDIANA
*	HOLTOM	PHILLIP L.	SGT	E	102ND INF	OHIO
*	HOOFNAIL	ABRAHAM	PVT	K	100TH INF	OHIO
*	HOOPER	JAMES H.	SGT	D	3RD CAV	TENNESSEE
*	HOOVER	WILLIAM C.	PVT	G	9TH CAV	INDIANA
	HOPE	JAMES W.	PVT	A	4TH CAV	KENTUCKY
	HORN	PHILLIP L.	PVT	I	102ND INF	OHIO
*	HORNBUGHER	WILLIAM C.	SGT	C	102ND INF	OHIO
	HORNER	IRA B.	CPL	K	65TH INF	OHIO
	HORNER	JACOB	PVT	A	102ND INF	OHIO
	HORNER	JAMES	PVT	B	MCLAUGHLIN'S	OHIO
*	HORTON	CHARLES E.	SGT	C	18TH INF	MICHIGAN
	HOTT	JOSEPH L.	PVT	C	102ND INF	OHIO
*	HOULSHOUSER	WILLIAM	PVT	H	6TH CAV	KENTUCKY
	HOUSER	ALEXANDER	PVT	A	3RD CAV	TENNESSEE
*	HOUSER	HENRY	PVT	A	3RD CAV	TENNESSEE
*	HOUSER	JAMES	CPL	B	3RD CAV	TENNESSEE
	HOUSER	LOUIS	PVT	A	3RD CAV	TENNESSEE
*	HOUSER	WILLIAM	PVT	A	3RD CAV	TENNESSEE
	HOUSTON	WILLIAM T.	PVT	A	4TH CAV	TENNESSEE
*	HOWARD	JOHN	PVT	C	40TH INF	INDIANA
*	HOWARD	TILMON A.	SGT	I	3RD CAV	TENNESSEE
	HOWELL	E.	PVT	F	3RD CAV	TENNESSEE
	HOYD	JEREMIAH	PVT	H	7TH CAV	OHIO
	HUBER	EVAN	PVT	A	32ND INF	INDIANA
*	HUCKINS	WARREN A.	PVT	C	9TH CAV	INDIANA
	HUDDLESTON	HENRY T.	PVT	H	6TH CAV	KENTUCKY
	HUDSON	HENRY	PVT	E	175TH INF	OHIO
*	HUDSON	JAMES	PVT	G	175TH INF	OHIO

* DIED
** BURIED AT THE MEMPHIS NATIONAL CEMETERY

*	HUDSON	JOHN	PVT	G	65TH INF	OHIO
*	HUDSON	PETER	PVT	G	3RD CAV	TENNESSEE
	HUFFAKER	JESSE M.	PVT	D	3RD CAV	TENNESSEE
	HUFFEY	JOHN	PVT	B	49TH INF	OHIO
*	HUFFMAN	WILLIAM H.	PVT	M	9TH CAV	INDIANA
*	HUGHES	HENRY	PVT	K	6TH CAV	KENTUCKY
	HUGHES	JOSEPH S.	PVT	C	3RD CAV	TENNESSEE
	HUGHES	WILLIAM	CPL		24TH INF	INDIANA
*	HULET	JAMES H.	PVT	K	6TH CAV	MICHIGAN
	HULETT	GEORGE W.	PVT	I	104TH INF	OHIO
	HULIT	WILLIAM A	PVT	A	64TH INF	OHIO
*	HUMBARGER	SAMUEL	PVT	H	111TH INF	OHIO
*	HUMES	FREEMAN L.	PVT	C	115TH INF	OHIO
	HUMPHREY	WILSON C.	PVT	B	50TH INF	OHIO
	HUMPHREYS	B.	PVT	H	4TH CAV	KENTUCKY
	HUNT	H.P.	PVT		36TH INF	INDIANA
*	HUNTER	ALBERT E.	PVT	M	10TH CAV	OHIO
*	HUNTSBERGER	JONAS	CPL	H	102ND INF	OHIO
	HURRY	J.	CPL	L	3RD CAV	TENNESSEE
	HUSTED	T.D.	PVT	C	11TH CAV	TENNESSEE
*	HUYCK	GEORGE B.	PVT	C	18TH INF	MICHIGAN
	HYSINGER	MADISON B.	WGNR	H	3RD CAV	TENNESSEE
	IMEVEG	G.H.		I	102D INF	OHIO
*	INNES	JAMES S.	PVT	I	24TH INF	MICHIGAN
*	IRONS	JACOB	CPL	E	102ND INF	OHIO
*	IRVINE	JAMES H.	PVT	A	MCLAUGHLIN'S	OHIO
*	ISENTREDGE	JAMES M.	PVT	L	9TH CAV	INDIANA
	IVES	EDWARD H.	PVT	D	1ST	MICHIGAN
	JACK	FRANCIS M.	PVT	K	3RD CAV	TENNESSEE
	JACKSON	G.	PVT	G	4TH CAV	KENTUCKY
*	JACKSON	J.H.	PVT	H	125TH INF	OHIO
**	JACKSON	JOHN F.	PVT	H	60TH INF	INDIANA
	JACKSON	JOHN W.	PVT	B	5TH CAV	KENTUCKY
*	JACKSON	TRUMAN	CPL	G	95TH INF	OHIO
	JACOBS	ALFORD	PVT	G	6TH CAV	KENTUCKY
*	JACOBS	JOHN A.	PVT	G	6TH CAV	KENTUCKY
	JAMES	JOHN HENRY	PVT	F	115TH INF	OHIO
*	JANNEY	JOHN H.	PVT	B	36TH INF	INDIANA

---

* DIED
** BURIED AT THE MEMPHIS NATIONAL CEMETERY

*	JARRETT	JOHN	PVT	H	102ND INF	OHIO
*	JEFFRIES	WILLIAM	PVT	A	3RD CAV	TENNESSEE
	JENKINS	SAMUEL W.	CPL	L	3RD CAV	TENNESSEE
	JENNINGS	IRA	PVT	B	10TH CAV	OHIO
*	JESSON	ROBERT	PVT	A	MCLAUGHLIN'S	OHIO
*	JOHNS	DIXON W.	CPL	G	102ND INF	OHIO
*	JOHNS	WILEY	PVT	I	3RD CAV	TENNESSEE
	JOHNSON	A.W.	PVT	H	2ND CAV	KENTUCKY
*	JOHNSON	ANDREW	PVT	H	3RD CAV	TENNESSEE
	JOHNSON	B.	PVT	A	2ND CAV	MICHIGAN
	JOHNSON	GEORGE J.	PVT	A	18TH	MICHIGAN
	JOHNSON	H.	PVT	M	7TH CAV	INDIANA
	JOHNSON	H.H.	PVT	A	4TH CAV	KENTUCKY
	JOHNSON	HENRY	SGT	I	6TH CAV	KENTUCKY
*	JOHNSON	HENRY H.	PVT	L	1ST ENG	MICHIGAN
*	JOHNSON	JACOB	PVT	L	3RD CAV	TENNESSEE
	JOHNSON	JAMES	PVT	L	9TH CAV	INDIANA
	JOHNSON	JAMES M.	CPL	E	3RD CAV	TENNESSEE
	JOHNSON	LEWIS	PVT	G	9TH CAV	INDIANA
	JOHNSON	M.W.	PVT	A	4TH CAV	KENTUCKY
	JOHNSON	SALEM	PVT	B	97TH INF	OHIO
	JOHNSON	T.B.	PVT	D	13TH CAV	INDIANA
	JOHNSON	V.A.	PVT		17TH	INDIANA
	JOHNSON	WILLIAM R.	PVT	C	3RD CAV	TENNESSEE
	JOHNSON	WILLIAM T.	PVT	L	9TH CAV	INDIANA
	JOHNSTON	BENJAMIN F.	PVT	A	5TH CAV	MICHIGAN
*	JOHNSTON	JOHN	PVT	D	2ND CAV	MICHIGAN
	JOLLEY	V.B.	SGT	E	5TH CAV	INDIANA
*	JONES	ALANSON	PVT	B	18TH INF	MICHIGAN
	JONES	ARTHUR A.	SGT	C	115TH INF	OHIO
	JONES	DOCK				TENNESSEE
	JONES	HARLEN C.	CPL	F	3RD CAV	TENNESSEE
	JONES	J.T.	PVT	K	10TH CAV	INDIANA
*	JONES	JAMES M.	SGT	H	3RD CAV	TENNESSEE
	JONES	JOSIAH W.	PVT	E	18TH INF	MICHIGAN
*	JONES	S.W.	PVT	I	6TH CAV	KENTUCKY
	JONES	STEPHEN	PVT	I	6TH CAV	KENTUCKY
	JONES	THOMAS F.	PVT	A	59TH INF	OHIO

* DIED
** BURIED AT THE MEMPHIS NATIONAL CEMETERY

*	JOPP	JOSEPH	CPL	D	9TH CAV	OHIO
*	JORDAN	HENRY	PVT	H	50TH INF	OHIO
	JORDAN	MONTGOMERY	PVT	G	3RD CAV	TENNESSEE
*	JOSEPH	MICHAEL	PVT	E	111TH INF	OHIO
*	KABLE	JOHN H.	PVT	A	3RD CAV	TENNESSEE
	KAGER	JAMES C.	PVT	H	3RD CAV	TENNESSEE
	KAMMER	THOMAS	PVT	C	9TH CAV	INDIANA
*	KANEY	WILLIAM	PVT	C	3RD CAV	INDIANA
	KARNS	NICHOLAS	SGT	B	18TH INF	OHIO
	KAUFFMAN	JOHN F.	PVT	K	102ND INF	OHIO
*	KAYWOOD	BENJAMIN F.	PVT	L	3RD CAV	TENNESSEE
*	KEARNS	JOHN	PVT	I	40TH INF	OHIO
	KEATING	JAMES	PVT	E	2ND CAV	MICHIGAN
*	KEEBLE	JOHN H.	PVT	A	3RD CAV	TENNESSEE
	KEEBLE	PLEASANT M.	PVT	H	3RD CAV	TENNESSEE
	KEELER	LEW L.	SGT	H	11TH CAV	INDIANA
*	KEELER	WILLIAM	PVT	F	102ND INF	OHIO
*	KEISTLER	JACOB	PVT	A	58TH INF	OHIO
	KELLAMS	MARTIUS	PVT	K	38TH INF	INDIANA
*	KELLEY	THOMAS	PVT	E	65TH INF	OHIO
	KELLUM	MARTIN	PVT	D	38TH INF	INDIANA
*	KELLY	GEORGE W.	PVT	H	10TH CAV	INDIANA
	KELLY	GRANDISON	PVT	L	9TH CAV	INDIANA
*	KELLY	JOHN	PVT	A	75TH INF	OHIO
	KENARD	A.	PVT	C	183RD INF	OHIO
	KENDALS	RENALDO	PVT	E	21ST	OHIO
*	KENDRICK	JAMES	PVT	E	2ND CAV	MICHIGAN
*	KENEAU	JAMES	PVT	D	3RD CAV	TENNESSEE
	KENNEDY	EDWARD J.	PVT	E	7TH CAV	OHIO
	KENNEDY	EDWIN J.	PVT	K	64TH INF	OHIO
	KENNEDY	ELIAS R.	PVT	K	4TH CAV	KENTUCKY
*	KENNEDY	GEORGE W.	PVT	C	3RD CAV	TENNESSEE
*	KENS	GEORGE	PVT	B	58TH INF	OHIO
*	KENT	GEORGE	SGT	D	40TH INF	OHIO
	KEORNEY	M.	PVT	C	3RD CAV	INDIANA
	KERNES	W.	PVT	A	59TH INF	OHIO
*	KERSTETTER	BENJAMIN	SADLR	M	3RD CAV	OHIO
	KESSLER	PHILLIP	PVT	K	9TH CAV	INDIANA

---

* DIED
** BURIED AT THE MEMPHIS NATIONAL CEMETERY

*	KETTERMAN	WILLIAM D.	CAPTAIN	A	7TH CAV	OHIO
	KIBBIN	JAMES H.	PVT	D	57TH INF	INDIANA
	KIDD	ALEXANDER	CPL	A	3RD CAV	TENNESSEE
*	KIDD	JAMES	SGT	E	3RD CAV	TENNESSEE
*	KIDD	JAMES W.	PVT	A	3RD CAV	TENNESSEE
	KIDD	LOUIS	PVT	A	3RD CAV	TENNESSEE
	KIMBERLIN	JAMES H.	SGT	C	124TH INF	INDIANA
	KING	ALBERT W.	CPL	D	100TH INF	OHIO
	KING	BARZILLA	PVT	B	64TH INF	OHIO
	KING	CARKINS	PVT	D	34TH INF	OHIO
*	KING	CHARLES	PVT	C	9TH CAV	INDIANA
*	KING	EDWARD	PVT	C	115TH INF	OHIO
	KING	GEORGE A.	PVT	B	2ND CAV	TENNESSEE
	KING	JOHN H.	PVT		9TH CAV	INDIANA
*	KING	LAWRENCE	PVT	D	50TH INF	OHIO
*	KING	SAMUEL	PVT	M	9TH CAV	INDIANA
*	KINNAMAN	SAMUEL	PVT	K	3RD CAV	TENNESSEE
*	KINNAMON	JAMES M.	PVT	F	3RD CAV	TENNESSEE
*	KINNEY	JOHN A.	PVT	F	8TH CAV	MICHIGAN
*	KINSER	CHRISTOPHER	PVT	A	58TH INF	OHIO
	KINSER	HUGH	PVT	E	50TH INF	OHIO
	KINSHA	G.S.	PVT	C	3RD CAV	TENNESSEE
	KIRK	WILLIIAM H.	PVT	F	72ND INF	OHIO
	KIRKER	WILLIAM J.	PVT	K	9TH CAV	OHIO
	KIRKPATRICK	JOHN R.	PVT	I	3RD INF	TENNESSEE
	KIRKPATRICK	WILLIAM C.	PVT	I	3RD CAV	TENNESSEE
	KISSELL	JACOB	PVT	K	62ND INF	OHIO
	KLINE	HENRY J.	PVT	G	9TH CAV	INDIANA
	KLINE	JACOB	PVT	C	58TH INF	OHIO
	KLIPPSTEIN	LEYMIER	PVT	B	7TH CAV	OHIO
*	KNAPP	ANDREW J.	CPL	A	18TH INF	MICHIGAN
	KNAPPS	CHARLES	PVT	G	115TH INF	OHIO
*	KNIGHT	JOHN D.	SGT	D	3RD CAV	TENNESSEE
	KOCH	LEWIS	PVT	D	28TH INF	OHIO
	KOCHENDERFER	JOHN H.	PVT	D	102ND INF	OHIO
	KOON	HENRICH	PVT	A	18TH INF	MICHIGAN
*	KREBBS	HENRY	CPL	B	102ND INF	OHIO
*	KRUSE	CHARLES T.	CPL	G	50TH INF	OHIO

* DIED
** BURIED AT THE MEMPHIS NATIONAL CEMETERY

KURTZ	JOHN J.	PVT	F	7TH CAV	OHIO
* LABOYTEAUX	THOMAS	PVT	E	9TH CAV	INDIANA
LACKEY	JOSEPH B.	PVT	B	3RD CAV	TENNESSEE
* LACKEY	PATRICK	PVT	G	18TH INF	MICHIGAN
* LACKLER	GEORGE	PVT	F	18TH INF	MICHIGAN
* LAHR	JACOB	PVT	F	51ST INF	OHIO
LAHUE	CHARLES J.	PVT	D	13TH CAV	INDIANA
LAMB	J.	PVT	B	33TH INF	OHIO
* LAMB	MARTIN	PVT	C	57TH INF	INDIANA
* LAMBERT	VELMORE	PVT	D	100TH INF	OHIO
LAMPSELL	H.	PVT		11TH CAV	OHIO
LAND	THOMAS	PVT	L	3RD CAV	TENNESSEE
LANDON	SIMEON	CPL	D	64TH INF	OHIO
* LANE	JAMES H.	PVT	C	22ND	MICHIGAN
LANG	JAMES B.	CPL	B	33RD	OHIO
LANGLEY	JAMES	PVT	K	3RD CAV	TENNESSEE
LANGLEY	WILLIAM F.	PVT	E	2ND CAV	MICHIGAN
* LARKEY	PAT	PVT	E	18TH INF	MICHIGAN
LARKIN	MILTON H.	LT	H	97TH INF	OHIO
LARSON	GEORGE M.	PVT	K	3RD CAV	TENNESSEE
LAS	A.M.	PVT		5TH CAV	INDIANA
* LAUGHETER	ALEXANDER	PVT	F	115TH INF	OHIO
LAUGHLIN	THOMAS B.	PVT	K	9TH CAV	INDIANA
LAULES	PATRICK	PVT	B	6TH CAV	VIRGINIA
* LAUTMEYER	JOHN B.	PVT	M	4TH CAV	OHIO
LAWHEAD	GEORGE W.	PVT	A	9TH CAV	OHIO
* LAWRENCE	ALBERT	SGT	D	18TH INF	MICHIGAN
LAWRENCE	H.K.	CPL	H	88TH INF	INDIANA
LAWSON	GEORGE M.	PVT	K	3RD CAV	TENNESSEE
LAWSON	HIRAM	PVT	G	5TH CAV	INDIANA
LAWLESS	GEORGE	PVT	G	6TH CAV	KENTUCKY
* LEAK	JAMES	PVT	B	3RD CAV	TENNESSEE
LEAKE	ADAM	CPL	B	3RD CAV	TENNESSEE
LEARNER	BENJAMIN F.	CPL	G	57TH INF	INDIANA
* LEAS	JOSEPH W.	CPL	F	95TH INF	OHIO
LEASURE	ANDREW J.	SGT	A	7TH CAV	OHIO
LEBEL	G.	SGT	B	6TH CAV	KENTUCKY
LEE	ASA	PVT	A	6TH CAV	INDIANA

* DIED
** BURIED AT THE MEMPHIS NATIONAL CEMETERY

LEE	E.C.	PVT	E	6TH CAV	INDIANA
* LEE	EDWARD	SGT	F	3RD CAV	TENNESSEE
LEE	J.W.	PVT	A	102ND INF	OHIO
* LEE	JAMES	PVT	G	3RD CAV	TENNESSEE
LEE	WESLEY	PVT	A	102ND INF	OHIO
* LEE	WILLIAM H.	SGT	E	50TH INF	OHIO
* LEEK	WILLIAM	PVT	K	3RD CAV	TENNESSEE
LEERS	C.H.	PVT	B	9TH CAV	INDIANA
LEHMAN	N.	PVT	G	50TH INF	OHIO
* LEIDIG	REUBEN	PVT	K	102ND INF	OHIO
LELIMAN	T.S.	PVT	I	18TH	INDIANA
LEMING	SAMUEL	CPL	L	3RD CAV	TENNESSEE
LEMONS	L.	CPL	L	3RD CAV	TENNESSEE
LEMONS	NATHAN	PVT		175TH INF	OHIO
LENNYSHAW	C.	PVT	C	7TH CAV	OHIO
LENTIMORE	J.B.	PVT	M	4TH CAV	OHIO
LEONARD	BENJAMIN F.			57TH INF	INDIANA
LEONARD	THOMAS J.	PVT	F	3RD CAV	TENNESSEE
LESLEY	JOHN	PVT	K	3RD CAV	TENNESSEE
* LEWIS	DANIEL C.	LT	M	3RD CAV	OHIO
* LEWIS	DAVID	PVT	A	7TH CAV	OHIO
LEWIS	JOHN B.	PVT	K	9TH CAV	INDIANA
LEWIS	WILLIAM	CPL	A	1ST ART	KENTUCKY
LEWIS	WILLIAM	PVT	E	16TH	INDIANA
LIBARKER	PORTER A.	CPL	L	2ND CAV	MICHIGAN
LICKLEITNER	JOSEPH	PVT	H	183RD INF	OHIO
LIDD	L.	PVT	D	2ND CAV	INDIANA
LIGHLAND	DANIEL	PVT	G	102ND INF	OHIO
LIGHTNER	J.	PVT	L	183RD INF	OHIO
LINCH	THOMAS	PVT	B	35TH INF	INDIANA
LINDLEY	HENRY C.	PVT	I	99TH INF	INDIANA
* LINDSAY	WILLIAM L.	PVT	E	2ND CAV	MICHIGAN
* LINDSEY	JOHN B.	PVT	I	3RD CAV	TENNESSEE
LINGINFELTER	GEORGE T.	PVT	A	3RD CAV	TENNESSEE
LINGINFELTER	HENRY TOLBERT	SGT	I	3RD CAV	TENNESSEE
* LINSON	SAMUEL	PVT	A	93RD INF	INDIANA
* LINSTED	HENRY	PVT	F	20TH	OHIO
* LINZIE	JOHN R.	PVT	I	3RD CAV	TENNESSEE

* DIED
** BURIED AT THE MEMPHIS NATIONAL CEMETERY

*	LITTLE	JOHN W.	SGT	F	95TH INF	OHIO
	LOCKE	JOHN H.	PVT	H	3RD CAV	TENNESSEE
	LOCKHART	WILLIAM	PVT	E	102ND INF	OHIO
*	LOCKMAN	BEAM	PVT	G	17TH	INDIANA
*	LOCKWOOD	DARIUS	PVT	A	2ND CAV	OHIO
	LOMER	J.B.	CPL	K	65TH INF	OHIO
	LONG	ABNER	PVT	D	3RD CAV	TENNESSEE
*	LONG	BARTHOLOMEW	PVT	C	114TH INF	OHIO
	LONG	GEORGE M.	CPL	F	21ST	OHIO
*	LONG	HENRY M.	PVT	E	11TH CAV	INDIANA
	LONG	JAMES B.	PVT	I	33RD CAV	OHIO
*	LONG	JOHN	PVT	D	3RD CAV	TENNESSEE
	LONG	MELVIN P.	PVT	F	3RD CAV	TENNESSEE
	LONG	ROBERT W.	SGT	D	65TH INF	OHIO
	LONGHOUSER	ANDREW	PVT	D	7TH CAV	OHIO
*	LONGSHORE	JEREMIAH	SGT	C	13TH CAV	OHIO
	LOPT	J.H.	PVT	H	3RD CAV	TENNESSEE
	LOST	D.M.	PVT	G	2ND CAV	TENNESSEE
	LOVE	J.H.	PVT	C	22ND	MICHIGAN
	LOW	O.W.	PVT	A	75TH INF	OHIO
	LOWDENBECKER	LAWRENCE	PVT	D	8TH CAV	MICHIGAN
*	LOWREY	DEMING N.	CAPTAIN	G	115TH INF	OHIO
	LOY	GEORGE C.	PVT	I	1ST CAV	VIRGINIA
*	LUCHANE	D.	PVT	F	25TH	MICHIGAN
*	LUDLAM	BENJAMIN F.	PVT	A	18TH INF	MICHIGAN
	LUDLUM	ALBERT E.	PVT	E	23RD	MICHIGAN
	LUES	GEORGE C.	PVT		1ST ART	VIRGINIA
	LUGENBEAL	WILLIAM	PVT	F	135TH INF	OHIO
	LUTTRELL	WILLIAM	CPL	G	3RD CAV	TENNESSEE
	LYBORGER	PORTER A.	CPL	L	2ND CAV	MICHIGAN
*	LYMAN	IRWIN J.	PVT	I	33TH INF	OHIO
	LYNCH	THOMAS	PVT	B	35TH INF	INDIANA
	LYONS	J.H.	CPL	B	6TH CAV	VIRGINIA
	MACKELROY	J.				UNKNOWN
	MADDEN	WILLIAM P.	PVT	F	8TH CAV	OHIO
	MADDIES	WILLIAM F.	PVT		3RD CAV	TENNESSEE
	MADDOX	JOHN C.	PVT	H	8TH CAV	INDIANA
	MADER	JOHN	SGT	C	81ST	OHIO

---

* DIED
** BURIED AT THE MEMPHIS NATIONAL CEMETERY

	MAES	JOTHAM W.	PVT	B	47TH INF	OHIO
	MAGGETT	ROBERT	PVT	L	2ND CAV	TENNESSEE
	MAHONEY	JEREMIAH	CPL	I	2ND CAV	MICHIGAN
**	MAIN	SEYMOUR H.	PVT	I	18TH INF	MICHIGAN
*	MALALEY	MORRIS	SGT		7TH CAV	KENTUCKY
	MALERY	HUGH	PVT	D	50TH INF	OHIO
	MALERY	JOHN	PVT	A	115TH INF	OHIO
*	MALEY	CHRISTOPHER	PVT	C	115TH INF	OHIO
*	MALLOTT	RICHARD A.	CPL	D	5TH CAV	INDIANA
	MALONE	VINCENT A.	PVT	C	115TH INF	OHIO
	MANIER	DARIUS	PVT	G	183RD INF	OHIO
*	MANIES	RILEY J.	PVT	B	3RD CAV	TENNESSEE
*	MANKIN	SILAS	PVT	H	9TH CAV	OHIO
	MANN	JAMES H.	PVT	K	18TH INF	MICHIGAN
*	MANN	WASHINGTON	PVT	D	18TH INF	MICHIGAN
	MANN	WILLIAM S.	PVT	C	3RD CAV	TENNESSEE
	MANNER	A.	PVT	A	1ST CAV	VIRGINIA
*	MANSFIELD	THOMAS MONROE	SGT	D	3RD CAV	TENNESSEE
	MANSFIELD	WILLIAM E.	SGT	D	3RD CAV	TENNESSEE
*	MANSFIELD	Z.M.	SGT	L	3RD CAV	TENNESSEE
*	MAPLES	HENRY	PVT	I	3RD CAV	TENNESSEE
	MARCUM	N.	PVT	B	4TH CAV	KENTUCKY
	MARITY	W.J.	SGT	H	9TH CAV	INDIANA
	MARK	CHARLES	PVT	F	79TH INF	OHIO
	MARKABEE	W.	PVT	B	8TH CAV	INDIANA
	MARKLAND	WILLIAM	PVT	D	8TH CAV	INDIANA
	MARR	BENJAMIN L.	PVT	F	3RD CAV	TENNESSEE
**	MARSHALL	JAMES T.	PVT	C	2ND CAV	KENTUCKY
	MARSLIN	F.	PVT	B	3RD CAV	KENTUCKY
	MARTIN	J.A.	PVT	C	17TH	INDIANA
*	MARTIN	JAMES A.	PVT	K	6TH CAV	KENTUCKY
	MARTIN	JESSE	PVT	D	35TH INF	INDIANA
	MARTIN	W.H.		C	115TH INF	OHIO
	MARVIN	WILLIAM	PVT	C	47TH INF	INDIANA
	MASLER	P.	PVT	K	9TH CAV	INDIANA
*	MASON	GEORGE R.	PVT	E	18TH INF	MICHIGAN
*	MASS	JOSEPH	PVT	C	7TH CAV	VIRGINIA
	MASSEY	JOHN J.	PVT	H	3RD CAV	TENNESSEE

---

 * DIED
** BURIED AT THE MEMPHIS NATIONAL CEMETERY

	MATCH	JOHN	PVT	K	6TH CAV	VIRGINIA
	MATHIAS	EPHRAIM	SGT	K	65TH INF	OHIO
*	MATLOCK	GEORGE W.	SGT	C	3RD CAV	TENNESSEE
	MATTER	F.	PVT	H	50TH INF	OHIO
*	MATTHEWS	JOHN	PVT	L	3RD CAV	TENNESSEE
	MATTHEWS	ORLO C.	PVT	D	41ST INF	OHIO
*	MATTISON	SIMON	PVT	H	18TH INF	MICHIGAN
	MATTLINGER	J.	PVT	F	10TH CAV	VIRGINIA
	MAUK	WILLIAM H.	CPL	H	102ND INF	OHIO
	MAURY	C.R.	PVT	I	6TH CAV	VIRGINIA
	MAVITY	URIAH J.	SGT	H	9TH CAV	INDIANA
	MAXAU	P.S.	PVT		102ND INF	OHIO
	MAXMON	MARSHALL	SGT	A	2ND CAV	MICHIGAN
	MAXWELL	GEORGE W.	SGT	F	3RD CAV	TENNESSEE
	MAXWELL	JOHN W.	PVT	B	7TH CAV	OHIO
*	MAY	CHARLES	PVT	G	40TH INF	INDIANA
*	MAY	JOHN T.	PVT	C	57TH INF	INDIANA
	MAY	MARTIN V.	PVT	E	3RD CAV	TENNESSEE
	MAYES	JOSEPH H.	PVT	C	40TH INF	INDIANA
*	MAYNARD	JOHN M.	PVT	G	9TH CAV	INDIANA
	MAYSE	JOSEPH	PVT	H	40TH INF	INDIANA
	MCALLISTER	CALVIN	PVT	A	7TH CAV	OHIO
*	MCBRIDE	GEORGE	PVT	L	5TH CAV	INDIANA
	MCCABBINS	J.C.	PVT		6TH CAV	KENTUCKY
*	MCCANE	ALBERT	PVT	I	3RD CAV	TENNESSEE
*	MCCARTNEY	LEANDER	PVT	L	9TH CAV	INDIANA
	MCCARTY	JAMES M.	CPL	D	76TH INF	OHIO
**	MCCELVEY	JOSEPH M.	PVT	I	102ND INF	OHIO
	MCCLANAHAN	DAVID B.	CPL	B	3RD CAV	TENNESSEE
	MCCLANAHAN	JOHN	PVT	G	3RD CAV	TENNESSEE
*	MCCLARY	DANIEL	PVT	B	96TH INF	OHIO
	MCCLAUSON	J.M.	PVT	G	3RD CAV	TENNESSEE
	MCCLELAND	JAMES A.	PVT	G	10TH CAV	INDIANA
	MCCLEVY	HUGH	PVT	D	50TH INF	OHIO
	MCCLINTOCK	WILLIAM G.	PVT	H	26TH INF	OHIO
	MCCLURAY	JAMES	PVT	K	13TH	OHIO
	MCCLURE	MARCUS D.	PVT	F	3RD CAV	TENNESSEE
	MCCORD	GEORGE B.	LT	F	111ST INF	OHIO

* DIED
** BURIED AT THE MEMPHIS NATIONAL CEMETERY

MCCORDY	JAMES	PVT	K	13TH CAV	OHIO
MCCORMICK	ANDREW	PVT	E	9TH CAV	INDIANA
MCCOWAN	JAMES M.	CAPTAIN	K	6TH CAV	KENTUCKY
* MCCOY	WILLIAM H.	CAPTAIN	F	175TH INF	OHIO
* MCCREA	JOHN	CPL	B	102ND INF	OHIO
MCCRORY	LEWIS W.	PVT	A	100TH INF	OHIO
MCCUBBER	J.B.	PVT	K	6TH CAV	VIRGINIA
MCCULLOUGH	SIMON A.	SGT	H	5TH CAV	INDIANA
MCCURDY	JAMES	CPL	E	115TH INF	OHIO
MCCUTCHEON	W.	PVT	C	2ND CAV	INDIANA
* MCDANIEL	FRANCIS M.	PVT	I	6TH CAV	KENTUCKY
MCDANIEL	G. M.	PVT	D	124TH INF	OHIO
MCDANIEL	ISAAC	PVT	A	7TH CAV	OHIO
MCDANIEL	JAMES W.	PVT	I	6TH CAV	KENTUCKY
* MCDANIEL	JOSEPH W.	PVT	I	6TH CAV	KENTUCKY
MCDONAL	GRANVILLE M.	PVT	I	124TH INF	OHIO
MCDONNELL	JAMES M.	PVT	I	6TH CAV	KENTUCKY
MCDOWELL	WILLIAM	LT	A	4TH CAV	TENNESSEE
* MCELDOWNEY	ANDREW J.	PVT	K	18TH INF	MICHIGAN
MCFALLS	JAMES	PVT	B	2ND MTD INF	TENNESSEE
MCFARLAND	WILLIAM	PVT	A	42ND INF	INDIANA
* MCGINLEY	JOHN	PVT	E	93RD INF	INDIANA
* MCGINNES	LUTHER	PVT	A	102ND INF	OHIO
MCGINNIS	SAMUEL	PVT	M	9TH CAV	INDIANA
MCGLINCEY	PATRICK	PVT	A	7TH CAV	OHIO
* MCGLINCEY	WILLIAM	PVT	A	7TH CAV	OHIO
MCHENRY	JAMES	PVT	D	1ST CAV	VIRGINIA
MCINTOSH	EPENETUS W.	PVT	A	14TH	ILLINOIS
* MCINTYRE	BYRON E.	PVT	B	72ND INF	OHIO
* MCINTYRE	WILLIAM F.	SGT	B	72ND INF	OHIO
MCKANN	ADAM	PVT	M	7TH CAV	INDIANA
MCKEEHAN	THOMAS J.	LT	B	175TH INF	OHIO
MCKENZIE	JOHN W.	PVT	G	10TH CAV	INDIANA
* MCKINLEY	DANIEL	PVT	I	64TH INF	OHIO
MCKINNEY	ROBERT	PVT	A	6TH CAV	KENTUCKY
MCKINNEY	ROBERT	PVT	A	7TH CAV	KENTUCKY
MCKINNEY	WILLIAM	SGT	G	115TH INF	OHIO
MCKNIGHT	JOHN	PVT	L	7TH CAV	KENTUCKY

* DIED
** BURIED AT THE MEMPHIS NATIONAL CEMETERY

	MCLELLAND	JAMES	PVT	G	10TH	INDIANA
*	MCMANNIS	MILES	PVT	I	6TH CAV	OHIO
	MCMILLEN	DAVID E.	PVT	B	95TH INF	OHIO
	MCMURRAY	WILLIAM	PVT	A	4TH CAV	TENNESSEE
	MCMURRY	BARTLEY R.	PVT	F	3RD CAV	TENNESSEE
	MCMURTRY	DAVID	CPL	A	6TH CAV	KENTUCKY
	MCNEAL	DAVID	PVT	H	7TH CAV	MICHIGAN
*	MCPHAIL	DAVID M.	CPL	C	3RD CAV	TENNESSEE
	MCPHAIL	BIRD N.	WGNR	C	3RD CAV	TENNESSEE
*	MCPHERSON	JOHN A.	PVT	A	3RD CAV	TENNESSEE
	MCQUEEN	A.	PVT	D	4TH CAV	KENTUCKY
	MCQUIRE	MICHAEL	PVT	G	35TH INF	INDIANA
	MCTEAG	D.	PVT	I	3RD CAV	TENNESSEE
	MCWETSY	CHARLES	PVT	M	3RD CAV	OHIO
*	MEADE	GEORGE	PVT	F	21ST	MICHIGAN
	MEAKER	F.	PVT	E	50TH	OHIO
	MEDSHER	JACOB	PVT	A	79TH INF	INDIANA
*	MEEKER	CLARK	PVT	H	8TH CAV	MICHIGAN
*	MEEKER	TIMOTHY	PVT	E	175TH INF	OHIO
	MEEKS	RHEUBEN	PVT	G	2ND CAV	TENNESSEE
	MEHER	DENNIS	MUSICIAN	I	124TH INF	INDIANA
	MEINSEL	C.	CPL	E	3RD CAV	TENNESSEE
*	MELLVILLE	ZACHARIAS	PVT	M	8TH CAV	MICHIGAN
*	MELTON	WILLIAM	PVT	F	3RD CAV	TENNESSEE
	MENINALD	EDWIN G.	PVT	G	18TH	MICHIGAN
*	MERCER	JAMES M.	PVT	B	102ND INF	OHIO
*	MERCHAND	LEANDER	PVT	A	102ND INF	OHIO
*	MERKEL	ORLANDO	PVT	F	102ND INF	OHIO
	MERRELL	F.	PVT	K	4TH CAV	KENTUCKY
	MERRIFIELD	EDWIN	PVT	G	18TH INF	MICHIGAN
**	MERRIMAN	THOMAS	PVT	I	3RD CAV	MICHIGAN
*	MERRIT	BAXTER	PVT	C	6TH CAV	KENTUCKY
	MERSHEN	G.	PVT	E	22ND INF	OHIO
*	METTE	ANTHONY R.	PVT	K	18TH	MICHIGAN
	MEYERS	H.	PVT	A	59TH INF	OHIO
	MEYERS	J.	PVT	H	40TH INF	INDIANA
	MILLARD	ELCANA	PVT	G	3RD CAV	TENNESSEE
	MILLER	ELIAS	PVT	L	9TH CAV	INDIANA

* DIED
** BURIED AT THE MEMPHIS NATIONAL CEMETERY

	MILLER	HENRY	PVT	C	124TH INF	INDIANA
	MILLER	JEROME	PVT	C	52ND INF	OHIO
*	MILLER	JOHN F.	PVT	C	3RD CAV	TENNESSEE
	MILLER	JOHN R.	CPL	D	26TH INF	OHIO
	MILLER	JOHN W.	CPL	E	3RD CAV	TENNESSEE
	MILLER	JOSEPH	SGT	D	183RD INF	OHIO
*	MILLER	PETER	PVT	E	95TH INF	OHIO
	MILLER	ROBERT	PVT	K	1ST CAV	KENTUCKY
	MILLIGAN	THEOPHILUS W.	SGT	G	72ND INF	INDIANA
*	MILLIKEN	ERSKINE	PVT	C	8TH CAV	INDIANA
	MILLS	C. W.	SGT	K	10TH CAV	INDIANA
*	MILLS	WILLIAM	PVT	H	3RD CAV	TENNESSEE
	MILLSAPS	JESSE	PVT	B	3RD CAV	TENNESSEE
	MILLSAPS	WILLIAM	PVT	B	3RD CAV	TENNESSEE
	MILLSAPS	JAMES	CPL	B	3RD CAV	TENNESSEE
*	MILLSPAUGH	DAVID	PVT	E	18TH	MICHIGAN
*	MILNER	REASON	PVT	C	97TH INF	OHIO
*	MILTON	WILLIAM	PVT	F	3RD CAV	TENNESSEE
	MINCEY	ROBERT	PVT	B	8TH CAV	TENNESSEE
	MINCEY	WILLIAM	PVT	B	8TH CAV	TENNESSEE
	MINIER	DARIUS	PVT	G	183RD INF	OHIO
*	MISENER	HENRY M.	TEAMSTER	F	3RD CAV	TENNESSEE
	MISKOQUON	LOUIS	PVT	K	1ST S.S.	MICHIGAN
*	MITCHELL	JAMES	PVT	A	13TH CAV	INDIANA
*	MITCHELL	JOSEPH R.	PVT	A	102ND INF	OHIO
*	MOARY	CHARLES R.	PVT	I	6TH CAV	KENTUCKY
	MOFFATT	JAMES	PVT	C	2ND CAV	TENNESSEE
	MOFFORD	JOSEPH T.	PVT	C	6TH CAV	KENTUCKY
	MOHIRR	J.T.		C	6TH CAV	KENTUCKY
	MONDAY	J.	PVT	K	12TH CAV	VIRGINIA
*	MONGER	GILLEM	PVT	G	3RD CAV	TENNESSEE
	MONSORT	R.	CPL	A	40TH INF	INDIANA
	MONTGOMERY	C.	PVT	A	8TH CAV	TENNESSEE
*	MONTGOMERY	JOHN M.	CPL	L	3RD CAV	TENNESSEE
	MONTGOMERY	WILLIAM	PVT		6TH CAV	KENTUCKY
	MOON	WASHINGTON	PVT	C	115TH INF	OHIO
	MOONEY	JOHN	PVT	B	9TH CAV	INDIANA
	MOORE	BILLY	PVT		7TH CAV	KENTUCKY

* DIED
** BURIED AT THE MEMPHIS NATIONAL CEMETERY

*	MOORE	JACOB	SGT	C	18TH INF	MICHIGAN
	MOORE	JAMES	PVT	A	175TH INF	OHIO
	MOORE	THOMAS D.	CPL	F	50TH INF	OHIO
*	MOORHOUSE	ROBERT A.	COL	L	9TH CAV	INDIANA
	MOPPIN	JOHN T.	PVT	C	5TH CAV	KENTUCKY
	MORAN	F.	PVT	D	2ND CAV	MICHIGAN
*	MOREIL	HENRY O.	PVT	K	99TH INF	INDIANA
*	MORGAN	JOB E.	PVT	B	10TH CAV	OHIO
	MORGAN	LEVI G.	PVT	D	121ST INF	OHIO
	MORGAN	F.	PVT	F	11TH CAV	INDIANA
*	MORGANTHALER	JACOB	PVT	A	7TH CAV	OHIO
	MORRELL	OLIVER O.	PVT	H	57TH INF	INDIANA
*	MORRIS	JAMES	PVT	H	6TH CAV	KENTUCKY
	MORRIS	S.	PVT	D	30TH INF	INDIANA
*	MORRIS	STACY	PVT	G	175TH INF	OHIO
**	MORRISON	GILFORD C.	PVT	L	3RD CAV	TENNESSEE
*	MORRISON	ISAAC A.	PVT	L	3RD CAV	TENNESSEE
	MORROW	WILLIAM M.	PVT	B	50TH INF	OHIO
	MORSE	VALOISE H.	PVT	E	6TH CAV	MICHIGAN
	MORTON	JAMES	PVT	K	35TH INF	INDIANA
*	MORTON	JAMES A.	PVT	C	124TH INF	INDIANA
*	MOSS	JOSEPH	PVT		7TH CAV	KENTUCKY
	MOTTIER	FAFOR Z.	PVT	H	50TH INF	OHIO
	MOULTON	DALLAS	PVT	I	104TH INF	OHIO
*	MOULTON	WILLIAM P.	PVT	F	9TH CAV	OHIO
*	MOWRY	JOHN	PVT	B	58TH INF	OHIO
*	MOYER	PHILIP	SGT	A	7TH CAV	OHIO
	MULLEN	JESSEE	PVT	L	5TH CAV	INDIANA
*	MULLER	DAVID S.	PVT	D	13TH CAV	OHIO
	MULLER	JOHN	CPL	D	22ND INF	OHIO
	MULLICK	JOHN	PVT		36TH INF	INDIANA
*	MULVANY	PETER	PVT	B	35TH INF	INDIANA
**	MUNDAY	WILLIAM H.	SGT	G	6TH CAV	KENTUCKY
	MUNROE	FRANCIS	PVT	F	2ND CAV	MICHIGAN
	MURPHREY	JOHN	CPL	I	3RD CAV	TENNESSEE
*	MURPHY	EBENEZER A.	PVT	E	3RD CAV	TENNESSEE
*	MURPHY	JOHN M.	PVT	E	3RD CAV	TENNESSEE
	MURPHY	CHRISTOPHER	PVT	H	50TH INF	OHIO

---

* DIED
** BURIED AT THE MEMPHIS NATIONAL CEMETERY

	MURSHORN	GEORGE	PVT	E	72ND INF	OHIO
	MUSSELMAN	JOHN	PVT		22ND ART	OHIO
*	MUSSER	BENJAMIN	CPL	H	102ND INF	OHIO
	MUSSIN	H. M.	PVT	F	3RD CAV	TENNESSEE
*	MYERS	CHARLES W.	PVT	G	15TH	OHIO
*	MYERS	DANIEL	PVT	G	115TH INF	OHIO
	MYERS	JACOB	PVT	C	3RD CAV	TENNESSEE
	MYERS	JOHN L.	PVT	A	18TH INF	MICHIGAN
*	MYERS	LESLEY	PVT	G	3RD CAV	TENNESSEE
*	MYERS	WILLIAM O.	PVT	D	175TH INF	OHIO
	NAILOR	PETER	PVT	C	28TH INF	KENTUCKY
	NALER	T. H.	PVT	K	84TH INF	INDIANA
	NAPP	CHARLES	PVT	G	115TH INF	OHIO
	NASH	THOMAS	PVT	H	38TH INF	INDIANA
*	NATION	ENOCH K.	CPL	G	9TH CAV	INDIANA
	NEALY	WILLIAM L.	PVT	C	3RD CAV	TENNESSEE
*	NELSON	LEMON	PVT	D	18TH INF	MICHIGAN
	NELSON	N.	PVT	K	13TH CAV	OHIO
*	NELSON	WILLIAM	CPL	C	33RD INF	OHIO
	NEMIER	JAMES	PVT	C	7TH CAV	INDIANA
*	NEUSTADT	DAVID	PVT	B	58TH INF	OHIO
	NEVINS	JOEL FRANK	PVT	F	18TH INF	MICHIGAN
	NEVINS	L.	PVT	A	8TH CAV	TENNESSEE
*	NEWBERN	ELAM	PVT	C	57TH INF	INDIANA
*	NEWMAN	GARRETT	PVT	C	3RD CAV	TENNESSEE
*	NEWTON	HENRY O.	PVT	K	9TH CAV	INDIANA
*	NICHOLAS	DANIEL H.	PVT	K	3RD CAV	TENNESSEE
	NICHOLS	C.	PVT	G	7TH CAV	INDIANA
*	NICHOLS	CONANT	PVT	H	18TH INF	MICHIGAN
	NICHOLS	D.	CPL	D	3RD CAV	TENNESSEE
*	NICHOLS	JOHN	PVT	I	3RD CAV	TENNESSEE
	NICKERSON	C.H.	SGT	E	31ST INF	OHIO
*	NICKERSON	CHARLES	SGT	E	65TH INF	OHIO
	NICKERSON	HENRY	CPL	C	115TH INF	OHIO
	NIHART	ADDISON	HOS. S.	G	90TH INF	OHIO
	NILES	ALBERT G.	PVT	C	55TH INF	OHIO
	NISLEY	CHRISTIAN M.	SGT	D	40TH INF	INDIANA
*	NOBLE	JOHN A.	PVT	B	8TH CAV	MICHIGAN

* DIED
** BURIED AT THE MEMPHIS NATIONAL CEMETERY

*	NOE	WILLIAM	PVT	A	3RD CAV	TENNESSEE
	NOG	H.H.	PVT	G	6TH CAV	KENTUCKY
	NOLAN	JOSEPH	PVT	H	4TH CAV	OHIO
	NOLEN	D.	PVT	E	2ND CAV	MICHIGAN
	NOORIER	J.	PVT	F	3RD CAV	INDIANA
	NORCUTT	JOHN W.	PVT	D	18TH INF	MICHIGAN
*	NORMAN	JAMES	PVT	F	3RD CAV	INDIANA
	NORMAN	JOHN A.	PVT	H	4TH CAV	TENNESSEE
	NORRIS	ALBERT	PVT	A	76TH INF	OHIO
*	NORRIS	DANIEL	PVT	I	57TH INF	INDIANA
	NORRIS	JOSEPH B.	PVT	C	51ST INF	OIIIO
*	NORTON	HENRY	PVT	B	8TH CAV	MICHIGAN
	NORTON	JOHN E.	PVT	A	5TH CAV	MICHIGAN
	NORTON	WILLIAM H.	CPL	C	115TH INF	OHIO
*	NORVELL	ELIJAH M.	BUGLER	F	3RD CAV	TENNESSEE
	NOSS	A. J.	PVT	B	101ST INF	INDIANA
	NOTCOMER				58TH INF	OHIO
*	NUTT	JAMES W.	PVT	A	5TH CAV	INDIANA
*	O'BRIEN	PATSEY	PVT	D	6TH CAV	INDIANA
	O'NEAL	JOHN A.	PVT	C	115TH INF	OHIO
*	O'SULLIVAN	RICHARD T.	PVT	A	3RD CAV	TENNESSEE
*	OAKLEY	ELIJ.	PVT	C	18TH INF	MICHIGAN
	OAKS	WILLIAM	PVT	I	6TH CAV	KENTUCKY
	ODUM	PLEASANT H.	PVT	A	4TH MTD INF	TENNESSEE
*	OFFIT	ALBERT	PVT	G	10TH CAV	OHIO
*	OGDEN	CHARLES P.	PVT	K	102ND INF	OHIO
	OGDEN	WILLIAM	PVT	E	97TH INF	OHIO
*	OKEY	EMANUEL	PVT	F	116TH INF	OHIO
*	OLIVER	THOMAS	PVT	K	183RD INF	OHIO
	OLLENDICK	JOHN	PVT	K	72ND INF	OHIO
*	OLLOM	JAMES C.	PVT	G	9TH CAV	INDIANA
**	OMWIG	GODFRED H.	SGT	D	102ND INF	OHIO
	OTTINGER	MORGAN	CPL	E	3RD CAV	TENNESSEE
	OWEN	WARRET	PVT	E	95TH INF	OHIO
*	OWENS	GEORGE F.	PVT	K	3RD CAV	TENNESSEE
	OWENS	MICHAEL J.	SGT	I	13TH CAV	INDIANA
	OXLEY	STEWART	PVT	I	51ST INF	OHIO
*	OYSTER	SIMON	PVT	C	102ND INF	OHIO

---

* DIED
** BURIED AT THE MEMPHIS NATIONAL CEMETERY

*	PADYOT	B.	PVT	G	3RD CAV	TENNESSEE
	PAIN	JAMES T.	PVT	A	3RD CAV	TENNESSEE
	PALLER	W.	PVT	C	6TH CAV	KENTUCKY
	PALMER	DAVID	PVT	K	124TH INF	INDIANA
*	PALMER	GEORGE N.	CPL	G	18TH INF	MICHIGAN
*	PALMER	WILLIAM N.	PVT	C	3RD CAV	TENNESSEE
	PANEL	ARTHUR	PVT	A	9TH CAV	INDIANA
	PANGLE	THOMAS	PVT	K	3RD CAV	TENNESSEE
	PAPERS	J.	PVT	E	4TH CAV	KENTUCKY
	PARKER	E.D.	PVT	B	9TH CAV	INDIANA
	PARKER	ISAAC N.	PVT	G	95TH INF	OHIO
*	PARKER	JACOB	PVT	C	18TH INF	MICHIGAN
	PARKER	JAMES R.	PVT	I	6TH CAV	KENTUCKY
	PARKER	JERRY	SGT	E	2ND CAV	MICHIGAN
*	PARMAN	EPHRAIM B.	PVT	B	9TH CAV	MICHIGAN
*	PARRISH	EDMUND H.	CAPTAIN	C	6TH CAV	KENTUCKY
	PASSE	JAMES A.	PVT	A	4TH MTD INF	KENTUCKY
	PATRICK	MOSES	PVT	H	22ND	INDIANA
*	PATTA	JOSIAH A.	PVT	A	3RD CAV	TENNESSEE
*	PATTERSON	JAMES	CPL	G	115TH INF	OHIO
	PATTERSON	JOSHUA S.	PVT	F	104TH INF	OHIO
	PATTERSON	MATTHEW	PVT	A	93RD INF	INDIANA
*	PATTERSON	ROBERT	PVT	I	18TH INF	MICHIGAN
	PATTERSON	THOMAS	PVT	L	4TH CAV	KENTUCKY
	PATTERSON	W.J.	LT	E	9TH CAV	MICHIGAN
	PATTON	R. E.	PVT	K	2ND CAV	TENNESSEE
	PAUGH	THOMAS	PVT	F	3RD CAV	TENNESSEE
**	PAUL	ARTHUR H.	PVT	A	9TH CAV	INDIANA
*	PAXTON	JOHN Q.	PVT	E	7TH CAV	INDIANA
*	PAYNE	GEORGE	PVT	D	175TH INF	OHIO
	PAYNE	JAMES	PVT	C	124TH INF	INDIANA
*	PAYNE	JAMES	PVT	D	175TH INF	OHIO
	PEACHIN	EDWARD				UNKNOWN
	PEACOCK	WILLIAM H.	CPL	G	9TH CAV	INDIANA
	PEASE	B.	PVT	E	35TH INF	OHIO
	PECHHAM	T.J.	CPL	F	17TH	MICHIGAN
	PECK	CHARLES	PVT	E	6TH CAV	MICHIGAN
	PECKHAM	PAUL R.	PVT	A	102ND INF	OHIO

---

* DIED
** BURIED AT THE MEMPHIS NATIONAL CEMETERY

	PECKINS	IRA	PVT	K	3RD CAV	OHIO
	PEER	JAMES B.	CPL	D	2ND CAV	OHIO
	PEERY	ANDREW	SGT	B	3RD CAV	TENNESSEE
	PEESE	JAMES B.	CPL	D	2ND CAV	OHIO
	PENDER	ANDREW	PVT	K	50TH INF	OHIO
	PENDERGAST	NATHANIEL A.	PVT	G	3RD CAV	TENNESSEE
	PENSON	ANDERSON	PVT	F	9TH CAV	INDIANA
	PENSTER	J.	CPL	B	93RD INF	INDIANA
**	PENTICUFF	JOHN	PVT	A	3RD CAV	KENTUCKY
	PERKINS	FRANCIS M.	SGT	E	2ND CAV	MICHIGAN
	PETERSON	ISAAC	PVT	A	MCLAUGHLIN'S	OHIO
	PETITT	MARTIN	CPL	E	2ND CAV	MICHIGAN
**	PETREE	DAVID	SGT	C	93RD INF	INDIANA
*	PETTIJOHN	CYRUS	PVT	E	50TH INF	OHIO
	PETTINGER	WILLIAM	PVT	B	130TH INF	OHIO
	PHELPS	J. W.	PVT	G	4TH CAV	KENTUCKY
	PHELPS	JOHN M.	PVT	A	3RD CAV	TENNESSEE
*	PHELPS	THOMPSON W.	PVT	A	3RD CAV	TENNESSEE
	PHENECIS	JOHN M.	CPL		4TH CAV	INDIANA
	PHILLIPS	FRANCIS M.	PVT	M	1ST CAV	MICHIGAN
	PHILLIPS	JOHN M.	PVT	L	5TH CAV	TENNESSEE
	PHILLIPS	WILLIAM	PVT	C	2ND CAV	INDIANA
	PHILLIPS	WILLIAM	PVT	B	51ST INF	OHIO
	PHINCE	JAMES M.	PVT	A	49TH INF	INDIANA
	PICK	C.	PVT	E	6TH CAV	MICHIGAN
	PICKENS	I.	PVT	K	3RD CAV	OHIO
	PICKENS	NEWTON	PVT	D	13TH	TENNESSEE
	PICKENS	SAMUEL	PVT	A	3RD CAV	TENNESSEE
*	PICKENS	WILLIAM C.	PVT	B	3RD CAV	TENNESSEE
*	PICKETT	EUGENE	CPL	D	50TH INF	OHIO
	PIERCE	JOSEPH J.	CPL	F	3RD CAV	TENNESSEE
	PIERCE	RICHARD M.	PVT	D	3RD CAV	TENNESSEE
	PIERCE	RICHARD R.	PVT	C	12TH CAV	TENNESSEE
*	PIERCE	WILLIAM	PVT	C	6TH CAV	KENTUCKY
	PIKE	L.	SGT	G	37TH INF	INDIANA
	PILKINGTON	ALBERT	PVT	K	2ND CAV	TENNESSEE
*	PLANK	HARRISON D.	CPL	H	18TH	MICHIGAN
	PLEMONS	THOMAS J.	PVT	A	3RD CAV	TENNESSEE

* DIED
** BURIED AT THE MEMPHIS NATIONAL CEMETERY

*	POLAND	JAMES L.	SGT	B	97TH INF	OHIO
	POLAR	GEORGE W.	CPL	E	183RD	OHIO
*	POLLY	WILLIAM	PVT	C	6TH CAV	KENTUCKY
	POPE	JAMES	PVT		4TH CAV	MICHIGAN
*	PORTER	COSTAN	PVT	E	7TH CAV	INDIANA
	PORTER	WALTER G.	PVT	C	18TH INF	MICHIGAN
	POST	CHRISTOPHER	PVT	C	115TH INF	OHIO
	POTOT	JOSEPH	PVT	A	102ND INF	OHIO
*	POTTER	JAMES B.	PVT	C	18TH INF	MICHIGAN
	POTTER	PETER	PVT	K	2ND CAV	TENNESSEE
	POTTER	SILAS R.	PVT	B	102ND INF	OHIO
	POTTERFIELD	WILLIAM	PVT	C	6TH CAV	INDIANA
	POTTLE	WINFIELD SCOTT	PVT	G	54TH INF	OHIO
*	POUCH	ASA	PVT	K	2ND CAV	OHIO
	POUPARD	SAMUEL	PVT	G	15TH INF	MICHIGAN
	POWDER	ANDREW	PVT	K	50TH INF	OHIO
	POWELL	JOHN	PVT	A	2ND CAV	TENNESSEE
*	POYSELL	SAMUEL	PVT	E	95TH INF	OHIO
*	POYSELL	WILLIAM W.	PVT	E	95TH INF	OHIO
*	PRATT	JOSIAH	PVT	H	9TH CAV	INDIANA
*	PRICE	ALFRED E.	PVT	A	50TH INF	OHIO
*	PRICE	SIMEN P.	PVT	G	102ND INF	OHIO
*	PRICE	WILLIAM D.	PVT	C	115TH INF	OHIO
	PRINDLE	ROMEO	PVT	H	10TH CAV	INDIANA
	PRIOR	JAMES	CPL	B	3RD CAV	TENNESSEE
	PRIOR	WILLIAM M.	PVT	B	3RD CAV	TENNESSEE
	PROPPER	GEORGE W.	PVT	A	18TH INF	MICHIGAN
	PROSSER	A. SIDNEY	LT		2ND CAV	TENNESSEE
*	PROVINES	ELI FINLEY	PVT	A	MCLAUGHIN'S	OHIO
	PRYER	FRANCIS	PVT	F	92ND INF	OHIO
	PURGER	WILLIAM	PVT	B	3RD CAV	TENNESSEE
	QUIRK	JAMES E.	PVT		5TH CAV	MICHIGAN
	RAGAN	JAMES T.	PVT		3RD CAV	TENNESSEE
	RAGSDALE	ROBERT	PVT	C	7TH CAV	VIRGINIA
	RAINA	WILLIAM	PVT	C	4TH CAV	INDIANA
	RAMSEY	MCPHERSON	PVT	I	3RD CAV	TENNESSEE
	RAMSEY	WILLIAM	PVT	K	3RD CAV	TENNESSEE
	RANDALL	ANSON	PVT	E	18TH INF	MICHIGAN

---

* DIED
** BURIED AT THE MEMPHIS NATIONAL CEMETERY

	RANKS	F.	PVT	D	3RD CAV	MICHIGAN
	RASS	C.P.	PVT	A	34TH INF	INDIANA
	RAUDEBAUGH	SAMUEL H.	PVT	K	65TH INF	OHIO
	RAWLEY	JOHN	PVT	C	80TH INF	INDIANA
	RAWLINS	WILLIAM	PVT		4TH CAV	TENNESSEE
	RAY	CHRISTIAN	PVT	C	50TH INF	OHIO
	RAY	PATTERSON	SGT	I	3RD CAV	TENNESSEE
	RAYMOND	W.H.	CPL		124TH INF	INDIANA
	RAYSOR	W.	PVT	H	3RD CAV	KENTUCKY
*	REA	WILLIAM T.	PVT	K	9TH CAV	INDIANA
	REACH	JONATHAN	PVT	M	1ST CAV	ALABAMA
	READ	WILLIAM P.	PVT	B	9TH CAV	INDIANA
	REAM	JOSEPH H.	PVT	K	75TH INF	OHIO
	REASE	L.	PVT		3RD CAV	TENNESSEE
*	REASONER	JOHN R.	PVT	G	9TH CAV	INDIANA
*	REDMAN	JAMES B.	PVT	A	10TH CAV	INDIANA
	REDMAN	W.	PVT	H	4TH CAV	KENTUCKY
*	REED	JOHN	PVT	I	3RD CAV	TENNESSEE
	REED	OLIVER H.	PVT	A	95TH INF	OHIO
*	REED	ROBERT	PVT	F	3RD CAV	TENNESSEE
	REED	WILLIAM M.	PVT	K	3RD CAV	TENNESSEE
	REESE	WILLIAM	SGT	G	2ND MTD INF	TENNESSEE
	REEVER	JOSEPH H.	PVT	K	102ND INF	OHIO
*	REEVES	THOMAS B.	LT	C	10TH CAV	INDIANA
	REGNEY	MICHAEL	PVT	I	4TH CAV	KENTUCKY
*	REIBEL	WILLIAM	PVT	A	7TH CAV	OHIO
	RENCHAN	WILLIAM	SGT	C	4TH CAV	INDIANA
*	RENEAU	JOHN C.	PVT	D	3RD CAV	TENNESSEE
*	RENNINGTON	LUCIUS	PVT	G	102ND INF	OHIO
	REX	ALFRED	PVT	G	2ND CAV	MICHIGAN
	REYNOLDS	MARCELUS	PVT	C	80TH INF	INDIANA
	RHON	JACOB	PVT	H	101ST INF	OHIO
	RICE	JOHN	SGT	E	3RD CAV	TENNESSEE
*	RICE	JONATHAN	SDLER	D	3RD CAV	TENNESSEE
*	RICE	MARTIN L.	PVT	A	175TH INF	OHIO
*	RICH	MILO	PVT	B	8TH CAV	MICHIGAN
*	RICHARD	REUBEN H.	SGT	B	102ND INF	OHIO
	RICHARDSON	AUTEBRIDGE	PVT	L	5TH CAV	INDIANA

* DIED
** BURIED AT THE MEMPHIS NATIONAL CEMETERY

	RICHARDSON	T. W.	PVT	A	1ST CAV	OHIO
*	RICHMOND	WILLIAM	PVT	D	175TH INF	OHIO
	RICHTER	H.	PVT	C	3RD CAV	TENNESSEE
*	RIDDLE	FRANCIS	PVT	L	3RD CAV	TENNESSEE
*	RIDDLE	JOHN M.D.	PVT	C	3RD CAV	TENNESSEE
*	RIDLEY	FRANKLIN	PVT	M	9TH CAV	INDIANA
	RILEY	JOHN	PVT	C	7TH CAV	VIRGINIA
	RILEY	WILLIAM	PVT	A	9TH CAV	INDIANA
	RINEHART	J.	SGT		22ND ART	OHIO
	RIRIE	JOHN	PVT	C	115TH INF	OHIO
*	ROATH	ROBERT W.	PVT	F	115TH INF	OHIO
*	ROBB	ROBERT D.	PVT	A	7TH CAV	OHIO
*	ROBBINS	JONATHAN	PVT	A	18TH INF	MICHIGAN
	ROBERSON	HIRAM	PVT	C	3RD CAV	TENNESSEE
	ROBERSON	JAMES	PVT	C	3RD CAV	TENNESSEE
	ROBERTS	CHARLES A.	PVT	H	23RD INF	OHIO
	ROBERTS	J. R.	PVT	L	7TH CAV	VIRGINIA
*	ROBERTS	JOHN	PVT	A	50TH INF	OHIO
	ROBERTSON	JAMES	PVT	I	3RD CAV	TENNESSEE
	ROBINSON	GEORGE F.	PVT	C	2ND CAV	MICHIGAN
*	ROBINSON	JOHN A.	PVT	A	121ST INF	OHIO
*	ROBSON	HENRY S.	LT	G	6TH CAV	KENTUCKY
*	RODEPOUCH	MARTIN V.	PVT	G	9TH CAV	INDIANA
	RODES	ABRAHAM	PVT	I	6TH CAV	KENTUCKY
	RODGERS	JAMES A.	FIFER	I	3RD CAV	TENNESSEE
*	ROGERS	MADISON H.	CPL	A	3RD CAV	TENNESSEE
*	ROGERS	TEDFORD	PVT	B	3RD CAV	TENNESSEE
	ROGERS	THOMAS	PVT	G	99TH INF	INDIANA
	ROGERS	WILLIAM	PVT	L	3RD CAV	TENNESSEE
*	ROGERS	WILLIAM	BLKSM	I	3RD CAV	TENNESSEE
	ROHLAND	PETER	PVT	C	183RD INF	OHIO
	ROHRER	JACOB	PVT	H	101ST INF	OHIO
	ROLING	ROBERT W.	PVT	B	3RD CAV	TENNESSEE
*	ROLLINS	GEORGE H.	PVT	E	95TH INF	OHIO
	ROME	F.	PVT	K	3RD CAV	OHIO
**	ROMINES	DAVID R.	PVT	I	3RD CAV	TENNESSEE
*	ROMINES	JOHN	PVT	I	3RD CAV	TENNESSEE
*	ROMINES	TATEN	PVT	I	3RD CAV	TENNESSEE

---

* DIED
** BURIED AT THE MEMPHIS NATIONAL CEMETERY

*	ROMINES	SAMUEL L.	PVT	I	3RD CAV	TENNESSEE
	ROON	J.	PVT	K	6TH CAV	INDIANA
*	ROOT	URIAH O.	SGT	C	6TH CAV	KENTUCKY
*	ROSE	JACOB	PVT	A	102ND INF	OHIO
	ROSE	JOSIAH N.	PVT	G	40TH INF	INDIANA
	ROSELOT	PETER	CPL	E	50TH INF	OHIO
	ROSS	WILLIAM	PVT	A	102ND INF	OHIO
	ROWALT	DANIEL H.	PVT	E	102ND INF	OHIO
	ROWE	DAVID P.	PVT	C	7TH CAV	INDIANA
*	ROWLEY	ORSON B.	PVT	A	18TH INF	MICHIGAN
*	ROWLEY	WARREN	PVT	A	18TH INF	MICIIIGAN
	ROYAL	L.S.	PVT	K	1ST S.S.	MICHIGAN
	ROYALTY	D.B.	PVT	A	4TH CAV	KENTUCKY
	RUE	ANDREW JOHN	PVT	F	3RD CAV	TENNESSEE
*	RUE	THOMAS	SGT	F	115TH INF	OHIO
	RULE	ANDREW	SGT	A	3RD CAV	TENNESSEE
	RULE	CALEB	PVT	K	3RD CAV	TENNESSEE
*	RULE	JOHN	CPL	K	3RD CAV	TENNESSEE
	RULE	ROBERT	SGT	A	3RD CAV	TENNESSEE
*	RUMMELL	ADOLPHUS W.	PVT	E	80TH INF	INDIANA
	RUPEL	CHARLES	PVT	G	1ST CAV	VIRGINIA
	RUSH	JACOB W.	PVT	L	3RD CAV	OHIO
	RUSSELL	ADAM	PVT	G	5TH CAV	MICHIGAN
	RUSSELL	ADAM	PVT	C	3RD CAV	TENNESSEE
	RUSSELL	CALVIN	PVT	A	3RD CAV	TENNESSEE
	RUSSELL	G.S.	PVT	G	2ND CAV	OHIO
	RUSSELL	JAMES	PVT	K	18TH	MICHIGAN
	RUSSELL	NICHOLAS R.	PVT	A	3RD CAV	TENNESSEE
	RUSSELL	O'CONNELLY	PVT	C	3RD CAV	TENNESSEE
*	RUSSELL	RICHARD T.	CPL	I	3RD CAV	TENNESSEE
	RUTMAN	ADAM	PVT	F	115TH INF	OHIO
*	RYAN	JOHN	PVT	K	64TH INF	OHIO
*	RYMAN	WILLIAM H.H.	PVT	C	124TH INF	INDIANA
	SACKETT	ALEXANDER				IOWA
	SADDLER	M.	PVT	G	6TH CAV	KENTUCKY
	SAFFIN	JAMES	PVT		7TH CAV	OHIO
	SAFFORD	GEORGE M.	PVT	H	10TH CAV	INDIANA
	SAHL	F.	PVT	G	51ST INF	INDIANA

* DIED
** BURIED AT THE MEMPHIS NATIONAL CEMETERY

SAMPS	HENRY	PVT	G	80TH INF	INDIANA
SAMPSON	HENRY	PVT		69TH INF	OHIO
SAMPSON	RICHARD H.	CPL	I	17TH INF	INDIANA
SAMSHOWER	ARRON	PVT		36TH INF	INDIANA
SANDERS	SAMUEL F.	PVT	I	137TH INF	ILLINOIS
* SANDERS	DAVID N.	PVT	D	3RD CAV	TENNESSEE
SANDERSON	JOHN	PVT	K	58TH INF	OHIO
SANDS	WILLIAM H.	PVT	F	45TH INF	OHIO
SANFORD	G. W.	PVT	H	10TH CAV	INDIANA
SANKER	AUGUST	PVT	C	183RD INF	OHIO
SARASON	HIRAM	PVT	G	5TH CAV	INDIANA
SASSELL	C.A.	PVT	K	3RD CAV	OHIO
SATTIN	LEMUEL H.	PVT	K	18TH INF	MICHIGAN
SAUNDERS	IGNATIOUS		F	102ND INF	OHIO
SAWANT	J.	PVT	K	9TH CAV	INDIANA
SAYER	SAMUEL K.	SGT	H	51ST INF	OHIO
SAYLOR	JOHN	PVT	D	3RD CAV	TENNESSEE
SCADDEN	JAMES	PVT	E	2ND CAV	MICHIGAN
* SCAGGS	ISHAM	PVT	F	3RD CAV	TENNESSEE
SCAGGS	JAMES C.	PVT	F	3RD CAV	TENNESSEE
SCAN	W.	PVT	C	54TH INF	OHIO
SCHIRMEYERRE	ALOISIOUS	PVT	A	32ND INF	INDIANA
SCHMIDT	JOSEPH	PVT	K	7TH CAV	INDIANA
SCHMUTZ	GEORGE S.	PVT	I	102ND INF	OHIO
* SCHNEIDER	ADAM	PVT	C	183RD INF	OHIO
* SCHRADER	JOHN	PVT	G	102ND INF	OHIO
SCHULTZ	ERNEST	PVT	A	9TH CAV	OHIO
SCOLE	R.	PVT	D	6TH CAV	INDIANA
SCOTT	JAMES	PVT	C	3RD CAV	TENNESSEE
SCOTT	JAMES R.	PVT	C	3RD CAV	TENNESSEE
SCOTT	LOUIS	PVT	L	5TH CAV	INDIANA
SCOTT	P.	PVT	G	4TH CAV	OHIO
SCOTT	ROBERT	PVT	B	9TH CAV	INDIANA
* SCOTT	WILLIAM W.	PVT	K	7TH CAV	INDIANA
SCOTT	THOMAS	PVT	L	7TH CAV	VIRGINIA
* SCRIMPSCHER	GEORGE	PVT	L	3RD CAV	TENNESSEE
SEABURY	CHARLES G.	PVT	B	8TH CAV	MICHIGAN
SEAHL	BENJAMIN	PVT	I	26TH INF	OHIO

* DIED
** BURIED AT THE MEMPHIS NATIONAL CEMETERY

SEARS	C.H.	PVT	B	9TH CAV	INDIANA
* SEELEY	FREDERICK	PVT	G	18TH INF	MICHIGAN
SEOGHENS	LOUIS	PVT		1ST CAV	MICHIGAN
* SESSLER	CONRAD	PVT	D	37TH INF	OHIO
SEWARD	R. W.	PVT	F	21ST	MICHIGAN
* SEWIL	GEORGE W.	PVT	A	6TH CAV	KENTUCKY
SEYMOR	GEORGE V.	PVT	B	4TH CAV	KENTUCKY
SHACHER	J.	PVT	E	42ND INF	OHIO
* SHAFER	DELASCUS B.	PVT	I	18TH INF	MICHIGAN
SHAFER	JOHN A.	PVT	F	101ST INF	OHIO
SHAFFER	JACOB N.	SGT	F	115TH INF	OHIO
SHAL	F.	PVT	G	6TH CAV	INDIANA
* SHARETTZ	ZEBULON	PVT	E	93RD INF	OHIO
SHARITS	JAMES M.	CPL	C	3RD CAV	TENNESSEE
* SHARP	EDWARD	CPL	E	55TH INF	OHIO
SHARP	JOHN C.	PVT	G	7TH CAV	OHIO
SHARP	THOMAS	PVT	F	2ND CAV	VIRGINIA
SHAUL	WILLIAM R.	PVT	E	95TH INF	OHIO
* SHAVER	JOHN M.	PVT	H	3RD CAV	TENNESSEE
SHAW	CHARLES M.	PVT	B	81ST INF	OHIO
* SHAW	DELOS	PVT	E	103RD INF	OHIO
SHAW	WILLIAM W.	PVT	G	54TH INF	OHIO
SHEAFFER	I.N.	PVT	E	115TH INF	OHIO
* SHEARER	GEORGE W.	PVT	B	50TH INF	OHIO
SHELTON	OLYNTHUS G.	PVT	E	6TH CAV	TENNESSEE
* SHELTON	WILLIAM	PVT	D	175TH INF	OHIO
SHEMIRE	L.	PVT	K	32ND INF	INDIANA
SHENLER	T.D.	PVT	K	9TH CAV	INDIANA
* SHEPARD	WILLIAM H.	PVT	E	34TH INF	OHIO
SHEPHARD	S.	PVT	D	1ST CAV	MICHIGAN
SHEPPARD	GEORGE M.	PVT	H	10TH CAV	INDIANA
* SHEPPERLY	GEORGE	PVT	F	102ND INF	OHIO
* SHERRICK	SAMUEL A.	PVT	A	7TH CAV	OHIO
SHERWOOD	S.	PVT	I	175TH INF	OHIO
SHETTLEROE	ISADORE	PVT	K	18TH INF	MICHIGAN
SHETTLEROE	JOHN	PVT	K	18TH INF	MICHIGAN
SHEWARD	SILAS	PVT	C	189TH INF	OHIO
SHIELDS	PAYTON	PVT	D	31ST INF	OHIO

* DIED
** BURIED AT THE MEMPHIS NATIONAL CEMETERY

*	SHILLING	PETER	PVT	K	50TH INF	OHIO
	SHINNYFIELD	SYDNEY	PVT	C	124TH INF	INDIANA
*	SHIVELY	WILLIAM H.	SGT	B	21ST	OHIO
*	SHOCKLEY	GEORGE H.	PVT	K	9TH CAV	INDIANA
	SHOE	EMANUEL	PVT	E	72ND INF	OHIO
	SHOEMAKER	ALEXANDER	PVT	E	72ND INF	OHIO
	SHOEMAKER	JOSEPH	PVT	C	70TH INF	OHIO
	SHOEMAKER	PHILIP	PVT	D	32ND INF	INDIANA
	SHOEMAKER	W.	PVT	E	72ND INF	OHIO
	SHOLEY	P.	PVT	C	7TH CAV	INDIANA
	SHORTZ	J. W.	CPL	C	3RD CAV	TENNESSEE
*	SHOUP	CHARLES W.	PVT	F	102ND INF	OHIO
	SHULER	THOMAS D.	SGT	K	9TH CAV	INDIANA
*	SHULL	JOHN W.	PVT	H	9TH CAV	INDIANA
	SHULTON	WILLIAM	PVT	D	50TH INF	OHIO
	SHULTZ	E.	PVT	A	9TH CAV	OHIO
	SHUMARD	WILLIAM T.	PVT	A	7TH CAV	OHIO
	SHUTTLERNS	SAMUEL	PVT		18TH INF	MICHIGAN
*	SIDLE	HENRY	PVT	D	102ND INF	OHIO
*	SIEMER	FREDERICK	PVT	C	37TH INF	OHIO
	SIMKINS	CHARLES E.	PVT	C	4TH CAV	INDIANA
	SIMMERMON	M.B.	PVT		24TH	INDIANA
*	SIMONS	JAMES	PVT	C	102ND INF	OHIO
*	SIMPSON	ADAM A.	PVT	I	3RD CAV	TENNESSEE
	SIMPSON	JOHN H.	PVT	I	3RD CAV	TENNESSEE
*	SIMPSON	JOSEPH	PVT	E	3RD CAV	TENNESSEE
*	SINGER	JEREMIAH	PVT	K	102ND INF	OHIO
	SKEON	WILLIAM	PVT	E	34TH INF	OHIO
	SLATTING	J.W.H.	PVT	H	38TH INF	INDIANA
*	SLEGGLE	EZRA K.	PVT	G	102ND INF	OHIO
	SLICK	JACOB L.	PVT	A	18TH INF	MICHIGAN
	SLOAN	ELZYE	PVT	D	102ND INF	OHIO
	SLOAN	TILDON W.	PVT	I	40TH INF	INDIANA
	SMALL	ANDREW J.	PVT	H	7TH CAV	TENNESSEE
*	SMATHERS	WILLIAM	PVT	C	115TH INF	OHIO
*	SMEAD	REUBAN	PVT	H	21ST INF	MICHIGAN
	SMEETS	J.U.	PVT	I	102ND INF	OHIO
	SMITH	ALONZO	PVT	K	22ND INF	MICHIGAN

* DIED
** BURIED AT THE MEMPHIS NATIONAL CEMETERY

	SMITH	ANDREW	PVT	C	57TH INF	INDIANA
	SMITH	B. F.	PVT	I	105TH INF	OHIO
	SMITH	C.	PVT	D	27TH INF	KENTUCKY
	SMITH	CHARLES	PVT	M	8TH CAV	INDIANA
	SMITH	COMMODORE	PVT	F	18TH INF	MICHIGAN
*	SMITH	CYRUS	PVT	H	102ND INF	OHIO
*	SMITH	DAVID	PVT	D	23RD INF	INDIANA
	SMITH	E.J.	PVT	D	23RD	INDIANA
*	SMITH	FREDERICK G.	PVT	H	57TH INF	INDIANA
	SMITH	FREEMAN M.	PVT	B	8TH CAV	MICHIGAN
	SMITH	GEORGE	PVT		87TH INF	ILLINOIS
	SMITH	GEORGE G.	PVT	D	1ST ART	VIRGINIA
	SMITH	GOSHENER F.	PVT	D	18TH INF	MICHIGAN
*	SMITH	HENRY	PVT	I	175TH INF	OHIO
	SMITH	J.	CPL	A	42ND INF	INDIANA
	SMITH	J.	PVT	G	11TH CAV	KENTUCKY
	SMITH	JAMES	PVT	D	27TH	KENTUCKY
*	SMITH	JAMES P.	PVT	K	3RD CAV	TENNESSEE
*	SMITH	JOHN	PVT	D	3RD CAV	TENNESSEE
*	SMITH	JOHN ROBINSON	PVT	D	3RD CAV	TENNESSEE
	SMITH	JOHN W.	PVT	A	7TH CAV	TENNESSEE
	SMITH	JOSEPH	PVT	K	7TH CAV	INDIANA
*	SMITH	ORSON W.	PVT	B	18TH INF	MICHIGAN
	SMITH	THOMAS	PVT	E	18TH INF	MICHIGAN
	SMITH	TRUMAN M.	PVT	B	8TH CAV	MICHIGAN
*	SMITH	WILLIAM B.	CPL	C	10TH CAV	INDIANA
	SMITH	WILLIAM B.	PVT	G	3RD CAV	TENNESSEE
	SMITH	WILLIAM D.	PVT	D	3RD CAV	TENNESSEE
	SMITH	WILLIAM H.	SGT	K	4TH CAV	OHIO
*	SMITH	WILLIAM H.H.	SGT	F	115TH INF	OHIO
*	SMITH	WILLIAM R.	PVT	D	51ST INF	OHIO
	SMITH	WILLIAM V.	PVT	B	104TH INF	OHIO
	SMITH	LORENZO	PVT	M	9TH CAV	INDIANA
	SMUTZ	JOHN C.	PVT	I	102ND INF	OHIO
*	SNIDER	F.	PVT	H	8TH CAV	MICHIGAN
*	SNODGRASS	WILLIAM P.	PVT	G	2ND CAV	OHIO
*	SNYDER	DAVID	PVT	H	18TH INF	MICHIGAN
*	SNYDER	HENRY F.	PVT	C	8TH CAV	MICHIGAN

* DIED
** BURIED AT THE MEMPHIS NATIONAL CEMETERY

	SNYDER	JACOB	PVT	F	83RD INF	OHIO
	SOHLY	CHRISTIAN	PVT	C	7TH CAV	INDIANA
	SOLLENBERGER	SETH	SGT	A	58TH INF	OHIO
	SORGEN	EDWARD	PVT	G	4TH CAV	OHIO
	SOULIER	SAMUEL	PVT	K	18TH	MICHIGAN
*	SOUTHWICK	EUGENE	PVT	C	18TH	MICHIGAN
	SPACY	OSCAR F.	PVT	M	9TH CAV	INDIANA
	SPADES	JACOB	SGT	A	9TH CAV	INDIANA
	SPAFFER	HENRY	PVT		102ND INF	OHIO
	SPAFFORD	HARRISON	PVT	B	102ND INF	OHIO
	SPENCER	A.	SGT	C	4TH CAV	KENTUCKY
	SPENCER	D.D.		B	5TH CAV	MICHIGAN
	SPENCER	EZRA E.	PVT	H	8TH CAV	MICHIGAN
*	SPENCER	THOMAS	PVT	G	115TH INF	OHIO
*	SPILANE	JOHN A.	PVT	A	3RD CAV	TENNESSEE
	SPINKLE	M.H.	PVT	B	16TH	OHIO
*	SPRAGUE	FRANKLIN	PVT	B	18TH INF	MICHIGAN
*	SPRING	JEREMIAH	CPL	A	18TH INF	MICHIGAN
	SPRINGER	S.	PVT	E	16TH CAV	VIRGINIA
	SPRINKLE	MICHAEL H.	SGT	K	102ND INF	OHIO
	SPRONGLE	G.	PVT	F	3RD CAV	TENNESSEE
	SQUIRE	ELBERT J.	LT	D	101ST INF	OHIO
	SQUIRES	ALBERT	PVT	C	115TH INF	OHIO
	STACKER	SAMUEL	PVT	B	102ND INF	OHIO
	STAFFORD	S.D.L.	PVT	L	3RD CAV	VIRGINIA
	STAHUM	HENRY V.	SGT	A	4TH MTD INF	TENNESSEE
	STALL	W. M.	PVT		2ND CAV	TENNESSEE
*	STALLINGS	JAMES W.H.	PVT	G	38TH INF	INDIANA
	STANLEY	H.H.	PVT	I	3RD CAV	TENNESSEE
	STANY	MONTERVILLE	PVT	L	3RD CAV	TENNESSEE
*	STARRITT	JOHN H.	CPL	F	7TH CAV	OHIO
	STATER	M.	SGT	D	72ND INF	OHIO
*	STATON	GEORGE W.	PVT	E	175TH INF	OHIO
*	STEINAUR	JOHN W.	PVT	A	MCLAUGHLIN'S	OHIO
*	STEINMETZ	GEORGE	PVT	K	102ND INF	OHIO
	STELLE	J.N.	PVT	C	5TH CAV	VIRGINIA
	STENDEVANT	T.	PVT	D	53RD INF	INDIANA
	STEPHENS	A.	PVT	D	1ST CAV	VIRGINIA

* DIED
** BURIED AT THE MEMPHIS NATIONAL CEMETERY

*	STEPHENS	ANDREW JOHN	PVT	I	3RD CAV	TENNESSEE
*	STEPHENS	CHARLES S.	CPL	C	115TH INF	OHIO
*	STEPHENS	JEPTHA B.	PVT	K	3RD CAV	TENNESSEE
	STEPHENS	JOSEPH	SGT	E	IST S.S.	MICHIGAN
*	STEPHENS	SAMUEL S.	PVT	G	102ND INF	OHIO
*	STEPHENS	THOMAS M., JR.	PVT	G	6TH CAV	KENTUCKY
	STEPHENS	WILLIAM	CPL	C	97TH INF	OHIO
*	STEPHENS	WILLIAM	PVT	C	115TH INF	OHIO
*	STEVENS	DARIUS	PVT	K	9TH CAV	INDIANA
*	STEVENS	WILLIAM	PVT	D	2ND CAV	INDIANA
*	STEWARD	JOHN	PVT	B	9TH CAV	INDIANA
	STEWART	GEORGE W.	PVT	D	40TH INF	INDIANA
*	STEWART	PERRY	SGT	B	6TH CAV	KENTUCKY
	STHERHER	T.J.		G	6TH CAV	KENTUCKY
	STILES	JOHN M.	CPL	F	8TH CAV	INDIANA
*	STINE	DAVID G.	PVT	F	102ND INF	OHIO
	STOCKDALE	LINDSEY	PVT	E	93RD INF	INDIANA
	STOCKER	JAMES	PVT	K	9TH CAV	INDIANA
	STOCKMAN	B.	PVT	G	17TH	INDIANA
*	STOCKWELL	ELEAZOR B.	PVT	E	100TH INF	OHIO
	STOKES	JAMES	PVT	K	9TH CAV	INDIANA
	STONE	JAMES	PVT	D	76TH INF	OHIO
	STONE	WILLIAM M.	PVT	F	3RD CAV	TENNESSEE
	STOOPS	HERMON B.	PVT	H	9TH CAV	INDIANA
*	STOTLER	MICHAEL	PVT	E	72ND	OHIO
*	STOUT	CHARLES	PVT	C	115TH INF	OHIO
*	STRAWSBAUGH	SAMUEL	PVT	D	102ND INF	OHIO
	STREMP	GEORGE	PVT	K	18TH INF	MICHIGAN
*	STRICKLAND	MADISON	PVT	I	3RD CAV	TENNESSEE
	STROUD	JAMES N.	PVT	C	3RD CAV	TENNESSEE
	STROUSER	LOUIS	PVT	K	2ND CAV	MICHIGAN
	STUBBERFIELD	SAMUEL	PVT	F	18TH	MICHIGAN
*	STUCKEY	JOHN	PVT	I	64TH INF	OHIO
*	STUFF	FREDRICK	PVT	E	102ND INF	OHIO
*	STULLER	JAMES	PVT	A	58TH INF	OHIO
	STUMP	GEORGE	PVT	K	18TH INF	MICHIGAN
*	STURDEVANT	JAMES	PVT	D	53RD INF	INDIANA
	SUGDER	A.	PVT	C	183RD INF	OHIO

* DIED
** BURIED AT THE MEMPHIS NATIONAL CEMETERY

	SULCER	LUCIUS B.	PVT	K	183RD INF	OHIO
	SUMMERSON	L.V.	PVT	C	80TH INF	INDIANA
	SUMMERVILLE	PERRY S.	PVT	K	2ND CAV	INDIANA
	SUMMERS	JAMES B.	PVT	A	4TH MTD INF	TENNESSEE
*	SUMMY	JAMES A.	PVT	A	3RD CAV	TENNESSEE
*	SUMNEY	JAMES	PVT	I	3RD CAV	TENNESSEE
*	SURBER	JAMES I.	LT	G	6TH CAV	KENTUCKY
*	SURVANT	JOSEPH	PVT	K	9TH CAV	INDIANA
	SUTENBAKER	LAWRENCE	PVT	D	8TH CAV	MICHIGAN
	SUTTON	WILLIAM	PVT	A	13TH CAV	INDIANA
	SWAGERTY	VANCE	PVT	L	3RD CAV	TENNESSEE
*	SWAGGERTY	CLAIBORNE	PVT	E	3RD CAV	TENNESSEE
	SWAGGERTY	WILLIAM S.	PVT	B	3RD CAV	TENNESSEE
	SWAIN	ELIHUE H.	LT	G	9TH CAV	INDIANA
*	SWARM	JOHN L.	PVT	K	111ST INF	OHIO
	SWINEFORD	OSCAR	SGT	B	102ND INF	OHIO
*	SWORDS	ELISHA	PVT	I	7TH CAV	INDIANA
	TAGGART	HENRY A.	CAPTAIN	I	101ST INF	OHIO
*	TAHAN	JAMES	PVT	C	124TH INF	INDIANA
	TALENTINE	J.				UNKNOWN
	TALKINGTON	ROBERT	PVT	A	9TH CAV	INDIANA
	TALMADGE	J.	PVT	H	6TH CAV	VIRGINIA
	TANAM	M.O.	SGT	B	35TH INF	INDIANA
*	TANTLINGER	JAMES H.	PVT	I	17TH	INDIANA
	TAYLOR	A.	PVT	G	10TH CAV	OHIO
*	TAYLOR	CHARLES	PVT	A	10TH CAV	OHIO
	TAYLOR	F.	PVT		1ST CAV	TENNESSEE
	TAYLOR	JOHN	PVT	C	6TH CAV	KENTUCKY
	TAYLOR	JOHN	PVT		3RD CAV	TENNESSEE
	TAYLOR	JOSEPH D.	PVT	C	6TH CAV	KENTUCKY
	TAYLOR	SQUIRE A.	CPL	G	37TH INF	INDIANA
*	TEAGUE	PLEASANT	PVT	I	3RD CAV	TENNESSEE
	TEARNE	CHARLES W.	PVT	C	72ND INF	OHIO
	TEASURE	A.J.		A	7TH CAV	OHIO
	TERRELL	HENRY	PVT	A	MCLAUGHIN'S	OHIO
*	TEST	JOSEPHUS	PVT	C	153RD INF	OHIO
	TETTERS	WASHINGTON W.	PVT	G	102ND INF	OHIO
	THACKER	JOHN	PVT	E	46TH INF	OHIO

* DIED
** BURIED AT THE MEMPHIS NATIONAL CEMETERY

	THAGE	WILLIAM	PVT	E	18TH INF	MICHIGAN
	THAHBONGER	J.W.	PVT	A	17TH	INDIANA
*	THAYER	CHARLES	PVT	B	18TH	MICHIGAN
	THAYER	WILLIAM	PVT	C	18TH	MICHIGAN
*	THEVENIN	ANTHONY	CPL	E	5TH CAV	INDIANA
	THOMAS	H.	PVT	L	4TH CAV	TENNESSEE
	THOMAS	J.P.	PVT	E	2ND CAV	MICHIGAN
	THOMAS	LINNAUS A.	PVT	F	115TH INF	OHIO
	THOMAS	MARION	PVT	E	3RD CAV	TENNESSEE
	THOMAS	NATHAN	PVT	G	75TH INF	OHIO
	THOMAS	NOAH	PVT	A	3RD CAV	TENNESSEE
*	THOMAS	THOMAS	PVT	H	76TH INF	OHIO
*	THOMPSON	ELI	SGT	G	115TH INF	OHIO
*	THOMPSON	HENRY	PVT	G	18TH INF	MICHIGAN
	THOMPSON	JAMES	PVT	A	76TH INF	OHIO
*	THOMPSON	JOHN	PVT	G	40TH INF	INDIANA
	THOMPSON	JOHN B.	PVT	H	6TH CAV	KENTUCKY
	THOMPSON	JOHN W.	PVT	C	124TH INF	INDIANA
	THOMPSON	MADISON	PVT	I	3RD CAV	TENNESSEE
	THOMPSON	MARTIN	PVT	I	3RD CAV	MICHIGAN
**	THOMPSON	RUSSELL W.	SGT	K	3RD CAV	TENNESSEE
	THOMPSON	WILEY J.	PVT	C	4TH CAV	MICHIGAN
*	THOMPSON	WILLIAM M.	PVT	M	7TH CAV	INDIANA
	THORN	THOMAS J.	PVT	A	40TH INF	INDIANA
*	THORNBURGH	NATHAN	LT	G	9TH CAV	INDIANA
	THRASHER	SAMUEL J.	PVT	G	6TH CAV	KENTUCKY
*	TIDD	LEONARD G.	PVT	D	2ND CAV	INDIANA
*	TIDWELL	CHARLES B.	PVT	A	MCLAUGHIN'S	OHIO
	TIFT	H.				OHIO
*	TILSON	WILLIAM	PVT	L	3RD CAV	TENNESSEE
*	TIPTON	ANDREW	SGT	B	3RD CAV	TENNESSEE
	TIPTON	CASWELL C.	PVT	B	3RD CAV	TENNESSEE
	TIPTON	JAMES	PVT	B	3RD CAV	TENNESSEE
	TIPTON	PETER H.	PVT	B	3RD CAV	TENNESSEE
*	TIRE	JACKSON	BUGLER	C	6TH CAV	KENTUCKY
	TOLBERT	ROMULUS	PVT	H	8TH CAV	INDIANA
*	TORBET	ROBERT	PVT	F	102ND INF	OHIO
	TORWELL	H.	PVT	K	3RD CAV	OHIO

* DIED
** BURIED AT THE MEMPHIS NATIONAL CEMETERY

	TOT	D.S.	PVT	G	40TH INF	INDIANA
	TRACEY	WILSON S.	PVT	H	102ND INF	OHIO
	TRAVIS	BENJAMIN B.	PVT	H	3RD CAV	TENNESSEE
	TRAXLER	WILLIAM	SGT		102ND INF	OHIO
	TRENOL	I.	PVT	A	7TH CAV	OHIO
	TRENT	ROBERT A.	SGT	B	1ST CAV	TENNESSEE
	TRIMBLE	ARTHUR	SGT	F	4TH CAV	INDIANA
	TRIMMER	WILLIAM	PVT	E	72ND INF	OHIO
*	TROBOUGH	ALLEN	PVT	C	3RD CAV	TENNESSEE
*	TROBOUGH	JOHN	PVT	C	3RD CAV	TENNESSEE
	TRUBY	ABRAM	PVT	C	115TH INF	OHIO
	TUBBS	HIRAM	PVT	B	2ND CAV	MICHIGAN
	TUCKER	GEORGE W.	CPL	I	6TH CAV	KENTUCKY
	TURNER	ROBERT	SGT	G	3RD CAV	TENNESSEE
*	TWIGG	ALEXANDER G.	LT	K	10TH CAV	INDIANA
	TYSON	CHARLES S.	PVT	C	115TH INF	OHIO
*	UHLER	NELSON	PVT	B	21ST INF	OHIO
*	UHLICK	GEORGE W.	PVT	D	102ND INF	OHIO
*	UNDERWOOD	JAMES	PVT	D	102ND INF	OHIO
	UPTON	HARVEY W.	PVT	I	18TH INF	MICHIGAN
*	UPTON	WARNER S.	PVT	I	18TH INF	MICHIGAN
*	USRY	JOHN R.	PVT	F	3RD CAV	TENNESSEE
*	VAN COURT	HARRISON	PVT	D	18TH INF	MICHIGAN
*	VAN COUVER	A.	PVT	E	23RD INF	MICHIGAN
*	VAN EMAN	MATTHEW T.	SGT	G	175TH INF	OHIO
	VAN FLEET	HENRY C.	PVT	I	14TH	OHIO
	VAN HORN	BOROUGHS	PVT	F	95TH INF	OHIO
**	VAN HOSIER	THOMAS	PVT	C	3RD CAV	KENTUCKY
	VAN NUYS	ISAAC	PVT	D	57TH INF	INDIANA
	VAN OVER	J.	PVT	C	99TH INF	INDIANA
	VAN VLACK	ALONSO A.	PVT	F	18TH INF	MICHIGAN
*	VANANDA	ALBERT H.	CPL	E	50TH INF	OHIO
*	VANATTA	JASON	PVT		18TH INF	MICHIGAN
*	VANGORDER	GEORGE W.	PVT	F	18TH INF	MICHIGAN
*	VANOVERR	JAMES	PVT	C	99TH INF	INDIANA
*	VANOY	WILLIAM	PVT	C	6TH CAV	KENTUCKY
	VANSCOYNE	J.W.	CPL	A	64TH INF	OHIO
	VARNELL	ALBERT P.	PVT	I	3RD CAV	TENNESSEE

---

  * DIED
** BURIED AT THE MEMPHIS NATIONAL CEMETERY

	VEATCH	COLUMBUS W.	PVT	H	28TH	INDIANA
	VEAZY	JOHN	PVT	D	53RD INF	INDIANA
	VEMEY	JOHN	PVT		63RD INF	INDIANA
	VENANT	HENRY	PVT	K	50TH INF	INDIANA
	VESSER	SAM	PVT	K	26TH INF	INDIANA
	VETREC	DAVID			93RD INF	INDIANA
*	VICKERY	JOSEPH	PVT	C	3RD CAV	TENNESSEE
	VINCENT	H.	PVT	H	4TH CAV	KENTUCKY
*	VINEYARD	WILLIAM T.	PVT	A	3RD CAV	TENNESSEE
	VOGELSONG	NELSON D.	SGT	F	18TH	MICHIGAN
	WACHTEL	HENRY	PVT	G	102ND INF	OHIO
*	WADDEL	SAMUEL M.	CPL	L	3RD CAV	TENNESSEE
*	WADE	BENJAMIN F.	SGT	A	102ND INF	OHIO
	WADE	GABRIEL	PVT	F	57TH INF	INDIANA
	WADE	JAMES	PVT	B	27TH INF	KENTUCKY
	WADE	JAMES P.	CPL	C	3RD CAV	TENNESSEE
	WADE	MARION F.	PVT	G	8TH CAV	MICHIGAN
	WADE	SILAS W.	CPL	C	3RD CAV	TENNESSEE
	WADE	WILLIAM D.	SGT	C	3RD CAV	TENNESSEE
*	WADE	WILLIAM H.	CPL	K	1ST CAV	OHIO
	WADFORD	W.	PVT	M	13TH CAV	INDIANA
*	WAGNER	JOHN	PVT	A	MCLAUGHLIN'S	OHIO
*	WAGNER	JOSEPH	CPL	G	64TH INF	OHIO
*	WAIT	HENRY	PVT	L	1ST ENG	MICHIGAN
	WAITS	ANTHONY W.	PVT	E	7TH CAV	OHIO
	WALDORF	WILLIAM C.	PVT	H	102ND INF	OHIO
*	WALKER	DANIEL B.	PVT	G	3RD CAV	TENNESSEE
	WALKER	JOHN L.	PVT	B	50TH INF	OHIO
	WALLACE	ARTHUR F.	PVT	D	3RD CAV	KENTUCKY
	WALLACE	HENRY B.	PVT	A	124TH INF	OHIO
	WALLACE	WILLIAM H.	PVT	G	102ND INF	OHIO
	WALLER	BENJAMIN J.	PVT	B	9TH CAV	INDIANA
	WALLICK	ELIJAH	CPL	G	102ND INF	OHIO
	WALTERMIER	JAMES T.	PVT	B	57TH INF	OHIO
	WALTZ	MOSES	PVT	H	75TH INF	OHIO
	WANNUM	THOMAS	SGT	A	7TH CAV	OHIO
	WARD	ARTEMUS	PVT	A	15TH	MICHIGAN
	WARD	JONATHAN	CPL	I	3RD CAV	TENNESSEE

* DIED
** BURIED AT THE MEMPHIS NATIONAL CEMETERY

	WARDEN	DAVID C.	BUGLER	H	2ND CAV	MICHIGAN
	WARLS	B.	PVT	G	8TH CAV	MICHIGAN
	WARMLY	M.	PVT	D	102ND INF	OHIO
*	WARNER	HARVEY D.	PVT	H	9TH CAV	MICHIGAN
	WARNER	WILLIAM C.	PVT	B	9TH CAV	INDIANA
	WARREN	HENRY F.	SGT	G	5TH CAV	MICHIGAN
	WASHBURN	GEORGE	PVT	B	75TH INF	OHIO
	WASHINGTON		PVT		115TH INF	OHIO
	WASSON	WILLIAM H.H.	SGT	I	102ND INF	OHIO
	WATENBERGER	THOMAS	PVT	C	3RD CAV	TENNESSEE
*	WATERBURY	AARON V.	SGT	H	17TH INF	MICHIGAN
	WATERMAN	JAMES		B	52ND INF	OHIO
*	WATERMAN	WILLIAM			115TH INF	OHIO
	WATERS	LUCIUS W.	PVT	H	125TH INF	OHIO
*	WATKINS	JAMES	PVT	D	18TH INF	MICHIGAN
	WATSON	JOSEPH H.	PVT	M	1ST CAV	MICHIGAN
	WATSON	JOSIAH	PVT	M	9TH CAV	INDIANA
	WATSON	ROBERT F.	PVT	C	115TH INF	OHIO
*	WATSON	WILLIAM	PVT	M	13TH CAV	INDIANA
	WATTS	GEORGE W.	PVT	E	97TH INF	OHIO
	WATTS	STEPHAN J.	CPL	C	6TH CAV	KENTUCKY
*	WAY	CHARLES W.	PVT	C	115TH INF	OHIO
*	WAYLAND	SAMUEL A.	SGT	F	3RD CAV	TENNESSEE
	WEAVER	A.C.	CPL	K	10TH CAV	INDIANA
*	WEAVER	PETER W.	PVT	C	115TH INF	OHIO
	WEBB	WILLIAM J.	PVT	G	3RD CAV	TENNESSEE
	WEBSTER	ASA	PVT	B	102ND INF	OHIO
*	WEBSTER	CHARLES H.	CPL	I	3RD CAV	TENNESSEE
	WEBSTER	L.F.	PVT	K	3RD CAV	OHIO
	WEBSTER	P.	PVT	E	4TH CAV	KENTUCKY
	WEEDS	MATT	PVT	E	103RD INF	OHIO
	WELCH	EDMOND C.	PVT		18TH INF	MICHIGAN
	WELCHER	JOHN	PVT	C	37TH INF	OHIO
*	WELLS	DANIEL A.	PVT	E	1ST S.S.	MICHIGAN
	WELLS	HIRAM C.	SGT	E	8TH CAV	MICHIGAN
*	WELLS	JOSEPH	PVT	B	102ND INF	OHIO
*	WELLS	MILES	PVT	H	102ND INF	OHIO
*	WELLS	WILLARD	PVT	H	15TH	MICHIGAN

---

* DIED
** BURIED AT THE MEMPHIS NATIONAL CEMETERY

*	WELLS	WILLIAM	PVT	A	58TH INF	OHIO
	WELSH	JOHN	PVT	C	40TH INF	INDIANA
	WENDT	WILLIAM	PVT	L	8TH CAV	MICHIGAN
	WESCOTT	SAMUEL W.	PVT	B	MCLAUGHIN'S	OHIO
*	WEST	ALLISON	PVT	E	79TH INF	INDIANA
*	WEST	CHARLES A.	PVT	G	18TH INF	MICHIGAN
	WESTRIP	GEORGE	PVT	E	23RD	MICHIGAN
*	WHEATLY	LUCIEN	SGT	A	6TH CAV	KENTUCKY
*	WHEELER	DANIEL	PVT	E	102ND INF	OHIO
	WHEELER	WILLIAM	PVT	D	100TH INF	OHIO
	WHETMORE	ALSON A.	PVT	C	115TH INF	OHIO
*	WHETMORE	CHARLES H.	PVT	C	115TH INF	OHIO
	WHISEMORE	ABRAHAM	PVT	B	102ND INF	OHIO
	WHITE	GEORGE	PVT	B	8TH CAV	MICHIGAN
	WHITE	J.W.	PVT	D	50TH INF	OHIO
	WHITE	JAMES E.	CPL	D	11TH CAV	TENNESSEE
	WHITE	JEREMIAH	PVT	H	7TH CAV	OHIO
	WHITE	JOSEPH	PVT	E	75TH INF	OHIO
	WHITE	JOSHUA	PVT	E	78TH INF	OHIO
*	WHITE	LEWIS K.	PVT	F	115TH INF	OHIO
	WHITE	MANLY C.	PVT	B	8TH CAV	MICHIGAN
*	WHITE	ROBERT	SGT	I	64TH INF	OHIO
	WHITE	THOMAS	PVT	C	124TH INF	INDIANA
	WHITE	WILLIAM H.	PVT	K	10TH CAV	OHIO
	WHITE	WILLIAM H.	PVT	H	19TH	OHIO
	WHITESOLL	J.	PVT	K	13TH CAV	INDIANA
*	WHITMAN	RILEY	PVT	F	3RD CAV	TENNESSEE
	WHYLER	L.	PVT	D	35TH	OHIO
	WHYLER	S.E.		D	55TH INF	OHIO
	WIIYLER	SEBASTIAN	PVT	D	55TH INF	OHIO
*	WIBLE	LEVI	SGT	G	63RD INF	OHIO
	WIECARD	ABRAM B.	PVT	K	18TH INF	MICHIGAN
*	WIGGINS	MICHAEL C.	CPL	L	3RD CAV	TENNESSEE
	WILCOX	JOHN A.	PVT	C	3RD CAV	TENNESSEE
	WILCOX	LEMUEL N.	PVT	C	115TH INF	OHIO
*	WILCOX	MARVIN	PVT	F	95TH INF	OHIO
	WILES	ALBERT G.	PVT	C	55TH INF	OHIO
	WILLARD	CHARLES	PVT	E	93RD INF	INDIANA

* DIED
** BURIED AT THE MEMPHIS NATIONAL CEMETERY

WILLHELM	C.	PVT	C	7TH CAV	VIRGINIA
WILLIAMS	DAVID M.	CPL	G	3RD CAV	TENNESSEE
* WILLIAMS	EDMOND	PVT	K	3RD CAV	TENNESSEE
* WILLIAMS	JAMES T.	PVT	D	102ND INF	OHIO
WILLIAMS	JESSEE	CPL	G	3RD CAV	TENNESSEE
WILLIAMS	JOHN H.	PVT	G	102ND INF	OHIO
WILLIAMS	JOHN W.	SGT	H	3RD CAV	TENNESSEE
WILLIAMS	MARTIN	PVT	G	102ND INF	OHIO
WILLIAMS	NATHAN S.	PVT	B	5TH CAV	INDIANA
WILLIAMS	NATHAN S.	PVT	M	2ND CAV	MICHIGAN
* WILLIAMS	NATHANIEL G.	PVT	K	3RD CAV	TENNESSEE
WILLIAMS	ROBERT	PVT		3RD CAV	TENNESSEE
* WILLIAMS	SPENCER H.	CPL	E	3RD CAV	TENNESSEE
WILLIAMS	W.T.	PVT	K	4TH CAV	KENTUCKY
WILLIAMS	WILLIAM H.	PVT	F	18TH INF	MICHIGAN
* WILLIS	WILLIAM W.	PVT	E	102ND INF	OHIO
* WILLSON	SAMUEL	PVT	A	58TH INF	OHIO
WILSON	ADAM	PVT	A	3RD CAV	TENNESSEE
WILSON	ANDREW	PVT		3RD CAV	MICHIGAN
WILSON	GEORGE P.	PVT	B	9TH CAV	INDIANA
* WILSON	HENRY B.	CPL	E	16TH INF	KENTUCKY
WILSON	J.P.	PVT	H	6TH CAV	VIRGINIA
WILSON	ROBERT	PVT	F	95TH INF	OHIO
* WILSON	THOMAS A.	CPL	H	6TH CAV	KENTUCKY
WINDORSTT	JONATHAN	PVT	K	9TH CAV	INDIANA
WINDSER	WILLIAM H.	PVT	L	9TH CAV	INDIANA
WINHASNER	THOMAS	PVT	G	3RD CAV	KENTUCKY
WINKLE	SAMUEL L.	PVT	B	79TH INF	INDIANA
WINKLEMAN	JOHN	PVT	H	104TH INF	OHIO
WINSLOW	W.H.	PVT	L	7TH CAV	TENNESSEE
WINSOR	WILLIAM H.	PVT	L	9TH CAV	INDIANA
* WINSTARD	JOHN	PVT	G	6TH CAV	KENTUCKY
WINTERHOST	T.	PVT	K	9TH CAV	INDIANA
WINTERS	ERASTUS	CPL	K	50TH INF	OHIO
WISLER	W.	SGT	C	102ND INF	OHIO
WITENBARGER	DREWEY A.	PVT	E	3RD CAV	TENNESSEE
* WITSIL	JOHN	PVT	M	13TH CAV	INDIANA
WOLCOMMER	JOHN	PVT	A	58TH INF	OHIO

* DIED
** BURIED AT THE MEMPHIS NATIONAL CEMETERY

	WOLFAMER	JOHN	PVT	B	58TH INF	OHIO
	WOLUM	JOHN	PVT	K	4TH CAV	KENTUCKY
	WOLVERTON	JAMES T.	SGT	G	6TH CAV	TENNESSEE
	WOOD	E.	PVT	E	9TH CAV	INDIANA
	WOOD	HENRY C.	CPL	D	18TH INF	MICHIGAN
*	WOOD	ISAAC J.	PVT	C	115TH INF	OHIO
	WOOD	JAMES E.	PVT	C	3RD CAV	TENNESSEE
	WOOD	JOHN	PVT	C	3RD CAV	TENNESSEE
*	WOOD	LANDON	PVT	C	3RD CAV	TENNESSEE
*	WOOD	WILLIAM H.H.	PVT	D	9TH CAV	INDIANA
*	WOODRUFF	STEPHEN B.	PVT	B	6TH CAV	KENTUCKY
	WOODS	MATTHEW	PVT	B	102ND INF	OHIO
*	WOODWARD	THEORDORE	PVT	A	7TH CAV	OHIO
	WOODWARD	TAYLOR	PVT	A	4TH CAV	VIRGINIA
*	WOOLEY	WILLIAM	PVT	I	6TH CAV	KENTUCKY
	WORD	J.W.	CPL	C	3RD CAV	TENNESSEE
	WRESTLER	JOHN	PVT	H	175TH INF	OHIO
*	WRIGHT	BENJAMIN	PVT	M	9TH CAV	OHIO
**	WRIGHT	DAVID	SGT	F	7TH CAV	KENTUCKY
	WRIGHT	FRANCIS	SGT	B	18TH INF	MICHIGAN
	WRIGHT	FRANK	PVT	M	9TH CAV	OHIO
	WRIGHT	H.W.	PVT	F	10TH CAV	OHIO
	WRIGHT	HOMER	PVT	F	15TH INF	MICHIGAN
	WRIGHT	J.C.	CPL	C	124TH INF	INDIANA
	WRIGHT	NELSON D.	PVT	D	18TH INF	MICHIGAN
	WRIGHT	W.	PVT	F	15TH	MICHIGAN
	WRIGHT	WILLIAM	PVT	I	3RD CAV	TENNESSEE
*	WRINKLE	ANDREW J.	PVT	E	3RD CAV	TENNESSEE
	WUBE	LEVI	SGT	G	83RD INF	OHIO
*	WYLERS	L.	PVT	G	3RD CAV	TENNESSEE
*	WYNN	THOMAS J.	PVT	H	102ND INF	OHIO
*	YEISLEY	E.H.	PVT	A	76TH INF	OHIO
	YEISLEY	WILLIAM	PVT	E	102ND INF	OHIO
	YEKK	J.A.	PVT	B	57TH INF	INDIANA
	YORK	ANDREW J.	PVT	G	99TH INF	INDIANA
*	YOUNG	FREDERICK	PVT	C	58TH INF	OHIO
	YOUNG	GEORGE N.	PVT	A	95TH INF	OHIO
	YOUNG	J.	PVT	C	2ND CAV	INDIANA

* DIED
** BURIED AT THE MEMPHIS NATIONAL CEMETERY

	YOUNG	JOHN	PVT	I	53RD INF	INDIANA
*	YOUNG	WILLIAM	MUSICIAN	D	18TH INF	MICHIGAN
	ZACHARIA	M.	PVT	M	8TH CAV	MICHIGAN
	ZACHARY	ALEXANDER K.	SGT	K	7TH CAV	MICHIGAN
	ZAISER	JOHN J.	PVT	F	115TH INF	OHIO
*	ZEHFUSS	GUSTAVE	SGT	H	183RD INF	OHIO
*	ZEIDLER	FRANK	PVT	C	18TH	MICHIGAN
*	ZIMMER	CASPER	PVT	B	64TH INF	OHIO
	ZIMMERMAN	JACOB	PVT	C	115TH INF	OHIO
*	ZIX	MATTHEW	PVT	K	9TH CAV	INDIANA
*	ZOLER	GEORGE A.	SGT	B	6TH CAV	KENTUCKY

---

* DIED
** BURIED AT THE MEMPHIS NATIONAL CEMETERY

Glossary of Abbreviations Contained in the List of Soldiers

RANK

BLKSM	BLACKSMITH
CPL	CORPORAL
HOS. S.	HOSPITAL STEWARD
LT	LIEUTENANT
PVT	PRIVATE
SGT	SERGEANT
SDLER	SADDLER
WGNR	WAGONER

REGIMENT

CAV	CAVALRY
ENG	ENGINEERS
INF	INFANTRY
MTD INF	MOUNTED INFANTRY
S.S.	SHARPSHOOTERS
U.S.C.T	UNITED STATES COLORED TROOPS

NOTES

1. Robert A. Hereford, *The Old Man River—The Memories of Captain Louis Rosche, Pioneer Steamboatman* (Caldwell, Idaho, 1943), pp. 82–83.

2. J. W. Rutter, "Bewitching News," *S & D Reflector*, Vol. 2, No. 3 (September, 1965), p. 12; and Cincinnati *Daily Commerce*, February 4, 1863, p. 4.

3. Funk and Wagnalls *Standard College Dictionary*, Text Edition (New York, 1966), p. 1,340.

4. Frederick Way, Jr., *Directory of Western River Packets* (Sewickley, Pa., 1950), p. 279.

5. Cincinnati *Daily Commerce*, February 4, 1863, p. 4.

6. Way, pp. 279–280; and Cincinnati *Daily Commerce*, February 4, 1863, p. 4.

7. Louis C. Hunter, *Steamboats on the Western Rivers* (New York, 1969), pp. 157–158.

8. Cincinnati *Daily Commerce*, February 4, 1863, p. 4.

9. *Ibid.*

10. *Report of the Board of Supervising Inspectors of Steamboats*, House Executive Document 3, 39th Congress, First Session, 1865–1866, p. 216. (Hereafter referred to as *Inspectors' Report*.)

11. U.S. War Department, *War of the Rebellion: A Compilation of the Official Records of the Union and Confederate Armies* (Washington, 1880-1901), Series I, Vol. 48, Part 1, p. 217. (Hereafter referred to as *O.R.*)

12. Cincinnati *Daily Commerce*, February 4, 1863, p. 4.

13. Way, p. 280.

14. Frank R. Levstik, "The Sinking of the Sultana," *Civil War Times Illustrated*, XII (January, 1974), p. 18.

263

15. U.S. Navy Department, *War of the Rebellion: The Official Records of the Union and Confederate Navies in the War of the Rebellion* (Washington, 1894–1922), Series I, Vol. 25, p. 4.

16. Ray Samuel, Leonard V. Huber, and Warren C. Ogden, *Tales of the Mississippi* (New York, 1955), p. 128.

17. *The Official Records of the Union and Confederate Navies in the War in the Rebellion*, p. 339.

18. St. Louis *Daily Missouri Democrat*, April 29, 1865, p. 4; and The *Sultana* License, Records of the Judge Advocate General's Office, Record Group 153, National Archives, Washington, D.C.

19. E. W. Gould, *Fifty Years on the Mississippi or Gould's History of River Navigation* (St. Louis, 1889), pp. 693–694.

20. St. Louis *Daily Missouri Democrat*, April 29, 1865, p. 4.

21. William Hyde and Howard L. Conard, eds., *Encyclopedia of the History of St. Louis* (New York, 1899), pp. 595–596.

22. *The Official Records of the Union and Confederate Navies in the War of the Rebellion*, Series I, Vol. 25, pp. 332–337, 420–421, 426–427, 546; William O. Bryant, *Cahaba Prison and the Sultana Disaster* (Tuscaloosa, 1990), pp. 122–123; and St. Louis *Daily Missouri Democrat*, April 29, 1865, p. 4.

23. *Transcript of the Courtmartial of Capt. Frederic Speed*, pp. 294–295, Records of the Judge Advocate General's Office, Record Group 153, National Archives, Washington, D.C. (Hereafter referred to as *Courtmartial*.)

24. Robert Selph Henry, *"First With the Most" Forrest* (Wilmington, 1987), pp. 347–352.

25. *Ibid.*, p. 353.

26. *O.R.*, Series I, Vol. 39, Part 1, pp. 523–524.

27. *Ibid.*

28. *Ibid.*; and Henry, p. 354.

39. *O.R.*, pp. 513–514; and Henry, p. 354.

30. *O.R.*, p. 514; and Henry, pp. 355–356.

31. Henry, pp. 355–356.

32. *O.R.*, p. 523.

33. Chester D. Berry, *Loss of the Sultana and Reminiscences of Survivors* (Lansing, 1892), pp. 144–145.

34. James Lee McDonough and Thomas L. Connelly, *Five Tragic Hours— The Battle of Franklin* (Knoxville, 1983), p. 157.

35. Shelby Foote, *The Civil War—A Narrative* (New York, 1974), Vol. 3, p. 673.

36. Berry, pp. 112–113.

37. *Ibid.*, p. 45.

38. *Ibid.*, p. 73 and p. 80.

39. *O.R.*, Series II, Vol. 1, p. 166.

40. E. Merton Coulter, *The Confederate States of America* (Baton Rouge, 1950), p. 478; and *O.R.*, Series II, Vol. 7, pp. 606–607.

41. John Ransom, *John Ransom's Andersonville Diary* (New York, 1963), p. XV.

42. Bruce Catton, *Short History of the Civil War* (New York, 1960), p. 213.

43. William B. Hesseltine, *Civil War Prisons* (Kent, 1962), p. 6.

44. *O.R.*, Series II, Vol. 7, pp. 606–607.

45. *Ibid.*, Series II, Vol. 8, pp. 595–596.

46. *Ibid.*, pp. 596–597.

47. *Ibid.*, p. 597.

48. *Ibid.*, p. 617.

49. *Ibid.*, p. 602.

50. Ransom, p. 111.

51. *O.R.*, p. 604.

52. *Ibid.*

53. *Ibid.*, p. 619.

54. Ovid Futch, *History of Andersonville* (Gainesville, 1968), p. 98.

55. Bruce Catton, "Prison Camps of the Civil War," *American Heritage*, Vol. X, August, 1959, p. 96.

56. Clement Eaton, *A History of the Southern Confederacy* (New York, 1954), p. 109.

57. Jesse Hawes, *Cahaba—A Story of Captive Boys in Blue* (New York, 1888), pp. 13–14; and John L. Walker, *Cahaba Prison and the Sultana Disaster* (Hamilton, 1910), pp. 4–5.

58. Hawes, pp. 159–160.

59. *Ibid.*, pp. 13–14.

60. *Ibid.*, pp. 16–17.

61. *Ibid.*, pp. 201–202.

62. Walker, p. 14; Pension records of Joseph Hines, National Archives, Washington, D.C.; and Bryant, pp. 112–113.

63. Catton, *Short History of the Civil War*, p. 244.

64. *O.R.*, Series II, Vol. 8, p. 170.

65. Catton, p. 249.

· 66. Joseph Taylor Elliott, "The Sultana Disaster," *Indiana Historical Society Publication*, Vol. V, No. 3 (1913), p. 163.

67. Berry, p. 114.

68. Elliott, pp. 163–164.

69. *O.R.*, Series II, Vol. 8, p. 492.

70. Berry, p. 114.

71. Elliott, p. 164.

72. J. S. Newberry, *The U.S. Sanitary Commission in the Valley of the Mississippi River* (Cleveland, 1871), pp. 180–181.

73. C. M. Eldridge, "Some Events at the Close of the Civil War," *The National Tribune*, August 1, 1929, p. 6.

74. Testimony of H. A. Henderson, *Courtmartial*, p. 276.

75. Berry, p. 190.

76. Bruce Catton, *A Stillness At Appomattox* (New York, 1953), p. 424.

77. *Annual Reunion of the Association of the Graduates of the United States Military Academy at West Point, New York* (New York, 1907), pp. 30–35.

78. Testimony of Gen. Morgan L. Smith, *Washburn Commission*, Records of the Adjutant General's Office, Record Group 153, National Archives, Washington, D.C. (Hereafter referred to as *Washburn Commission.*)

79. *Military Records of Gen. Morgan L. Smith*, Records of the Adjutant General's Office, 1780's–1917, Record Group 94, National Archives, Washington, D.C. (Hereafter referred to as *Smith's Records.*)

80. St. Louis *Post Dispatch*, January 2, 1875, p. 2.

81. *Smith's Records.*

82. *Military Records of Capt. William Franklin Kerns*, Records of the Adjutant General's Office, Record Group 94, National Archives, Washington, D.C.

83. *Military Records of Capt. George Augustus Williams*, United States Military Academy Archives, United States Military Academy, West Point, New York.

84. George W. Cullum, *Biographical Register of the Officers and Graduates of the United States Military Academy at West Point, New York* (Cambridge, 1891), Vol. II, pp. 503–504.

85. *Military Records of Capt. George Augustus Williams*, Records of the Adjutant General's Office, Record Group 94, National Archives, Washington, D.C.

86. John Y. Simon, ed., *The Papers of Ulysses S. Grant* (Carbondale, 1967), Vol. 7, pp. 59–60.

87. *Records of Capt. George Augustus Williams*, Record Group 94, National Archives.

88. *O.R.*, Series II, Vol. 7, p. 404.

89. *Ibid.*

90. *Ibid.*, p. 405.

91. *Ibid.*, p. 406.

92. *Ibid.*, p. 407.

93. *Ibid.*

94. Testimony of Frederic Speed, *Washburn Commission*; and Special Order No. 125, April 7, 1865, *Courtmartial*, p. 341.

95. The Goodspeed Publishing Co., *Biographical and Historical Memoirs of Mississippi* (Chicago, 1891), Vol. II, pp. 805–806.

96. *Ibid.*

97. *Military Record of Col. Reuben B. Hatch*, Records of the Adjutant General's Office, Record Group 94, National Archives, Washington, D.C. (Hereafter referred to as *Hatch's Records*.)

98. United States House of Representatives, 37th Congress, 2nd Session, House Reports, part 2, p. 1090 and p. 1130. (Hereafter referred to as *Cairo Fraud Reports*.)

99. *Chicago Tribune*, December 12, 1861, p. 5.

100. Simon, III, p. 325.

101. *Ibid.*, pp. 325–326; and *Cairo Fraud Reports*, p. 1109.

102. *Cairo Fraud Reports*, pp. 1133–1135.

103. Simon, IV, p. 80.

104. *Ibid.*, III, p. 325 and IV, pp. 46–47.

105. *Ibid.*, IV, p. 47.

106. *Ibid.*, IV, pp. 79–80, *Ibid.*, III, p. 362; and *Personal Histories of Volunteer Officers of the Quartermaster Department 1861–1865*, Military Archives Division, National Archives, Washington, D.C., p. 144. (Hereafter referred to as *Personal Histories*.)

107. *Personal Histories*, p. 144.

108. Simon, IV, p. 82.

109. *Ibid.*, p. 80.

110. Reinhard H. Luthin, *The First Lincoln Campaign* (Cambridge, 1944), p. 139; Harry E. Pratt, *The Personal Finances of Abraham Lincoln* (Springfield, 1943), p. 110; and Shelby Foote, *The Civil War—A Narrative* (New York, 1958), Vol. I, p. 749.

111. Luthin, p. 139; Pratt, p. 110; and Simon, IV, p. 83.

112. Simon, IV, p. 83.

113. *Ibid.*

114. *Ibid.*

115. *Ibid.*, pp. 83–84; and Charles A. Dana, *Recollections of the Civil War* (New York, 1963), pp. 11–14.

116. *Personal Histories*, III, p. 146.

117. *Hatch's Records.*

118. *Ibid.*; Simon, VII, p. 297; Bruce Catton, *Grant Moves South* (Boston, 1960), p. 98.

119. *Hatch's Records.*

120. *Ibid.*

121. *Ibid.*

122. *Ibid.*

123. *Ibid.*

124. *Ibid.*; and Simon, VII, p. 298.

125. *Hatch's Records.*

126. Pratt, p. 110.

127. *Hatch's Records.*

128. *Personal Histories*, III, p. 147; and *Hatch's Records.*

129. *Hatch's Records.*

130. *Ibid.*

131. *Ibid.*

132. *Ibid.*

133. *Ibid.*

134. *Ibid.*

135. Letter from Reuben Hatch to O. M. Hatch, January 4, 1865, O. M. Hatch Collection, Illinois Historical Society Library, Old State Capitol Building, Springfield, Illinois.

136. *Personal Histories*, III, p. 148.

137. *Ibid.*

138. *Ibid.*

139. *Ibid.*

140. St. Louis *Daily Missouri Democrat*, April 10, 1865, p. 4.

141. Inspector's Certificate of *Sultana*, April 12, 1865, *Courtmartial.*

142. St. Louis *Daily Missouri Democrat*, April 15, 1865, p. 4.

143. James W. Elliott, *Transport to Disaster* (New York, 1962), p. 7.

144. Levstik, p. 20.

145. Memphis *Daily Bulletin*, April 16, 1865, p. 3.

146. St. Louis *Daily Missouri Democrat*, February 22, 1865, p. 4.

147. Berry, p. 47.

148. License issued to *Sultana*, March 20, 1865, National Archives, Washington, D.C., courtesy of Gene Salecker, Chicago, Illinois; St. Louis *Daily Missouri Democrat*, April 29, 1865, p. 4; and Testimony of Capt. L. C. Mitchell, *Dana Commission*, Records of the Adjutant General's Office, Record Group 153, National Archives, Washington, D.C.

149. Testimony of Miles Sells, *Courtmartial*, p. 121; and *O.R.*, Series I, Vol. 48, Part 1, p. 219.

150. Testimony of Miles Sells, *Courtmartial*, p. 121; and Testimony of Morgan L. Smith, *Washburn Commission*.

151. New Orleans *Picayune*, April 20, 1865, p. 10.

152. *Ibid.*, April 21, 1865, p. 1.

153. *Ibid.*, April 22, 1865, p. 8.

154. Memphis *Daily Bulletin*, April 28, 1865, p. 1.

155. *Inspectors' Report*, p. 216.

156. St. Louis *Daily Missouri Democrat*, April 29, 1865, p. 1.

157. Berry, p. 28.

158. Testimony of Nathan Wintringer, *Washburn Commission*.

159. Testimony of William Rowberry, *Washburn Commission*; and Testimony of Lieutenant Colonel Compton, *Courtmartial*, p. 148.

160. *O.R.*, p. 211.

161. *Ibid.*; and Report of General Dana to Gen. William Hoffman, May 8, 1865, *Dana Commission*.

162. Berry, pp. 252–254.

163. *O.R.*, p. 211.

164. *Ibid.*; and Report of General Dana to General Hoffman, May 8, 1865, *Dana Commission*.

165. Testimony of Capt. Frederic Speed, *Washburn Commission*.

166. Testimony of William Kerns, *Courtmartial*, p. 64; and Testimony of William Jones, p. 91.

167. Testimony of R. G. Taylor, *Washburn Commission*.

168. *Ibid.*

169. *O.R.*, p. 211.

170. *Ibid.*, p. 219; and Testimony of Miles Sells, *Courtmartial*, p. 121.

171. Testimony of Miles Sells, *Dana Commission*.

172. *Ibid.*

173. *Ibid.*, p. 127.

174. Testimony of Miles Sells, *Courtmartial*, pp. 121–122.

175. *Ibid.*, p. 119.

176. Testimony of Frederic Speed, *Washburn Commission*.

177. *Ibid.*; and Testimony of Miles Sells, *Courtmartial*, p. 123.

178. Testimony of Miles Sells, *Courtmartial*, p. 121.

179. Testimony of Miles Sells, *Dana Commission*.

180. Testimony of George Williams, *Courtmartial*, p. 24 and p. 41; and Testimony of Miles Sells, *Courtmartial*, p. 124.

181. Testimony of Frederic Speed, *Washburn Commission*.

182. Testimony of George Williams, *Courtmartial*, p. 25.

183. Special Order No. 139, April 23, 1865, *Courtmartial*, p. 361.

184. Testimony of William L. Friesner, *Courtmartial*, p. 115.

185. Testimony of E. L. Davenport, *Courtmartial*, p. 283.

186. *O.R.*, p. 211.

187. Testimony of H. H. Emmon, *Courtmartial*, p. 193.

188. Testimony of Frederic Speed, *Washburn Commission*.

189. Testimony of George Williams, *Courtmartial*, p. 13.

190. Testimony of Frederic Speed, *Washburn Commission*.

191. Testimony of E. L. Davenport, *Courtmartial*, pp. 294–295.

192. Testimony of George Williams, *Courtmartial*, p. 13; and *O.R.*, p. 211 and p. 214.

193. Testimony of E. D. Butler, *Courtmartial*, p. 154.

194. Testimony of William Kerns, *Courtmartial*, p. 47 and *Dana Commission*.

195. Testimony of Kerns, *Courtmartial*, p. 54, p. 58, and p. 80; Exhibits A and B, *Courtmartial*.

196. Testimony of Kerns, *Courtmartial*, pp. 47–48.

197. Testimony of William Kerns, *Washburn Commission*.

198. Testimony of Kerns, *Courtmartial*, p. 48.

199. Testimony of George Williams, *Courtmartial*, p. 13; and Testimony of Frederic Speed, *Washburn Commission*.

200. Berry, p. 57.

201. Testimony of Williams, *Washburn Commission*.

202. Testimony of Kerns, *Washburn Commission*.

203. Testimony of Williams, *Courtmartial*, p. 38 and *Washburn Commission*.

204. Tillinghast, *Washburn Commission*.

205. G. G. Adam, *Dana Commission*.

206. *O.R.*, p. 215.

207. E. B. Butler, *Courtmartial*, p. 152.

208. William Geins, *Washburn Commission*.

209. Kerns, *Dana Commission*.

210. George B. Denton, *Washburn Commission*; Kerns, *Courtmartial*, p. 49; and Speed, *Washburn Commission*.

211. Kerns, *Courtmartial*, p. 49.

212. *Ibid.*, pp. 49–50.

213. *Ibid.*

214. Deposition of Dr. George S. Kemble, Exhibit O, *Courtmartial*.

215. J. Warren Miller, *Courtmartial*, pp. 219–220.

216. *O.R.*, p. 211; and Williams, *Courtmartial*, p. 17.

217. Kerns, *Courtmartial*, pp. 50–51.

218. *Ibid.*

219. Morgan L. Smith, *Washburn Commission*.

220. Hatch, *Washburn Commission*.

221. H. C. Huntsman, *Courtmartial*, pp. 323–324.

222. George Williams, *Courtmartial*, p. 15; and James McCowan, *Courtmartial*, pp. 94–95.

223. Speed, *Washburn Commission*.

224. William Jones, *Courtmartial*, p. 86.

225. Kerns, *Courtmartial*, p. 51.

226. Speed, *Washburn Commission*.

227. Kerns, *Courtmartial*, p. 52.

228. Lewis Bean, *Dana Commission*.

229. J. L. McHarg, *Courtmartial*, p. 174.

230. *National Tribune*, June 15, 1923, p. 2.

231. J. Mahoney, Records of the Inquiry conducted by Gen. William Hoffman, Records of the Adjutant General's Office, Record Group 153, National Archives, Washington, D.C. (Hereafter referred to as *Hoffman*.)

232. Kerns, *Courtmartial*, p. 52.

233. *Ibid.*, pp. 52–53; and William H. Gaud, *Washburn Commission*.

234. William Jones, *Courtmartial*, p. 86.

235. William Butler, *Hoffman*.

236. *Ibid.*

237. McCowan, *Courtmartial*, p. 99.

238. Berry, p. 63.

239. Friesner, *Courtmartial*, p. 111.

240. Military Records of Lt. Harvey Annis, Record Group 94, National Archives, Washington, D.C.; and Testimony of Ann Annis, *Dana Commission*; and *O.R.*, p. 215.

241. McCowan, *Courtmartial*, p. 101.

242. William H. Gaud, *Washburn Commission*.

243. *Ibid.*

244. Speed, *Washburn Commission*.

245. Memphis *Daily Bulletin*, April 28, 1865, p. 1.

246. Berry, pp. 77 and 78.

247. McCowan, *Courtmartial*, p. 101.

248. *National Tribune*, June 14, 1923, p. 2.

249. Williams, *Courtmartial*, p. 14.

250. Williams, *Washburn Commission*, p. 14.

251. *O.R.*, p. 214; and Berry, p. 77 and p. 190.

252. Joseph Elliott, *Courtmartial*, p. 143; McCowan, *Courtmartial*, p. 103; and Mahoney, *Hoffman*.

253. Berry, p. 225.

254. Kerns, *Courtmartial*, p. 73; *O.R.*, p. 212; and Report of General Dana to General Hoffman, *Dana Commission*.

255. Washington, D.C. *National Tribune*, August 1, 1929, p. 6.

256. William F. Dixon, "Aboard the Sultana," *Civil War Times Illustrated*, 12 (February, 1974), p. 38.

257. McCowan, *Courtmartial*, p. 107.

258. Berry, pp. 62 and 65.

259. *Ibid.*, pp. 318–319.

260. *Ibid.*, pp. 285–286.

261. McCowan, *Courtmartial*, p. 100; and Lewis Bean, *Hoffman*.

262. McCowan, *Courtmartial*, p. 102; *O.R.*, p. 215; and Franklin Barker, *Hoffman*.

263. McCowan, *Washburn Commission*.

264. McCowan, *Courtmartial*, p. 101.

265. Lewis Bean, *Hoffman*.

266. Elbert J. Squire, *Hoffman*.

267. Lewis F. Hake, *Washburn Commission*.

268. McCowan, *Courtmartial*, p. 102; and Foote, Vol. III, pp. 996–997.

269. Memphis *Daily Bulletin*, April 29, 1865, p. 3.

270. Berry, p. 252.

271. Joseph Elliott, *Courtmartial*, p. 143.

272. Berry, pp. 247–249; and Bryant, pp. 98–99.

273. Lloyd B. Walton, "The Great Civil War Shipwreck," *The Indianapolis Star Magazine*, March 15, 1981, p. 29.

274. George Kayton, *Washburn Commission*; and Berry, p. 210.

275. Nathan Wintringer, *Washburn Commission*.

276. Elliott, p. 170.

277. Berry, p. 126.

278. William B. Floyd, "The Burning of the Sultana," *The Wisconsin Magazine of History*, XI (September, 1927), p. 70.

279. *Ibid.*; and Hawes, p. 183.

280. Berry, p. 149.

281. *Ibid.*, pp. 298–301.

282. *Portrait and Biographical Album of Jackson County, Michigan* (Chicago, 1890), pp. 600–601.

283. Richmond (Indiana) *Palladium-Item and Sun-Telegram*, January 8, 1969, p. 22.

284. Mark Twain, *Life on the Mississippi* (Hartford, 1883), p. 59.

285. Hunter, p. 278.

286. William C. Cochran, "Perils of River Navigation in The Sixties," *Proceedings of the Mississippi Valley Association*, Vol. X, 1919–1920, pp. 320–321; and Hunter, p. 278.

287. Hunter, p. 278.

288. *Ibid.*, p. 279.

289. *Inspectors' Certificate*.

290. Samuel Clemens, *Washburn Commission*.

291. William Rowberry, *Washburn Commission*.

292. Berry, p. 103.

293. J. J. Witzig, *Courtmartial*, p. 131.

294. Memphis *Commercial Appeal*, January 25, 1920, p. 18.

295. Berry, pp. 191–192.

296. William Rowberry, *Washburn Commission*; and George Kayton, *Washburn Commission*.

297. Berry, p. 169.

298. *National Tribune*, August 1, 1929, p. 6.

299. Berry, pp. 234–235.

300. Letter from Samuel Pickens to Cynthia Pickens and Mary Pickens, April 28, 1865, Courtesy of Helen A. Kerr, Knoxville, Tennessee.

301. Berry, p. 353.

302. *Ibid.*, p. 224.

303. *Ibid.*, pp. 319–320.

304. *Ibid.*, pp. 94–95; and St. Louis *Daily Missouri Democrat*, June 19, 1865, p. 4.

305. Maryville (Tennessee) *Enterprise*, April 30, 1975, p. 3.

306. Berry, pp. 174–175.

307. *Ibid.*, p. 117 and p. 256.

308. *Ibid.*, pp. 285–286.

309. *Ibid.*, pp. 265–266.

310. William S. Friesner, *Courtmartial*, pp. 112–113.

311. Berry, pp. 314–315.

312. Christian M. Nisley, *Washburn Commission*.

313. Joseph Taylor Elliott, p. 171.

314. Berry, pp. 115–117.

315. Letter from Gene Salecker to author, January 11, 1991.

316. Berry., pp. 117–118.

317. Walker, pp. 17–18.

318. Berry, pp. 274–275.

319. *Ibid.*, p. 126.

320. *Ibid.*, p. 249.

321. Hawes, p. 292.

322. *Ibid.*, p. 194.

323. Berry, p. 10.

324. *Ibid.*, p. 162.

325. Hawes, pp. 183–184.

326. *Ibid.*

327. Berry, pp. 299–301.

328. Memphis *Daily Bulletin*, April 28, 1865, p. 1.

329. Walker, pp. 20–21.

330. Berry, p. 51–52.

331. *National Tribune*, August 1, 1929, p. 6.

332. Berry, p. 79.

333. *Ibid.*, pp. 319–320 and p. 331.

334. *Ibid.*, p. 118.

335. Hawes, pp. 167–169.

336. Berry, p. 117.

337. Hawes, p. 177.

338. *Portrait and Biographical Album of Jackson County, Michigan* (Chicago, 1890), pp. 600–601.

339. J. H. Kimberlin, *The Destruction of the Sultana* (Hamilton, 1910), p. 19.

340. Elliott, p. 172.

341. Walker, p. 19.

342. Hawes, p. 167; and Jacob Rush, *Washburn Commission*.

343. Hawes, pp. 168–170.

344. *Ibid.*, pp. 192–193.

345. Berry, p. 341.

346. St. Louis *Daily Missouri Democrat*, May 1, 1865, p. 4.

347. Berry, pp. 186–187.

348. Memphis *Daily Bulletin*, April 28, 1865, p. 1.

349. Memphis *Press Scimitar*, May 28, 1969, p. 17.

350. Ann Annis, *Washburn Commission*.

351. Berry, p. 215.

352. *Ibid.*, p. 119.

353. *Ibid.*, pp. 225–226.

354. Elliott, p. 179.

355. *Ibid.*, pp. 173–176.

356. Account told to author by George Millsaps, April, 1988, Knoxville, Tennessee.

357. Berry, pp. 353–354.

358. Nellie Pickens Anderson, *John Pickens Family* (Knoxville, 1951), p. 188.

359. Hawes, pp. 185–187.

360. *Ibid.*, pp. 189–190.

361. Berry, p. 327.

362. Edgar Rhea Keeble, son of Pleasant Keeble, Unpublished manuscript, January 27, 1987, Knoxville, Tennessee.

363. Maryville (Tennessee) *Enterprise*, April 30, 1975, p. 2.

364. Floyd, p. 71.

365. *Log of Charles Ackley*, Inland River Library, Public Library of Cincinnati and Hamilton County, Cincinnati, Ohio, p. 103.

366. Memphis *Commercial Appeal*, January 25, 1920, p. 18.

367. *Ibid.*; and Letter of L. P. Berry, West Memphis (Arkansas) *Evening Times*, April 25, 1969.

368. William B. Alwood, *Washburn Commission*; and Memphis *Argus*, April 28, 1865, p. 3.

369. Records of the Judge Advocate General's Office, Record Group No. 153, National Archives, Washington, D.C.

370. Hawes, pp. 195–196.

371. *Kansas City Star*, May 14, 1905.

372. Walker, pp. 21–22.

373. *Ibid.*, pp. 22–23.

374. Berry, pp. 119–120.

375. Floyd, pp. 71–73.

376. Berry, p. 222.

377. *O.R.*, p. 220.

378. *Ibid.*, p. 221.

379. *Log of Charles Ackley*, pp. 103–104.

380. United States House of Representatives, House Bill 1160 (57–1) 4403.

381. *Ibid.*

382. Berry, p. 61.

383. Memphis *Daily Bulletin*, April 28, 1865, p. 1.

384. Berry, p. 27.

385. *Ibid.*, pp. 52–53.

386. *Ibid.*, pp. 194–195.

387. Hawes, pp. 170–171; Memphis *Daily Bulletin*, April 28, 1865, p. 1.

388. Dr. B. T. D. Irwin, *Courtmartial*, pp. 116–117.

389. *O.R.*, p. 221.

390. Hawes, pp. 178–179.

391. Berry, p. 80.

392. Hawes, p. 175.

393. *Ibid.*, pp. 170–171.

394. Memphis *Argus*, April 28, 1865, p. 3; and Berry, p. 166.

395. Memphis *Argus*, April 28, 1865, p. 3; and Letter of L. P. Berry, West

Memphis (Arkansas) *Evening Times*, April 25, 1969.

396. Hawes, pp. 172–173.

397. *Ibid.*, pp. 172–174.

398. Maryville (Tennessee) *Enterprise*, April 30, 1975, p. 3.

399. Memphis *Argus*, April 28, 1865, p. 3; and Memphis *Daily Bulletin*, April 28, 1865, p. 1.

400. Memphis *Argus*, April 28, 1865, p. 3; and West Memphis (Arkansas) *Evening Times*, April 25, 1969.

401. Memphis *Commercial Appeal*, January 25, 1920, p. 18.

402. Berry, p. 223.

403. *Ibid.*, p. 166.

404. Berry, pp. 121–122 and 256.

405. Colleen Morse Elliott and Louis Armstrong Moxley, eds., *The Tennessee Civil War Veterans Questionnaires* (Easley, 1985), Vol. 1, p. 142.

406. Berry, pp. 33–34.

407. *Ibid.*, p. 250.

408. *Ibid.*, pp. 54–55.

409. *Ibid.*, p. 379.

410. Memphis *Daily Bulletin*, April 28, 1865, p. 2.

411. Dr. Irwin, *Courtmartial*, p. 117.

412. Hawes, pp. 174–175.

413. *Ibid.*, p. 180.

414. Berry, p. 251.

415. *Ibid.*, p. 131.

416. Irwin, *Courtmartial*, p. 117.

417. Patricia M. LaPointe, "Military Hospitals in Memphis, 1861–1865," *Tennessee Historical Quarterly*, Vol. 43, no. 4, (1983), p. 341; and Hawes, p. 167.

418. Memphis *Daily Bulletin*, April 28, 1865, p. 2.

419. Memphis *Argus*, April 29, 1865, p. 3.

420. Berry, p. 166.

421. Letter to Cynthia Pickens and Mary Pickens from Samuel Pickens, April 28, 1865, Courtesy of Helen A. Kerr, Knoxville, Tennessee.

422. Summitt County (Ohio) *Beacon*, May 18, 1865, p. 1.

423. Irwin, *Courtmartial*, p. 118; and Memphis *Daily Bulletin*, April 28, 1865, p. 2.

424. Memphis *Argus*, April 29, 1865, p. 3.

425. Memphis *Daily Bulletin*, April 28, 1865, p. 2.

426. Memphis *Argus*, April 30, 1865, p. 3.

427. *Ibid.*, May 27, 1865, p. 3.

428. Berry, p. 252.

429. Hawes, p. 174.

430. Memphis *Argus*, May 7, 1865, p. 3; and Floyd, p. 74.

431. Memphis *Argus*, May 11, 1865, p. 3.

432. *Ibid.*, May 12, 1865, p. 3.

433. *Ibid.*, May 19, 1865, p. 3.

434. *National Tribune*, April 18, 1889, p. 1.

435. *Ibid.*

436. *The Confederate Veteran*, Vol. XXXIV, May, 1926, p. 180.

437. Memphis *Daily Bulletin*, May 27, 1865, p. 3 and May 2, 1865, p. 3.

438. Memphis *Daily Bulletin*, May 8, 1865, p. 3.

439. Memphis *Argus*, April 29, 1865, p. 3; Memphis *Daily Bulletin*, May 4, 1865, p. 3; and Letter to author from Gene Salecker, Chicago, Illinois, January 11, 1991.

440. Memphis *Argus*, May 11, 1865, p. 3; and Memphis *Daily Bulletin*, May 11, 1865, p. 3.

441. Records of the National Cemetery, 3568 Townes Avenue, Memphis, Tennessee.

442. Burial Records of the Elmwood Cemetery, 824 South Dudley Street, Memphis, Tennessee.

443. Memphis *Argus*, May 10, 1865, p. 3.

444. *Ibid.*, May 6, 1865, p. 3.

445. *Ibid.*, April 29, 1865, p. 3.

446. *Ibid.*, May 9, 1865, p. 3.

447. *Ibid.*, May 12, 1865, p. 3.

448. Memphis *Daily Bulletin*, May 5, 1865, p. 2.

449. St. Louis *Daily Missouri Democrat*, May 1, 1865, p. 4.

450. Memphis *Daily Bulletin*, May 5, 1865, p. 3.

451. *O.R.*, p. 217.

452. Way, *Directory of Western River Packets*, pp. 279–280.

453. *O.R.*, p. 217.

454. Hawes, p. 167.

455. *Washburn Commission Records*.

456. George Kayton, *Washburn Commission*.

457. William Snow, *Ibid.*
458. J. O. Lewis, *Ibid.*
459. Samuel Clemens, *Ibid.*
460. William Gaud, *Ibid.*
461. William Postal, *Ibid.*
462. John Curtis, *Ibid.*
463. Jacob Rush, *Ibid.*
464. George Denton, *Ibid.*
465. William Tillinghast, *Ibid.*
466. *Ibid.*
467. William Jones, *Ibid.*
468. R. G. Taylor, *Ibid.*
469. George Williams, *Ibid.*
470. *Ibid.*
471. *Ibid.*
472. Reuben Hatch, *Ibid.*
473. Frederic Speed, *Ibid.*
474. *Ibid.*
475. *Ibid.*
476. J. S. Nauson, *Ibid.*
477. J. S. Neal, *Ibid.*
478. George Williams, *Ibid.*
479. Morgan L. Smith, *Ibid.*
480. J. J. Witzig, *Ibid.*
481. Memphis *Daily Bulletin*, May 21, 1865, p. 4.
482. *Ibid.*
483. *Ibid.*
484. *O.R.*, pp. 212–213.
485. *Dana Commission Records.*
486. William Kerns, *Dana Commission Records.*
487. *Ibid.*
488. *Ibid.*
489. *Ibid.*
490. *Ibid.*
491. *Ibid.*
492. *Ibid.*

493. *Ibid.*

494. *Ibid.*

495. *Ibid.*

496. *Ibid.*

497. *Ibid.*

498. G. G. Adams, *Ibid.*

499. James McGuire, *Ibid.*

500. Miles Sells, *Ibid.*

501. *O.R.*, p. 211.

502. *Ibid.*

503. *Ibid.*, pp. 211–212.

504. *Ibid.*, p. 212.

505. *Ibid.*

506. William Butler, *Hoffman Investigation.*

507. William Kerns, *Ibid.*

508. Edward D. Butler, *Ibid.*

509. Lewis Bean, *Ibid.*

510. Nathan Wintringer, *Ibid.*

511. *Ibid.*

512. Frederic Speed, *Ibid.*

513. George Williams, *Ibid.*

514. Isaac West, *Ibid.*

515. J. Mahony, *Ibid.*

516. *O.R.*, p. 214.

517. *Ibid.*

518. *Ibid.*

519. *Ibid.*, p. 215.

520. *Ibid.*, p. 216.

521. *Ibid.*, p. 215.

522. *Ibid.*

523. *Ibid.*, pp. 215–216.

524. *Ibid.*, p. 217.

525. Memphis *Daily Bulletin*, April 28, 1865, p. 1.

526. William Postal and John Curtis, *Washburn Commission*; and Memphis *Daily Bulletin*, May 2, 1865, p. 3.

527. Memphis *Daily Bulletin*, May 2, 1865, p. 3.

528. Cochran, p. 319.

529. Memphis *Daily Appeal*, May 8, 1888, p. 1.

530. Memphis *Argus*, May 5, 1865, p. 3.

531. J. J. Witzig, *Courtmartial*, p. 131.

532. *O.R.*, p. 216.

533. Berry, pp. 25–26.

534. *Inspectors' Report*, p. 216.

535. *Ibid.*

536. J. J. Witzig, *Courtmartial*, p. 136.

537. *Ibid.*; and *Inspectors' Report*, pp. 216–217.

538. Frederick Way, Jr., *Way's Steamboat Directory Abridged*, Packet Edition (Sewickley, Pa., 1944), p. 212; and St. Louis *Daily Missouri Democrat*, June 19, 1865, p. 4.

539. St. Louis *Daily Missouri Democrat*, June 19, 1865, p. 4.

540. *Ibid.*

541. Way, p. 212.

542. Memphis *Daily Bulletin*, May 21, 1865, p. 4.

543. *O.R.*, p. 213.

544. *Ibid.*, p. 213.

545. Letter from General Meigs to the Adjutant General of the Army, June 16, 1865, Records of the Judge Advocate General's Office, Record Group 153, National Archives, Washington, D.C.

546. *Ibid.*; and L. W. Perce, *Courtmartial*, p. 158.

547. *Personal Histories of Volunteer Officers of the Quartermaster Department 1861–1865*, Vol. III, p. 148.

548. Letter from Quartermaster General to Adjutant General of the Army, January 24, 1872, Reuben Hatch's Military Records, Record Group 94, National Archives.

549. *Ibid.*

550. *Hatch's Records.*

551. *Courtmartial*, pp. 1 & 2.

552. Letter from Frederic Speed to Colonel Badeau, December 13, 1865, Courtesy of Bill Mason, Morehead City, North Carolina.

553. Military Record of Lt. William Tillinghast, Record Group 54, National Archives.

554. Letter from Frederic Speed to Colonel Badeau.

555. Deposition of Dr. Kemble, Exhibit O, *Courtmartial.*

556. *Courtmartial*, pp. 6–9.

557. *Ibid.*, p. 5.

558. George Williams, *Courtmartial*, pp. 12–13, and p. 20.

559. *Ibid.*, pp. 13–15.

560. *Ibid.*, p. 14.

561. *Ibid.*, p. 22.

562. *Ibid.*, p. 18.

563. *Ibid.*, pp. 18–19.

564. *Ibid.*, pp. 22–25.

565. *Ibid.*, p. 27.

566. William Kerns, *Courtmartial*, pp. 62–63.

567. *Ibid.*, pp. 48–52.

568. *Ibid.*, p. 62.

569. William Jones, *Courtmartial*, pp. 88–90.

570. *Ibid.*, p. 91.

571. *Ibid.*

572. Miles Sells, *Courtmartial*, pp. 120–123.

573. *Ibid.*, pp. 123–124.

574. *Ibid.*, p. 127.

575. *Ibid.*

576. J. J. Witzig, *Courtmartial*, pp. 129–130.

577. *Ibid.*, p. 130.

578. Elias Shull, *Courtmartial*, pp. 145–146.

579. E. D. Butler, *Courtmartial*, pp. 151–154.

580. *Courtmartial*, pp. 155–156.

581. *Ibid.*, pp. 155–159.

582. Nathan Wintringer, *Courtmartial*, pp. 163–164.

583. J. S. McHarg, *Courtmartial*, pp. 173–176.

584. *Ibid.*, p. 180.

585. *Courtmartial*, pp. 181–182.

586. *Ibid.*, pp. 183–188.

587. W. H. H. Emmon, *Courtmartial*, p. 193.

588. J. Warren Miller, *Courtmartial*, p. 219.

589. *Ibid.*, p. 219.

590. *Ibid.*, pp. 219 and 222.

591. *Courtmartial*, p. 226 and pp. 269–273.

592. H. A. Henderson, *Courtmartial*, p. 276 and p. 281.

593. E. L. Davenport, *Courtmartial*, p. 283.

594. *Ibid.*, p. 293.

595. *Ibid.*, p. 315.

596. Deposition of Dr. Kemble, Exhibit O, *Courtmartial*.

597. Deposition of Frank Miller, Exhibit P, *Courtmartial*.

598. *Courtmartial*, p. 366.

599. *Ibid.*, pp. 369–371; and *O.R.*, pp. 217–218.

600. *O.R.*, p. 218.

601. *Ibid.*, p. 219.

602. *Ibid.*, p. 220.

603. *Ibid.*, pp. 219–220.

604. *Ibid.*, p. 219.

605. *Ibid.*, p. 219.

606. *Ibid.*, p. 220.

607. Memphis *Daily Bulletin*, May 21, 1865, p. 4.

608. *O.R.*, p. 219.

609. *O.R.*, Series III, Vol. 5, p. 3.

610. *Annual Report of the Secretary of War for the Year 1865*, 39th Congress, First Session, House Executive Documents, Vol. 3, Part 1, no. 1, p. 226.

611. Records of Gen. Napoleon Dana, United States Military Academy Archives, West Point, New York.

612. *O.R.*, p. 216.

613. *Smith's Records*.

614. St. Louis *Post Dispatch*, January 1, 1875, p. 2.

615. *Ibid.*

616. *The New York Times*, December 30, 1874, p. 5.

617. St. Louis *Post Dispatch*, January 1, 1875, p. 2.

618. United States House of Representatives, *House Miscellaneous Documents*, 4 (43–2) 1653.

619. St. Louis *Post Dispatch*, January 9, 1875, p. 1.

620. *The New York Times*, January 12, 1875, p. 12.

621. United States House of Representatives, House Report 598(43–1) 1625, and *House Miscellaneous Documents* 4 (43–2) 1653.

622. *Personal Histories of Volunteer Officers of the Quartermaster Department*, p. 144.

623. Berry, pp. 47–48.

624. Letter from Mrs. Reuben Hatch to the Secretary of War, February 27, 1872, *Hatch's Records*, Record Group 94, National Archives, Washington, D.C.

625. Military Records of Capt. George Williams, Records of the Adjutant General's Office, Record Group 94, National Archives; and Records of Capt. George Williams, United States Military Academy Archives.

626. *Biographical and Historical Memoirs of Mississippi*, Vol. II (Chicago, 1891), p. 806; and William C. Harris, *The Day of the Carpetbagger: Republican Reconstruction in Mississippi* (Baton Rouge, 1979), pp. 269–70.

627. *Biographical and Historical Memoirs of Mississippi*, p. 806.

628. *Ibid.*, p. 807.

629. Records of the Old Court House Museum, Vicksburg, Mississippi.

630. *Way's Steamboat Directory Abridged*, p. 60.

631. Berry, p. 27.

632. Way, p. 60.

633. Power of Attorney executed on November 18, 1884, Records of Adjutant General's Office, Record Group 94, National Archives.

634. Letter from M. A. McDonald to the Secretary of War, March 11, 1884, *Ibid.*

635. Letter from the Secretary of War to McDonald, March 20, 1884, *Ibid.*

636. First endorsement by Quartermaster General of the Army to letter dated February 13, 1886 from War Department to John Glover, *Ibid.*

637. Hawes, p. 164.

638. Clement Eaton, *A History of the Southern Confederacy* (New York, 1954), p. 100.

639. Memphis *Argus*, May 5, 1865, p. 6.

640. Letter from Dorothy E. Bates, granddaughter of John Clark Ely to author, June 1, 1989.

641. Letters from Ruth Provines Isenogle to author, May 31, 1989 and June 20, 1989.

642. Letter to Survivors of the *Sultana* Association from Hannah Braunwart, April 24, 1901, Courtesy of Mrs. John Kerr, Knoxville, Tennessee and Gene Salecker, Chicago, Illinois. Interview with Pam Newhouse, Ann Arbor, Michigan, December 7, 1990.

643. Pension records of Michael Daly, courtesy of Patricia Tieszen, Sanger, Texas.

644. Hawes, p. 29.

645. *Ibid.*, p. 191.

646. Pension records of Joseph Hines, courtesy of Charles M. Jenkins, Fort Smith, Arkansas.

647. Berry, p. 11.

648. Kimberlin, p. 5.

649. *National Tribune*, April 18, 1889, p. 1.

650. Bill 3296, United States House of Representatives (January 6, 1896), First Session, 54th Congress.

651. *Ibid.*

652. Kimberlin, p. 5.

653. *Sultana Monument*, Mount Olive Cemetery, Knoxville, Tennessee.

654. *Knoxville Journal*, April 27, 1930, Section B, p. 1.

655. Kimberlin, p. 5.

BIBLIOGRAPHY

GOVERNMENT DOCUMENTS

National Archives, Washington, D.C., Dana Commission records, the Adjutant General's Office. Record Group 153

National Archives, Washington, D.C., Military records of Lt. Harvey Annis

National Archives, Washington, D.C., Military records of Col. Reuben B. Hatch

National Archives, Washington, D.C., Military records of Capt. William Franklin Kerns

National Archives, Washington, D.C., Military records of Gen. Morgan L. Smith

National Archives, Washington, D.C., Military records of Lt. William Tillinghast

National Archives, Washington, D.C., Military records of Capt. George Augustus Williams

National Archives, Washington, D.C., Pension records of Michael Daly

National Archives, Washington, D.C., Pension records of Joseph Hines

National Archives, Washington, D.C., Personal Histories of Volunteer Officers of the Quartermaster Department 1861–1865

National Archives, Washington, D.C., Transcript of the Courtmartial of Capt. Frederic Speed, Records of the Judge Advocate General's Office. Record Group 153

National Archives, Washington, D.C., Washburn Commission Records, Records of the Adjutant General's Office. Record Group 153

National Cemetery, Memphis, Tennessee. Burial records

United States Military Academy Archives, West Point, New York. Military records of Gen. Napoleon Dana

United States Military Academy Archives, West Point, New York. Military records of Capt. George A. Williams

United States Congress, Annual Report of the Secretary of War for the Year 1865, 39th Congress, First Session, House Executive Document Vol. 3, Part 1, No. 1

United States Congress, House Bill 1160 (57-1-) 4403, United States House of Representatives

United State Congress, House Report 598 (43-1) 1625, United States House of Representatives

United States Congress, House Misc. Documents, 4 (43-2) 1653

United States Congress, House Bill 3296, United States House of Representative, 54th Congress, First Session, January 6, 1896

United States Congress, Report of the Board of Supervising Inspectors of Steamboats, House Executive Document 3, 39th Congress, First Session, 1865–1866

United States Congress, Report of the Cairo Fraud Investigation, United States House of Representatives, 37th Congress, Second Session, House Reports, part 2

MAGAZINES

Catton, Bruce, "Prison Camps of the Civil War." *American Heritage*, X (August 1959)

Cochran, William C., "Perils of River Navigation in the Sixties." *Proceedings of the Mississippi Valley Association*, X (1919–1920)

Dixon, William F., "Aboard the Sultana." *Civil War Times Illustrated*, XII (February 1974)

Elliott, Joseph Taylor, "The Sultana Disaster." *Indiana Historical Society Publication*, V, No. 3 (1913)

Floyd, William B., "The Burning of the Sultana." *The Wisconsin Magazine of History*, XI (September 1927)

LaPointe, Patricia M., "Military Hospitals in Memphis. 1861–1865," *Tennessee Historical Quarterly*, 43, No. 4 (1983)

Levstik, Frank R., "The Sinking of the Sultana." *Civil War Times Illustrated*, XII (January 1974)

Rutter, J. W., "Bewitching News." *S & D Reflector*, 2, No. 3 (September 1965)

The Confederate Veteran, XXXIV (May 1926)

Walton, Lloyd B., "The Great Civil War Shipwreck." *The Indianapolis Star Magazine* (March 15, 1981)

NEWSPAPERS

Chicago Tribune, December 12, 1861

Cincinnati *Daily Commerce*, February 4, 1863

Kansas City Star, May 14, 1905

Knoxville Journal, April 27, 1930

Maryville (Tennessee) *Enterprise*, April 30, 1975

Memphis *Argus*, April and May, 1865

Memphis *Commercial Appeal*, January 25, 1920

Memphis *Daily Appeal*, August 8, 1888

Memphis *Daily Bulletin*, April and May, 1865

Memphis *Press Scimitar*, May 28, 1969

New Orleans *Picayune*, April 20–22, 1865

The New York Times, December 30, 1874 and January 12, 1875

Richmond (Indiana) *Palladium-Item and Sun-Telegram*, January 8, 1969

St. Louis *Daily Missouri Democrat*, February 22, 1865, April and May, 1865, and June 19, 1865

Saint Louis *Post Dispatch*, January 1, 1875, January 2, 1875, and January 9, 1875

Summitt County (Ohio) *Beacon*, May 18, 1865

Washington, D.C. *National Tribune*, April 1, 1889, June 14, 1923, and August 1, 1929

West Memphis (Arkansas) *Evening Times*, April 25, 1969

BOOKS

Anderson, Nellie Pickens, *John Pickens Family*. Knoxville: S. B. Newman Co., 1951

Annual Reunion of the Association of the Graduates of the United States Military Academy at West Point, New York. New York: Waldron & Payne, 1907

Berry, Chester D., *Loss of the Sultana and Reminiscences of Survivors*. Lansing, Michigan: Darius D. Thorp, 1892

Biographical and Historical Memoirs of Mississippi. Chicago: Goodspeed Publishing Company, 1891

Bryant, William O., *Cahaba Prison and the Sultana Disaster*. Tuscaloosa: The University of Alabama Press, 1990

Catton, Bruce, *A Stillness at Appomattox*. New York: Doubleday, 1953

Catton, Bruce, *Grant Moves South*. Boston: Little, Brown, 1960

Catton, Bruce, *Short History of the Civil War*. New York: American Heritage Publishing Co., Inc., 1960

Civil War Centennial Commission, *TENNESSEANS IN THE CIVIL WAR*. Nashville, 1965

Coulter, E. Merton, *The Confederate States of America*. Baton Rouge: Louisiana State University Press, 1950

Cullum, George W., *Biographical Register of the Officers and Graduates of the United States Military Academy, West Point, New York*. Cambridge: Riverside Press, 1891

Dana, Charles A., *Recollections of the Civil War*. New York: Collier Books, 1963

Eaton, Clement, *A History of the Southern Confederacy*. New York: Free Press, 1954

Elliott, Colleen Morse & Louis Armstrong Moxley, eds., *The Tennessee Civil War Veterans Questionnaires*. Easley, SC: Southern Historical Press, 1985, 3 vols.

Elliott, James W., *Transport to Disaster*. New York: Holt, Rinehart & Winston, 1962

Foote, Shelby, *The Civil War: A Narrative*. New York: Random House, 1958–1974, 3 vols.

Funk and Wagnalls Standard College Dictionary, Text Edition. New York: Harcourt, Brace and World, Inc., 1966

Futch, Ovid, *History of Andersonville*. Gainesville: University of Florida Press, 1968

Gould, E. W., *Fifty Years on the Mississippi or Gould's History of River Navigation*. St. Louis: Nixon-Jones Printing Co., 1889

Harris, William C., *The Day of the Carpetbagger: Republication Reconstruction in Mississippi*. Baton Rouge: Louisiana State University Press, 1979

Hawes, Jesse, *Cahaba: A Story of Captive Boys in Blue*. New York: Burr Printing House, 1888

Henry, Robert Selph, *"First With The Most" Forrest*. Wilmington: Broadfoot Publishing Co., 1987

Hereford, Robert A., *The Old Man River — The Memories of Captain Louis*

Rosche, Pioneer Steamboatman. Caldwell, Idaho: The Caxton Printing Ltd., 1943

Hesseltine, William B., *Civil War Prisons.* Kent, OH: Kent State University Press, 1962

Hunter, Louis C., *Steamboats on the Western Rivers.* New York: Octagon Books, 1969

Hyde, William, and Howard L. Conard, eds., *Encyclopedia of the History of St. Louis.* New York: The Southern History Company, 1899, 2 vols.

Luthin, Reinhard H., *The First Lincoln Campaign.* Cambridge: Harvard University Press, 1944

McDonough, James Lee, and Thomas L. Connelly, *Five Tragic Hours — The Battle of Franklin.* Knoxville: University Press, 1983

Newberry, J. S., *The U.S. Sanitary Commission in the Valley of the Mississippi River.* Cleveland: Fairbanks, Benedict and Co., 1871

Official Records of the Union and Confederate Navies in the War of the Rebellion. 30 vols. Washington, D.C.: Government Printing Office, 1894–1922

Portrait and Biographical Album of Jackson County, Michigan. Chicago: Chapman Bros., 1890

Pratt, Harry E., *The Personal Finances of Abraham Lincoln.* Springfield, IL: The Abraham Lincoln Association, 1943

Ransom, John, *John Ransom's Andersonville Diary.* New York: Berkley Books, 1963

Samuel, Ray; Leonard V. Huber, and Warren C. Odgen, *Tales of the Mississippi.* New York: Hastings House, 1955

Simon, John Y., ed., *The Papers of Ulysses S. Grant.* Carbondale, IL: Southern Illinois University Press, 1967–1982, 10 vols.

The War of The Rebellion: A Compilation of the Official Records of the Union and Confederate Armies. 128 vols. Washington, D.C.: Government Printing Office, 1880-1901

Twain, Mark, *Life on the Mississippi.* Hartford: American Publishing Company, 1883

Walker, John L., *Cahaba Prison and the Sultana Disaster.* Hamilton, OH: Brown & Whitaker, 1910

Way, Frederick, Jr., *Directory of Western River Packets.* Sewickley, PA: Frederick Way, Jr., 1950

Way, Frederick, Jr., *Way's Steamboat Directory Abridged.* Packet Edition. Sewickley, PA: Frederick Way, Jr., 1944

MISCELLANEOUS SOURCES

Ackley, Charles, *Log of Charles Ackley*. Inland River Library, Public Library of Cincinnati and Hamilton County, Cincinnati, Ohio

Braunwart, Hannah, Letter to Survivors of the *Sultana* Association, April 24, 1901

Bates, Dorothy E., Letter to Author from Dorothy E. Bates, June 1, 1989

Elmwood Cemetery, Memphis, Tennessee. Burial Records

Hatch, O. M., *O.M. Hatch Collection*. Illinois Historical Society Library, Springfield, Illinois

Isenogle, Ruth Provines, Letters to Author from Ruth Provine, May 31, 1989 and June 20, 1989

Keeble, Edgar Rhea, son of Pleasant Keeble, Unpublished Manuscript of Edgar Rhea Keeble, Knoxville, Tennessee 1987

Kimberlin, J. H., *The Destruction of the Sultana*, An Unpublished Manuscript by J. H. Kimberlin, Hamilton, Ohio, 1910

Millsaps, George, Knoxville, Tennessee. Interview by Author, April 1988

Newhouse, Pam, Ann Arbor, Michigan. Interview by Author, December 7, 1990

Pickens, Samuel, Letter from Samuel Pickens to Cynthia Pickens and Mary Pickens, Knoxville, Tennessee, April 28, 1865

Salecker, Gene, Letter to Author from Gene Salecker, Chicago, Illinois, January 11, 1991

Speed, Frederic, Letter to Colonel Badeau from Capt. Frederic Speed, December 13, 1865

INDEX

973.771   92-1220
P867s   Potter, Jerry O.
                The Sultana tragedy

Hartford Public Library
115 N. Main Street
Hartford, WI 53027
TELEPHONE: 673-8240

AUG

DEMCO